IMPROVING THE QUALITY OF
PUBLIC SCHOOL PROGRAMS

Improving the Quality of Public School Programs

APPROACHES TO CURRICULUM DEVELOPMENT

Harold J. McNally, Professor of Education
Teachers College, Columbia University

A. Harry Passow, Professor of Education
Teachers College, Columbia University

and **Associates**

BUREAU OF PUBLICATIONS
TEACHERS COLLEGE, COLUMBIA UNIVERSITY
1960

FOREWORD

DESCRIPTIONS and appraisals of organized efforts at curriculum improvement are essential to the constructive development of educational theory and practice. When field experience is thoughtfully analyzed, shortcomings become apparent and sound guidelines emerge for the future.

This book presents such materials. The first four chapters deal with the setting, which requires continuous curriculum improvement; and with administrative procedures and curriculum development techniques that are currently employed. Seven chapters then present descriptions of field programs with critical appraisals of strengths and weaknesses. A final chapter presents a formulation of central concepts which emerge from the field programs.

The plan and purposes of the book are based on one which I prepared in 1950: *Curriculum Improvement in Public School Systems*. The purposes stated for that book were to assist "in appraising new developments and spreading good practice." This book will serve the same purposes for the nineteen sixties. Curriculum problems and procedures of improvement have changed so rapidly during the past few years that it will meet a real need, both of field workers and of college classes studying the curriculum.

The authors possess unusual competence to prepare such a book. They have long been careful students of curriculum development and have a wealth of firsthand experience on which to base their analysis and appraisal.

HOLLIS L. CASWELL, *President*
Teachers College, Columbia University

PREFACE

As Dr. Caswell points out in his foreword, this book is a sequel to his *Curriculum Improvement in Public School Systems*. When copies of that publication were nearly exhausted, President Caswell's responsibilities prevented his revising the text and he invited us to do so.

In the Caswell volume, there was a discussion of organization and administration of curriculum improvement followed by a description of school programs. Although we have completely rewritten the text, we have kept the essential concept and structure of the original book.

The educators who have contributed Chapters 5 through 11 were chosen to participate because of their recognized leadership in curriculum programs which vary in size, organization, and geographic location. Each of the participants and programs is known personally by both of the authors. The seven chapters include descriptions of state, county, city programs; urban, suburban, and rural; large and small.

Having accepted the invitation to describe the way changes in educational programs are brought about in their school systems, the contributors were free to develop their chapters as they wished. A "Guide Sheet for Contributors" was prepared, with a suggestion that the writer include descriptions and analyses that he felt would be most significant for other curriculum workers. He was asked to keep in mind this question: "As a reader, what would I want to know about curriculum improvement in this school system that might help me in understanding my own situation better?" Each contributor was asked to give attention to program objectives, means of initiation, personnel involved, organization, and procedures. Each was requested to make whatever general observations he cared to with respect to the strengths and weaknesses of the program, the cautions recommended to others, and the major emphases in curriculum improvement activities in the foreseeable future. The contributors have responded to the "Guide Sheet" by providing a clear, concise picture of the program development in their systems. The variations in the chapters reflect both the individual differences among the authors and the ways in which the quality of education is being improved through these seven programs.

We, in turn, have attempted to provide a framework for the seven contributor chapters. The first four chapters discuss the social changes and forces which call impellingly for modifications in the nature and objectives of today's curriculum; in administrative and organizational considerations in the curriculum improvement program; in the nature of the curriculum improvement process and its relationship to underlying curriculum theory; and in the variety of procedures found in today's curriculum development programs. In Chapter 12, the concluding chapter, we have attempted to formulate a group of guidelines based on the seven curriculum program descriptions. By relating these guidelines closely to the descriptions of the programs, we hope that they may have a quality of practicality that curriculum discussions are often accused of lacking.

This, then, is an attempt to wed theory with practice in a manner that will be found helpful by administrators, curriculum workers, and those who offer instruction in curriculum development. We believe that it is illustrative of forward-looking practice in American public school systems.

We are indebted to President Caswell for permitting us to discuss our plans with him, and to draw on his ideas as freely as we wished.

A. HARRY PASSOW
HAROLD J. MCNALLY

Teachers College, Columbia University
January 1960

CONTENTS

Approaches to Curriculum Development

Reports of
Curriculum Programs

Appraising Curriculum
Improvement Programs

APPROACHES TO
CURRICULUM DEVELOPMENT

1

DEMANDS FOR CHANGE

EVERY curriculum worker is well aware that the American school curriculum has its roots deep in the past. Its nature is the composite result of mandates of history and tradition, as well as of the values and circumstances of time and place. Although it has kinship with education in Europe (a kinship it shares with other institutions of our nation), the specific nature and needs of the American society have forged it into a program unique in conception and organization.

One of the notable characteristics of the curriculum of American schools has been its protean nature; it has changed (often in laggardly fashion, it is true) with the changing needs of advancing time, and the different needs of different places. These changes have not taken place without protest. There have been voices, and persuasive ones, which have proclaimed that "true" education (by *their* definition) should be relatively unchanging, and essentially the same regardless of time and place. One of the foremost spokesmen of this viewpoint in recent years has been Hutchins, who once stated:

> One purpose of education is to draw out the elements of our common human nature. These elements are the same in any

time or place. The notion of educating a man to live in any particular time or place, to adjust him to any particular environment, is therefore foreign to a true conception of education. Education implies teaching. Teaching implies knowledge. Knowledge is truth. The truth is everywhere the same. Hence education should be everywhere the same . . . I suggest that the heart of any course of study designed for the whole people will be, if education is rightly understood, the same at any time, in any place, under any political, social or economic conditions.[1]

While this may represent an extreme position, current public discussions and criticisms of American schools are accompanied by a persistent obbligato, adjuring us to "return to the fundamentals," and to eschew the "nonintellectual" accretions and frills of today's curriculum.

There are others who take an opposite point of view. Kelley and Rasey, for example, disagree not only with Hutchins' conclusion, but with his premise of the immutable nature of truth.

When we get the concept of change into our organisms so that we can act as though it was so, we will not try to plan for eternity. This is the very point where we make the error set forth by Howard Mumford Jones when he says that the school curriculum is always planned for eternity instead of for time. It is not just in planning school programs that we do this. It permeates our whole lives.

While known answers serve as a foundation for creativity, they form an insecure base for continuous operation. Owing to the dynamic of change and the uncertainty of knowledge, they will not abide. They are the best we know at any given time, and they are all we can have to operate with at that time, but some of them are not true at any time, and some of them lose their validity in changed times . . . Certainties become uncertainties, verities become spurious, truth must be revised. This is the significance of change.[2]

Serious students of the curriculum of the public schools, including well-qualified curriculum workers in schools and school systems, for the most part have realized that there is no essential con-

---

[1] Robert M. Hutchins, *The Higher Learning in America* (New Haven: Yale University Press, 1936), p. 66.

[2] Earl C. Kelley and Marie I. Rasey, *Education and the Nature of Man* (New York: Harper and Brothers, 1952), pp. 18, 117–18.

flict between "eternal" values and the constant adaptation and improvement of the curriculum. They are aware that the curriculum worker must take account of the values of the society the curriculum is to serve, the needs of the children who are part of that society, and the practical realities of time, place, and circumstance that exist in the educational systems in which they work.

While some of these conditions are "basic" and change so slowly as to seem not to change at all, there are few today who will deny that important social changes call for changes in the curriculum. Otherwise, continuing attention to curriculum development would be largely unnecessary. If this is granted, it is obvious that the person charged with responsibility for curriculum development must provide leadership in (1) identifying valid reasons for curriculum change; (2) deciding what curriculum changes they imply; (3) bringing about appropriate changes; and (4) evaluating the effectiveness of change.

Not the least important of these responsibilities is the first one, namely, identifying those forces which seem to call for curriculum change, and deciding which of them are valid. It is readily apparent that, just as the mandates which determine the basic nature of the curriculum have several sources, so do the mandates for change have various origins.

For purposes of discussion, we can identify three closely interrelated sources of demands for change. The first comprises those cultural values and changes which have implications for the nature of education. The second is that group of research findings which change or clarify our understandings of how people learn, how teaching can be made more effective, or which throw light on the value of different learnings in today's world. The third is the voices of critics of education, with their variety of suggestions (some made with sincerity, others with ulterior motives) for the improvement of American education. Without attempting to approach exhaustive analysis, let us examine each of these for some important change pressures, or implications, existing at the time of this writing.

CULTURAL CHANGES

One does not have to be a close student of history to know that we are living in the midst of basic changes in world society. Indeed, today's American citizen has become so accustomed to astounding changes that he has become blasé—or benumbed, if you will—about them. It is probably safe to say that few Americans realize even the relatively simple and short-term significance of many of the revolutionary social and scientific changes which have occurred recently or are now in process. The most insightful among us are not vouchsafed foresight clear enough to reveal many of the long-term, more complex meanings of these changes.

Nevertheless, educators have a grave responsibility to be aware of important cultural changes, and to assess them carefully for curriculum implications. There are many specialists to help us identify significant changes: sociologists, economists, historians, social and political analysts, philosophers, to name a few.[3]

Among the many changes now taking place, there are a few which seem to the authors especially worthy of note by curriculum workers. While they may appear to be obvious, we believe that their implications are far from being realized in the schools of today.

No Place to Hide

One of the most striking phenomena of the past half century has been the startling increase in the world's population. The reasons for this development are complex, perhaps chief among them being increased productivity, and decreases in mortality rates brought about by medical science. This has resulted in a fact remarked upon by one authority, who makes the astonishing observation that, "Not only has the American birth rate approxi-

[3] It would be an egregious presumption to attempt to select the most important or most pertinent of the many writings by specialists in these fields, which deal with cultural changes. However, a few attempts by professional educators or groups to identify cultural changes with curriculum implications may be worth mentioning: Association for Supervision and Curriculum Development, *Forces Affecting American Education* (yearbook) (Washington, D.C.: National Education Association, 1953); George S. Counts, *Education and American Civilization* (New York: Bureau of Publications, Teachers College, Columbia University, 1952); Department of Elementary School Principals, *Contemporary Society: Background for the Instructional Program* (Washington, D.C.: National Education Association, 1957); Henry Harap (ed.), *The Changing Curriculum* (New York: D. Appleton-Century Company, 1937); Harold Rugg, *Foundations for American Education* (Yonkers-on-Hudson, N.Y.: World Book Company, 1947).

mately doubled since the 1930s, but the high birth rate and decreasing death rate throughout the world make it possible to say that *approximately half of all the adults who have ever lived in the world are still living.*[4]

Furthermore, unexplored, unsettled and unexploited geographic regions of the earth, seemingly so abundant a century or two ago, have all but disappeared. Almost none of us can any longer, like Daniel Boone, "leave the world behind and go and find a place that's known to God alone," as the words of a not so old song had it. In today's increasingly crowded world, "man's chief task in life is in adjustment to others. There is now no escape from this necessity, and one's success or failure in life depends largely upon this adjustment."[5]

There have been numerous accompaniments to this rapid population growth. One that is fundamental is that man is becoming an urban creature. "The census taken in 1920 was the first in which more than half the population of the United States (51.5 per cent) was reported as resident in urban areas. . . . By 1950, there were almost 5,000 urban places in the United States, with a population of some 96.5 million or almost two-thirds (64 per cent) of the entire population of the nation."[6] This fact alone would call for a reassessment of an educational program developed to serve a predominantly agrarian society. Have we made the adaptations necessary to educate for the role diffusion required in a complex urban industrial society? Do our educational objectives include the development of newly developing group membership roles? Are we educating for satisfying living patterns in the midst of our urban lonely crowds?[7] Are our children being helped to develop appropriate means of exercising individual responsibility in the midst of the impersonality of large population concentrations? Does our curriculum provide experiences designed to help children to learn constructive and rewarding patterns of living in close juxtaposition with people of diverse religions, races, eco-

[4] Ralph W. Tyler, "The Individual in Modern Society," *National Elementary Principal*, Vol. 36 (February 1957), p. 17. (Italics added.)

[5] Kelley and Rasey, *op. cit.*, p. 11.

[6] Philip M. Houser, "Population Facts and Figures," *National Elementary Principal*, Vol. 36 (February 1957), p. 14.

[7] The editors of *Fortune, The Exploding Metropolis*. Doubleday Anchor Books (Garden City, New York: Doubleday and Company, Inc., 1958).

nomic levels, national origins and interests? Are they being helped
to develop appropriate patterns of recreation in an urban culture?
Are our textbooks and other learning materials oriented to an
urban society? These are but a few of the problems posed for the
curriculum worker by developments attendant upon our current
rapid population growth.

The Individual in the Crowd

Another of the cultural developments which has implications
for education is the apparent growth of pressures toward conformity. Although the idealized view some contemporary critics
take of the halcyon days of "rugged individualism" is specious
and misleading, it is probably true that it is becoming increasingly
difficult to be different from "the crowd." Mass organization in
business and industry, though it may have many human and material values, is claimed by Whyte to be responsible for the emergence of "the organization man." [8] A group of sociologists tells
us that we are ceasing to be a people directed by our inner convictions, and are becoming a society whose members are "other-
directed." That is to say, we are tending more and more to model
our values and living patterns in accord with those of the majority
of our contemporaries.[9] These values and patterns, in turn, are
affected by other forces, of which mass education in our public
schools is probably not the least. Among other influences are the
revolutionized and multiplied mass media (i.e., electronic recordings, radio, television, motion pictures, comics, periodicals), mass
production (e.g., of homes, automobiles, clothes, art-form repro-
ductions, books, foods)[10] and the tremendous increase in our
spatial mobility, which tends to diminish regional differences. As
one writer comments, "The farmer's daughter now wears blue
jeans not as work clothes but because it is an urban fashion." [11]

[8] William H. Whyte, *The Organization Man* (New York: Simon and Schus-
ter, 1956).

[9] David Riesman, Nathan Glazer and Reuel Denney, *The Lonely Crowd*
(New Haven: Yale University Press, 1950).

[10] Bernard Rosenberg and David M. White (eds.), *Mass Culture* (Glencoe,
Ill.: Free Press, 1957).

[11] Gordon Blackwell, "Impact of New Social Patterns upon Education,"
Teachers College Record, Vol. 57 (March 1956), p. 393.

Such developments pose a threat to individuality and creativity, for these precious qualities can all too easily become submerged in a culture of "machine-made men." Conversely, they are a challenge to educators to develop a curriculum and a methodology that will result truly in what Benjamin has called "the cultivation of idiosyncrasy." [12] It is the differences among human beings that make life interesting; it is these differences which result in a Jonas Salk, a Leonard Bernstein, a Marian Anderson, a Thomas Jefferson, a Florence Nightingale. Few would deny that our schools fall short of their potential in enhancing desirable individual differences.

One of the major questions to be answered in the years ahead, therefore, is whether high quality individualized education is consistent with, and possible in, mass education. While the answer involves questions of school finance, teacher education, and administrative and supervisory leadership, all curriculum workers unquestionably share responsibility in its resolution.

Home Away from Home

Population growth, industrialization and urbanization have also had effects upon the nature of family life and responsibilities. There is an increasing proportion of gainfully employed married women,[13] and a large proportion of these are women with children of school age. In many cases this has resulted in what Hechinger has called "the doorkey kids," children who daily return to an empty house after school is out, who must prepare their own dinners, and who are unsupervised for long periods of time.[14]

Furthermore, there is a growing trend toward the state's assuming responsibilities that were formerly those of the home. The aged, the unemployed, and the mentally incompetent, for example, no longer need depend entirely on their families for support. This changing point of view with respect to family responsi-

[12] Harold Benjamin, *The Cultivation of Idiosyncrasy.* Inglis Lecture (Cambridge: Harvard University Press, 1949).

[13] Educational Policies Commission, *Manpower and Education* (Washington, D.C.: National Education Association, 1956), p. 45.

[14] Fred M. Hechinger, "Who's Looking After Today's Children?" *National Elementary Principal,* Vol. 36 (April 1957), pp. 8–10. Also reprinted in Department of Elementary School Principals, *op. cit.,* pp. 75–77.

bilities has had its impact on the school. Whereas the home once indisputably bore the primary responsibility for a child's moral and spiritual education, his sex education, social education, and his preparation for a vocation, a large measure of these responsibilities has been shifted to the school. And in many communities even children's nutrition is being subsidized through the school. While few educators question the desirability of giving attention in school to these varied aspects of children's growth, recognizing that "the whole child" comes to school, some have raised questions as to how far the shift in responsibilities from home to school should extend. Certainly currriculum workers need to face the question of what is the relative responsibility of the home and the school in the various aspects of the child's growth. What is the unique responsibility of the school? What is it that the school is equipped to do better than any other agency or institution in the community? What should be the relationship of the school, the home, and the other community agencies in the nurture of the community's children? The way in which curriculum workers answer these questions will have profound effects on the direction of curriculum development in the years ahead.

Men and Machines

In one of a provocative series of articles, Carskadon reports that whereas muscle power accounted for almost two-thirds of all productive power in the United States a century ago, today—only three generations later—it accounts for only a little over one per cent.[15] This is but one of the outcomes of the industrial revolution that marked a major change of direction in the engrossing history of man. The little-regarded, agrarian nation of 1800 has become a complex industrial giant, whose wide-ranging enterprise requires a host of vocational specializations. Today we are in a new phase of that revolution, or perhaps even another revolution.[16]

---

[15] Thomas R. Carskadon, "Economic Bases of Our Society," *National Elementary Principal,* Vol. 36 (December 1956), p. 13. (This article appears also in *Contemporary Society . . . Background for the Instructional Program* (Washington, D.C.: Department of Elementary School Principals, 1957), pp. 36–39.

[16] Charles Frankel, "The Third Great Revolution of Mankind," *New York Times Magazine,* February 9, 1958, p. 11.

Nuclear sources of energy are being developed, and electronic servo-mechanisms in complex automated production systems make it possible for a few men to operate a large productive enterprise. On the other hand, the manufacture, installation, maintenance, and repair of these complex systems call for a hitherto un-dreamed-of variety of technical skills. "Help Wanted" advertisements in today's newspapers call for such specializations as systems engineers, electromagnetic researchers, digital computer designers and analysts, product design engineers, specialists in avionics, guidance and control technicians, senior systems research engineers, and specialists in transistorizing and in microwave theory, techniques, and systems. "The . . . trend is illustrated by the fact that in 1900 about one industrial worker in 250 was an engineer, and that now about one in 50 is an engineer. The prospect of automation suggests that similar trends will continue." [17]

These and other remarkable products of our fertile inventiveness have resulted in an astonishing increase in our productivity. Carskadon observes that the United States, "with little more than 6 per cent of the world's population and less than 7 per cent of its land area, now produces and consumes well over one-third the world's goods and services, and turns out nearly one-half the world's factory-produced goods." [18] No longer must man live in an economy of scarcity, as he had done since his emergence from primordial life-forms; now there is enough so that none need go hungry. In fact, in some agricultural products we are faced with an embarrassment of plenty, so much so that we have not yet learned how to administer the surpluses.

Furthermore, our enhanced productivity has made leisure a possession of almost everybody—in its way, another kind of surplus. The past half-century has seen the number of hours in a working day in business and industry almost halved. One result has been that millions of the beneficiaries of this largesse do not know what to do with their new-found leisure time except "kill" it. Nor should this be surprising, since American education has, by and large, been devoted more to preparing us for making a

[17] Dael Wolfle, "Education and New Approaches to Manpower," *Teachers College Record*, Vol. 57 (February 1956), p. 291.
[18] Carskadon, *op. cit.*, p. 12.

living than to helping us to learn how to make a life. Thus, in our assiduous attention to the mastery of facts and in our ardor for the promotion of material success, we run the danger of neglecting the precious, humanizing "things of the spirit." [19]

Again, this would seem to call for attention on the part of those concerned with curriculum objectives and content. How should our educational program today and tomorrow differ from what it was when the 60-to-70-hour week prevailed? Do the more ascetic, intensified educational programs endorsed by some of education's critics provide our answer? Do these particular cultural changes raise questions as to what should be considered "essentials" of a sound contemporary program of education? What ingredients of an educational program can best help our pupils to learn how to use leisure most constructively? And for that matter, how do we define "worthy use of leisure," about which we have talked so glibly for the past three decades? What is the role of the schools in the learning and development of cultural values? The answers to these questions—or lack of them—are bound to have an impact on American society in the generations ahead.

The Family of Man

The opening of the earth's Pandora's box of energy sources with the key of scientific inquiry has had all kinds of unforeseen circumstances. Not the least important among these have been the development of a new, closer sense of community on the part of the diverse peoples of the world, and the hosts of problems which their increased interrelationships have spawned. Developments in communications make it possible to link almost any spot on earth with any other with practically the speed of light. Transportation developments make it possible to commute across oceans and continents. As one wag put it, "In the space of one day you can now have breakfast in London, lunch in New York, and indigestion in Los Angeles."

[19] See, for example, Joseph Wood Krutch, *Human Nature and the Human Condition* (New York: Random House, 1959); K. G. Saiyidain, *Education and the Art of Living*, The Julius and Rosa Sachs Endowment Fund Lectures (New York: Bureau of Publications, Teachers College, Columbia University, 1959).

The United States has been catapulted, willy-nilly, into a position of leadership in this world community. Whereas fifty years ago we were supremely unconcerned with the destinies of the peoples of the eastern and southern hemispheres, today we find that our lives may be profoundly altered, or even threatened, because of events in Tibet, in Laos, or in obscure tiny islands in the China Sea that we never before knew existed. With the emergence of regional and world political organization, Americans find themselves in role-conflict. To what degree can one be a "world citizen" without compromising one's national loyalty? How much responsibility should we assume for the buttressing of economies in far-off lands whose names we don't even know how to pronounce? What should be taught about the United Nations organization? Indeed, is teaching about the United Nations and UNESCO in our public schools a "subversive" practice, as a Los Angeles board of education implied? What kind of curriculum is best suited to the development of that international understanding so desperately required of Americans in this momentous period of the world's history? What should we be teaching about sovereignty, race, prejudice? Can history be so taught that our people can learn its lessons before it is too late for America? The dramatic change in the international picture in the past two generations demands significant curriculum changes. To ignore or to misconstrue this demand could be fatal for our nation's future.

Education—Threat or Promise?

H. G. Wells reports Stalin once to have said, "Education is a weapon, whose effect depends upon who holds it in his hand, and at whom it is aimed." Events today are grimly illustrative of this statement. Prior to the end of World War II, Americans were prone to think of education primarily as a necessity for citizenship and for making a living; and at its advanced levels, in some degree as a luxury and perhaps an adornment. Since the launching of the first earth satellite, all that has changed. In the minds of large numbers today, education is a weapon in the cold war. We are frantically adjured to raise standards and increase educational efficiency so that we may not be outstripped by the U.S.S.R. in scientific and technological achievement. In the onrushing Soviet economy we fear not only the eclipse of our world leadership, but even subjection to Soviet totalitarian arms and rule. In questioning why the Russians forestalled us in launching the first satellite, in launching the first successful moon shot, in outstripping us in intercontinental ballistic missiles, critics have found the schools a convenient scapegoat.

Certainly our leap into the space age is a historical turning point. It is a logical outcome of the new revolution previously referred to. As such, it underlines the expanding need for technically trained manpower, the need for a different look at the heavens in our educational program. But above all, it emphasizes the requirement for an education which will help our children to learn how to live in constructive amity with their no longer distant neighbors of other lands.

The foregoing is admittedly a cavalier treatment of the cultural mandates for change. We have tried to do no more than to call attention to some of the forces which have been—and are—at work in our culture, which call for some reorientation in the curriculum of our public schools. Most of these are implications for curriculum content, as distinguished from method (though it is fully recognized that method provides a kind of content itself). What the implications are will have to be decided by curriculum workers themselves. This is no easy task. Perhaps the words of Benjamin Franklin, in a letter written over two centuries ago still have pertinence today.

> As to their studies, it would be well if they were taught everything that is useful and everything that is ornamental. But art is long and time is short. It is therefore proposed that they learn those things that are likely to be *most* useful and *most* ornamental, regard being had for the several professions for which they are intended.

INSIGHTS FROM RESEARCH
IN THE BEHAVIORAL SCIENCES

Whereas cultural changes have implications primarily for the objectives and content of the educational program, curriculum organization and instructional method are affected more by research findings in the behavioral sciences. Cultural anthropology, sociology and the various fields of psychology have provided us with invaluable insights into the dynamics of human behavior. The full impact of these findings has yet to be felt in our schools.

We have learned, for example, that "human nature" is not the same for all humans, but that it is acquisitive or thriftless, enterprising or indolent, warlike or pacific, competitive or cooperative, dour or gay, depending on the living conditions and cultural mandates of the society in which it develops. In other words, "human nature" is acquired, and its most important determinants are the components of the cultural environment in which it develops. Hence, it is educable, and becomes, partially at least, a responsibility of the schools. One student of the behavioral sciences considers this to be the *principal* function of education: "We conclude that the function of education should be principally to help the individual realize his potentialities for being a healthy human being, that is to say, one who is able to relate himself in a harmonic and creative manner to others." [20]

How, then, should we educate human nature in our schools? What kind of curriculum will help develop more humane human beings? How should we go about curriculum development so as to enhance the achievement of appropriate goals and understandings in school classrooms? These questions gain in importance from our growing understanding of the implications of the fact that we learn what we do. Hence, the process by which we educate is also in a very real sense content; i.e., if we would teach humanity, we must teach in a humane manner. More than that, the learners must themselves have experiences in humane behavior, which would then be part of the curriculum.

From psychology we have gained further insights into the nature of learning. The Cartesian theory of the dichotomy of mind and body has been discredited, as has the related theory of mind as an aggregate of discrete faculties which, like muscles, could be strengthened (i.e., disciplined) by appropriately rigorous exercise in designated areas of study, which were accordingly called "disciplines." The fallacy of the correlative theory of the transfer of training has also been demonstrated. Yet there are many in

[20] Ashley Montagu, "Behavior as Viewed in the Behavioral Sciences and by American Education," *Teachers College Record*, Vol. 60 (May 1959), pp. 447–48.

education who continue to operate on the theory that the function of education is mind training.

In addition to correcting the misconceptions of prescientific formulations, psychological research has clearly demonstrated a number of other generalizations about human learning. The fact of the limitless variation in individual differences has been overwhelmingly documented. While we know this "intellectually," few would deny that we have fallen far short of developing an educational program suited to these differences, and well designed to enhance to the utmost those differences which are desirable.

Changes have already taken place in education in recognition of psychology's revelation of the role of motivation. In a real sense it can be said that children learn only that which they want to learn. We have far to go in devising a currriculum and method consonant with this fact. How best can we capitalize the needs and interests that children bring with them to school? How best can we use these to open doors to other inviting vistas of interests? How can we help children catch the excitement of learning about the multitude of fascinating things there are to learn, so that an active and intense desire to learn more extends throughout their lives? All too often, schooling results in an aversion to learning, so that the chief learning that results is skill in how to avoid learning and our students become skilled in incompetence. What do the answers to these questions mean for educational planning and practice?

Closely interrelated with motivation is the role of emotions in learning. We know that scholastic performance, for example, is determined only in small part by children's ability as indicated by ability tests. Their aspirations, fears, hopes, anxieties, aversions, preconceptions, affections and other emotional ingredients strongly affect their learning in school. Montagu strongly underlines this:

> I read all the relevant evidence as indicating that the satisfaction of the organism's need to love and to be loved is the key which opens all doors to its healthy development.[21]

These few are but illustrative of the findings about human nature and learning which are the products of scientific inquiry during this century. There is no questioning the fact that their

21 Montagu, *op. cit.*, p. 447.

implications are largely unrealized as yet in the classrooms of our schools. It seems obvious that such findings constitute clear mandates for change in our educational programs.

THE VOICE OF THE CRITIC

Perhaps the most clearly evident demands for change in education are those made by vocal critics of education, both friendly and hostile. While these do not constitute fundamental change mandates such as those discussed previously in this chapter, they are often reflections of cultural stresses. As such, they deserve careful assessment by educators.

Any such assessment will take into account the validity of the different criticisms of the schools, and the qualifications and possible motives of those making them. Some are patently ridiculous and irresponsible. It has been charged, for example, that educators are banded together in one vast subversive plot to poison or "capture" the minds of America's children.[22]

Others who have attacked the competence of educators and the quality of education in the schools have walked the shadow-line of irresponsibility, professing sincere concern for good education, but sprinkling their diatribes with half-truths, quotations out of context, and statistics that are misconstrued so as to seem to support untrue allegations.[23] Finally, there are those critics with no axe to grind but their sincere interest in the education of America's children. Their proposals have been both constructive and provocative.[24]

[22] For examples see Irene C. Kuhn, "Your Child Is Their Target," *American Legion Magazine*, June 1952; E. Merrill Root, *Brainwashing in the High Schools* (New York: Devin-Adair Company, 1958); and Representative John T. Wood (Idaho), "The Greatest Subversive Plot in History," *Congressional Record*, Vol. 97, Part 15 (82d Congress, 1st session), pp. 6550–52.

[23] As examples, see Arthur Bestor, "We Are Less Educated Than 50 Years Ago," *U.S. News & World Report*, November 30, 1956, p. 68; Rudolf Flesch, *Why Johnny Can't Read* (New York: Harper and Brothers, 1955); Albert Lynd, *Quackery in the Public Schools* (Boston: Little, Brown and Company, 1953).

[24] See, for example, James B. Conant, *The American High School Today* (New York: McGraw-Hill Book Company, Inc., 1959); Fred M. Hechinger, *An Adventure in Education* (New York: The Macmillan Company, 1956); Paul Woodring, *A Fourth of a Nation* (New York: McGraw-Hill Book Company, Inc., 1957); The President's Science Advisory Committee, "Education for the Age of Science" (Washington, D.C.: Government Printing Office, 1959).

From the barrage of criticism which has beset the public schools in the years following World War II, it is possible to cull a number which have significance for the curriculum worker. It will be obvious to the reader that the issues raised are intimately related to the social changes discussed elsewhere in this chapter. There seem to be four major categories of such criticisms and proposals.

1. *We are neglecting the individual.* Some of the critics look at this problem in proper perspective, but most of them focus their concern only on those individuals who are termed "gifted" or "talented." Extensive testing programs are proposed for the identification of school children of outstanding ability. There has been a recent upsurge of attention to the necessity for guidance of these children at the high school level, so that they may be steered into appropriate vocational channels. Various schemes have been put forward for the special grouping of such children— in special sections, special classes or in special schools. The more thoughtful critics have recognized (along with many professional educators) that the problem of the gifted is but a special case of the problem of how to help every individual realize his potential in the mass education system of a mass culture. Certainly this is a problem to challenge the ingenuity of all educators, and particularly those responsible for developing a curriculum appropriate to our world in the days ahead.

2. *We are not maintaining educational standards.* In a sense, most of the criticisms add up to the claim that our schools fail to maintain standards. Allegations are made that the schools are not educating as well as did those of former generations and that a high school diploma no longer attests to anything but twelve years spent in school classrooms. More responsible critics refuse to waste their time and that of the public on such barren and sensation-seeking charges. Rather, they charge that the existing educational program, while perhaps better in some respects than in former years, still fails to challenge children's abilities sufficiently. Some critics then go on to make constructive proposals for improvement. These proposals deserve careful appraisal, for they frequently raise questions of fundamental philosophy and policy in American education.

To some, improvement in education means "raising academic standards." A good example of how simple the problem can seem to one who apparently knows little about education is this quotation:

> All that basically needs to be done, therefore, is to put the emphasis back on the teaching of subjects. This means raising scholastic standards, strengthening curricula, eliminating most of the frills, requiring discipline, and permitting students to advance at the rate of their ability rather than according to arbitrary formulas.[25]

Frequently coupled with such criticism is the charge that the contemporary educational program is "soft." It is claimed that we spend too much time on activities of minor educational significance and too little on the training of the intellect. In an approach reminiscent of the now discredited belief in the dualism of mind and body, and the related theories of mental discipline, faculty psychology, and transfer of training, some critics urge that we place more emphasis on the "basic intellectual disciplines" of English, mathematics, science, history, and foreign languages. The curriculum should thus be "toughened up"; more homework should be required; and all children should be held to the same high standards in the basic subjects. In the present cold-war context it often appears that children are regarded as weapons in that war. Perhaps we should rechristen the primary grades "the infantry."

A number of highly respected voices have been heard in the controversy. Conant, for instance, suggests that in our high schools we do away with "clearly defined and labeled tracks such as 'college preparatory,' 'vocational,' 'commercial,'" and build a completely individualized program for each student. He proposes that students be grouped by ability, subject by subject, that the "academically talented" be held to a rigorous required program, that the top 3 per cent be given a special program, perhaps through tutorial work or special grouping, and that special help, particularly in reading, be given retarded students.[26] The Science Advisory Committee, established by President Eisenhower, urged that our schools foster and reward intellectual excellence by strengthening the teaching staff, doing away with "automatic pro-

[25] Editorial in *The Wall Street Journal*, March 19, 1958.
[26] James B. Conant, *op. cit.*

motion," updating textbooks, and reducing emphasis on "personal adjustment courses." [27]

A few of the suggestions seem to hint at a measure of federal control of the curriculum. Hechinger proposes a National Board of Education Advisers, to be appointed by the President of the United States, to set national minimum standards,[28] and Rickover advocates a privately financed national council of scholars, charged with establishing a national standard for the high school diploma and for "scholastic competence of teachers." [29] It has also been proposed that we establish a system of national tests as a means of unifying and upgrading standards of educational performance. All these proposals need to be examined critically for their consistency with American educational objectives and with our national philosophy, insofar as one may be said to exist. Furthermore, the experienced worker in the educational vineyard knows that the improvement of the excellence of instruction, and its consequent enhancement of learning, is a painstaking social process of changing human behavior, and one to which there is no attractively simple solution through the use of "gimmicks."

3. *We are not putting priorities on the most important learnings.* Throughout the criticisms of education of the past generation has run a persistent complaint to the effect that educators are neglecting the "fundamentals." The definition of just what these fundamentals are tends to vary from critic to critic, although by far the great majority tend to refer to reading, writing, and arithmetic. With the advent of the "Sputnik hysteria" has come a new definition of "fundamentals" in many quarters. Some maintain that modern foreign languages are now indispensable at both the elementary and secondary school levels. Others make a strong case for greater stress on mathematics and science at the secondary level. Conant, for example, deems it desirable that "academically talented" students be required to take four years of mathematics and four years of a foreign language. Others would require four years of history, or four years of science, and this in addition to the usual requirement of four years of English. With

[27] The President's Science Advisory Committee, *op. cit.*

[28] Fred M. Hechinger, *The Big Red Schoolhouse* (Garden City, New York: Doubleday and Company, Inc., 1959), pp. 207–08.

[29] Hyman G. Rickover, *Education and Freedom* (New York: E. P. Dutton and Company, 1959), pp. 218–20.

a "life is real, life is earnest" attitude, therefore, such critics would have us approach education grimly as a weapon in the cold war, or as a harsh and Spartan preparation for the grim vicissitudes and savage competition of a stern, ungraceful life.

Still another group deplores such a utilitarian approach (insisting that this is what educators mean when they refer to "pragmatism"), and wistfully lament the neglect of the humanities in American education. Critics such as Barzun, for example, claim that great literature, art, and music get short shrift in today's schools and colleges, being shouldered aside by studies more clearly suited to improving our national productivity, or to helping us best Russia in the technological race to oblivion.[30]

4. *We are not using the most effective forms of organization and instruction.* Finally, there are those critics who have put forward proposals relating primarily to the organization and methods of instruction in our schools. Woodring, for example, proposes a complete reorganization of education.[31] He would establish a three-year ungraded primary school; a four-year elementary school in which there would be little or no "grade failure"; ability grouping by subject in high school; elimination of specialization in the liberal arts college; and graduate schools to prepare for professional specializations. Another group proposes a reorganization of instruction in high schools. They would have students spend about 40 per cent of their time in large-class groups of 100 or more, another 40 per cent in individual study, and 20 per cent in discussion groups of 12 to 15 students in which the teacher would act as "counselor, consultant, and evaluator."[32] Stoddard proposes a "dual progress plan for elementary schools," which appears to be a combination of the old platoon plan, ability grouping and departmentalization at the elementary school level.[33] A number of sources, notably the Fund for the Advancement of Education, propose experimentation with instruction by television for large groups of children. The utilization of nonprofessionally trained

[30] Jacques Barzun, "The Educated Man," *Life* magazine, October 16, 1950.
[31] Paul Woodring, *op. cit.*
[32] J. Lloyd Trump, *Images of the Future* (Urbana, Ill.: Commission on the Experimental Study of Utilization of Staff in the Secondary School, 1959).
[33] New York University, Experimental Teaching Center, *Answers to Basic Questions on the Cooperative Study of the Dual Progress Plan* (New York: The Center, 1959).

teacher aides has been tried in Bay City, Michigan, and a few other places.

These and other proposals for modifications in our instructional organization and methodology are illustrative of the current ferment in education, brought about by the concatenation of forces such as those discussed in this chapter. In rounding out our discussion of demands for change, it may be helpful to identify some of the issues around which the controversy seems to center. It seems safe to say that the future course of American education will be determined in large part by the way in which they are resolved.

1. *Shall the schools place their greatest emphasis on social adjustment, or upon intellectual development?* This issue is highlighted by the criticisms of Bestor and Rickover, and by the report of the Rockefeller Brothers Fund.[34] Those concerned with curriculum development will make decisions which will determine the balance between these two points of view. This raises the question of what we consider to be the primary objectives of American education, and what we consider to be a sound psychology of learning. To raise this issue is not to imply that our emphasis should be entirely upon one or another of the objectives; rather, it is to suggest that we need to seek a sensible balance between the "practical" and the "cultural," between the sciences and the humanities, between education for making a living and education for making a life.

2. *Shall the schools organize so as to emphasize the interrelationships between and among the fields of knowledge and facilitate integration in the learning of them, or shall we organize to teach the various "disciplines" (i.e., subjects) separately?* For the past three decades, we have been moving toward "fused," "broad fields," "areas of living," and "core" types of organization of subject matter for learning. Problem-centered "units" have been advocated, and have been employed extensively at the elementary school level.

[34] See Arthur E. Bestor, *The Restoration of Learning* (New York: Alfred A. Knopf, 1956); Hyman G. Rickover, *op. cit.*; Rockefeller Brothers Fund, *The Pursuit of Excellence* (Garden City, N.Y.: Doubleday and Company, Inc., 1958).

A number of the current proposals suggest returning to some form of departmental organization in elementary schools. Here again, the answer arrived at by curriculum workers will depend on the educational objectives they consider to be paramount, and their conception of the learning process.

3. *Shall the schools concentrate on a curriculum of basic, relatively unchanging subject matter, or shall we continue to make significant curriculum changes designed to adapt education to a rapidly changing world?* While some of the participants in the contemporary educational controversy seem to state the issue in terms of these extremes, most curriculum workers will probably reject such an either/or approach. The issue is essentially a problem of perspective. In the long sweep of human existence—past, present, and conjectural future—what learnings are of paramount importance? What objectives, emphases, specific contents of the curriculum have become obsolete? What is still relevant and valid? What new ingredients or perspectives are necessitated by the revolutionary changes of our generation? This is as much a cultural question as it is an educational one, for our cultural choices as to what we hold most dear in life must inevitably leave their imprint on educational goals and content.[35]

4. *Shall all the schools adopt the same goals and the same curriculum, or shall there continue to be freedom to adapt goals and curriculum to local needs and conditions?* Proposals for a uniform national curriculum were mentioned earlier in this chapter. The same problem faces curriculum workers in school systems in another form: how much should the curriculum be permitted or encouraged to vary within a given school system? This is but another dimension of the problem posed in issue Number 3, above. Again, the manner in which this issue is resolved will depend on one's social and educational philosophy. It is related to the growing pressures toward conformity in today's world, to the question of whether or not we wish a strongly centralized

---

[35] Arthur W. Foshay, "Choice of Content," *Educational Leadership,* Vol. 14 (March 1956), pp. 340–43; Harold J. McNally, "What Shall We Teach, and How?" *National Elementary Principal,* Vol. 36 (May 1957), pp. 6–11.

society, and to conceptions of what learning is and how it takes place.

5. *Who shall make the curriculum?*   Underlying all the afore-mentioned issues is the question of who shall make the important decisions which determine the curriculum. From the many suggestions concerning how curriculum goals, content, and organization should be decided we can identify five different agencies, each of which is implied by someone to be the proper source of curriculum decisions: government; great foundations; liberal arts college professors; committees of laymen; and professional educators. We have already mentioned proposals which suggest that the federal government, in some manner or other, should establish a national curriculum and national standards of achievement. There are more subtle ways in which the federal government may control or strongly influence curriculum decisions. Cases in point are the Hatch Act and subsequent related acts, which exerted a strong influence on the internal programs of land-grant colleges; the Smith-Hughes Act and subsequent related acts, which brought about markedly expanded programs of vocational education in secondary schools; and the recently enacted National Defense Education Act, which provides strong encouragement for greater emphasis on certain segments of the curriculum through federal subsidy of programs in these subject areas.

Great philanthropic foundations have recently committed many millions of dollars to the advancement of their particular educational points of view.[36] Such groups have made definite and strongly worded proposals in the realms of teacher education and utilization, curriculum content and organization, school organization, teaching methods, and educational standards. Their prestige has won their proposals wide hearing, and they undoubtedly have had considerable impact on the program and operation of many schools. Corey's statement typifies the reaction of many professional educators to the activities of some of the foundations.[37]

[36] See, for example, The Rockefeller Brothers Fund, *op. cit.;* Alexander J. Stoddard, *op. cit.;* J. Lloyd Trump, *op. cit.*

[37] Stephen M. Corey, "Foundations and School Experimentation," *Educational Leadership,* Vol. 17 (December 1959), pp. 134–36.

Some college professors have been outspoken with respect to what they think we should be teaching, and how. Bestor and Conant are two studies in contrast from among this group.[38] In addition, it should also be noted that the college professor who authors textbooks used in the public schools influences to a very real degree what the children in classes using his textbook shall learn.

A fourth source of pressures influencing educational decisions is committees of laymen. The National Citizens' Commission for the Public Schools (recently disbanded) reported that in 1949 they knew of but seventeen state and local citizens' committees specifically concerned with schools. By May of 1959 this number had risen to 18,000.[39] Some of these have been groups appointed by, and working harmoniously with, boards of education, primarily in an advisory capacity. Some groups have operated independently as pressure groups on the board of education and school personnel. Still other groups have exerted pressure from the standpoint of some special interest, such as taxpayer groups, and groups of superpatriots. Functioning in a great variety of ways, they have often pressed their demands on local school boards and educators with respect to curriculum content.

Among all these pressures, the professional educator may well wonder what his role should be in deciding what should be taught. It can easily be seen that this is not as simple a question as it might appear at first blush. It is a question to which the answer will depend largely on which definition of "curriculum" we adopt. As this is dealt with in Chapter 3, we need not dwell on it here.

It is the view of the authors that decisions concerning the nature, content, and organization of the curriculum are properly matters for professional educators to decide. This is not to deny that laymen, as individuals and as independent groups, may have significant and extensive roles to play in assisting educators in establishing educational objectives, in making curriculum decisions, and in helping boards of education to develop sound policies. For curriculum develop-

---

[38] Cf. Bestor, *op. cit.*, and Conant, *op. cit.*
[39] *Better Schools*, May 1959.

ment is a many-faceted process. It takes place as parents confer with teachers, as parents assist teachers in classrooms and on field trips, in child-study groups, in PTA meetings and in workshops, as well as in organized curriculum development programs. Laymen can and should be enlisted to assist professionals when their particular resource is pertinent to the problem at hand. To accomplish this, public participation should be organized in what Collins and Brickell term "orderly patterns." [40] However, no group of laymen can usurp the policy-making prerogatives of the board of education. Further, it seems reasonable to maintain that, once the board of education has enunciated the major outcomes the community expects of its schools, and the policies governing the school system's operation, the decisions concerning curriculum content, organization, evaluation, and instructional method are properly the province of professional educators. Laymen may be invited to advise and assist in these decisions, but professionals should make them, and should be responsible for them.[41]

The reader will recognize that this is by no means an exhaustive listing of the issues in education; it is simply a statement of some issues the authors consider to be pertinent to the problem of curriculum development and to the task of improving the quality of education in our schools. They are important issues, and the manner of their resolution will affect the nature of American education in the critical years ahead. Hence, it behooves the educator to clarify his position on them, and to act upon it.

One is reminded of the perhaps apocryphal story told of Gertrude Stein as she lay on her deathbed. Looking into the faces of those gathered around her, she asked, "What are the answers?" Receiving no response, she smiled faintly and said, "Well, then, what are the questions?" With a knowledge of significant cultural changes, of significant findings from the behavioral sciences, and of criticisms and proposals related to education being made

[40] Raymond L. Collins and Henry M. Brickell, "Helping the Public Participate in Curriculum Development," *Educational Leadership,* Vol. 15 (April 1958), pp. 415–18.

[41] See Myron Lieberman, *Education as a Profession* (Englewood Cliffs, N.J.: Prentice-Hall, Inc., 1956), particularly Chapter 4, for a provocative but stronger position on professional autonomy than we would concur in.

by responsible members of our society, the curriculum worker is prepared to help those working with him to formulate the curriculum questions to which they should address themselves.

SELECTED READINGS

ALCORN, MARVIN D. and LINLEY, JAMES M., *Issues in Curriculum Development.* Yonkers-on-Hudson, New York: World Book Company, 1954.

ASSOCIATION FOR SUPERVISION AND CURRICULUM DEVELOPMENT, *Forces Affecting American Education.* Washington, D.C.: National Education Association, 1953.

————, *What Shall the High School Teach?* Washington, D.C.: National Education Association, 1956.

CONANT, JAMES B., *Education in a Divided World.* Cambridge, Mass.: Harvard University Press, 1949.

DEPARTMENT OF ELEMENTARY SCHOOL PRINCIPALS, *Contemporary Society: Background for the Instructional Program.* Washington, D.C.: National Education Association, 1957.

"Educational Leadership for a Free World," *Teachers College Record,* Vol. 57: 271–337, 347–424, February and March 1956.

EDUCATIONAL POLICIES COMMISSION, *Manpower and Education.* Washington, D.C.: National Education Association, 1956.

EHLERS, HENRY and LEE, GORDON C., ed., *Crucial Issues in Education* (rev. ed.). New York: Henry Holt and Company, 1959.

KANDEL, I. L., *American Education in the Twentieth Century.* Cambridge, Mass.: Harvard University Press, 1957.

"Ten Criticisms of Public Education," *NEA Research Bulletin,* 35: 131–74, December 1957.

SAYLOR, J. GALEN and ALEXANDER, WILLIAM M., *Curriculum Planning for Better Teaching and Learning.* New York: Rinehart and Company, 1954.

SCOTT, C. WINFIELD, *The Great Debate; Our Schools in Crisis.* Englewood Cliffs, N.J.: Prentice-Hall, Inc., 1959.

SMITH, B. O., STANLEY, WILLIAM O., and SHORES, J. H., *Fundamentals of Curriculum Development* (rev. ed.). Yonkers-on-Hudson: World Book Company, 1957.

STRATEMEYER, FLORENCE B., FORKNER, HAMDEN L., McKIM, MARGARET, and PASSOW, A. HARRY, *Developing a Curriculum for Modern Living* (2d ed. rev.). New York: Bureau of Publications, Teachers College, Columbia University, 1957.

SYMONDS, PERCIVAL M., *What Education Has to Learn from Psychology.* New York: Bureau of Publications, Teachers College, Columbia University, 1958.

2

THE PROCESS OF IMPROVING
THE CURRICULUM

SINCE their beginnings, American schools have been exposed to recurring reappraisals and constant program modification. The current reevaluations had their counterparts in yesteryears. But the urgency of the present, together with new means of communication, has made the quality of education an agitating topic of national concern. Always reflecting and influencing the society which maintains them, the schools have reacted—sometimes rapidly, but more often slowly—to new conditions and requirements. Change has been a prominent feature of American schools, an integral part of a unique educational system.

In the mid-eighteenth century, Franklin's plan for the academy represented one of the earliest proposals for major curriculum change. Modern languages, English, history, and natural sciences were to be added to the curriculum of the Latin grammar school, a school patterned on the traditional English plan. Since then, educational reformers—some of them visionary and influential—have criticized existing programs and practices and have set forth proposals for change. Much more recent is the systematic organization all good schools maintain today for continuous curriculum study and revision. The idea that the process of curriculum improvement might itself be studied to better the empirical activities is a notion scarcely four decades old.[1]

When the curriculum is perceived as all those experiences which children and youth have under the school's jurisdiction, then curriculum improvement may involve any of the many dimensions of the educational process influencing the nature and quality of these experiences. Curriculum modifications in America have ranged from the development of a new institution (such as the academy and, later, the high school) to the rewriting of a textbook. Administrative arrangements, content, methods, instructional materials, class organization, school services—all have been modified in various ways to raise educational quality and to provide more appropriate learning. The processes by which these modifications have been brought about have been diverse. The evolution of planned programs for curriculum development began slowly but accelerated rapidly after World War I.

EARLY CURRICULUM IMPROVEMENT EFFORTS

From the period of the common-school revival to the close of World War I, the curriculum in American schools changed greatly. The changes were, however, frequently piecemeal and haphazard. The resulting curriculum was characterized by one observer as "the amorphous product of generations of tinkering." The patchwork of courses—fragmented and disjointed, crowded and full—had evolved from a process described as the "scissors and pastepot" approach to curriculum building. New subjects were introduced and new topics added to existing courses, usually without consideration of the curriculum as a whole. The conception of the curriculum as a collection of subjects guided the approaches used to improve programs generally. There were a few individual reformers who saw the educational program whole but the textbook writers preparing publications in a single subject area had the last word.

[1] The first book dealing with the curriculum in comprehensive terms was published in 1918. See J. F. Bobbitt, *The Curriculum* (Boston: Houghton Mifflin Company, 1918). The National Society for the Study of Education yearbook in 1927 was another pioneer publication. See Twenty-sixth *Yearbook*, Part I—"Curriculum-making: Past and Present"; Part II—"The Foundations of Curriculum-making" (Chicago: The Society, 1927).

It was the textbook writers who, by their selection and arrangement of content, both influenced and created the curriculum of the schools from the time of graded classes in the 1840s. Where the lawmakers fixed the subjects to be taught, the textbook writers prescribed the lessons in these subjects. When new subjects were introduced, the publishers produced the necessary textbooks. Even when courses of study and syllabi appeared later in the nineteenth century, these tended to follow the content in available textbooks rather than vice versa. One obvious means of curriculum improvement was the production of better textbooks.

Increasing numbers of students had necessitated the graded school. Various administrative reforms were tailored to the instructional problems which arose from the growing heterogeneity and size of the student population. In 1867, for example, the St. Louis public schools initiated a program of accelerated promotion for rapid learners; this was soon followed by other administrative modifications in schools from Cambridge, Massachusetts, to Santa Barbara, California.[2] Administrative changes constituted another means of curriculum change through alteration of the conditions for teaching and learning.

Another avenue for upgrading instruction was the teachers' institutes. Designed as antidotes to substandard training, the institutes offered regularly organized classes in varied subjects. By the end of the nineteenth century, the institutes had become embedded in legislation and had assumed a structure which no longer met the needs of the times. They were now following the same forms even though the teachers were coming to them differently prepared and needing different kinds of help. The institutes were the forerunners of many present in-service programs, particularly where the purposes were gradually modified to meet new purposes and new demands.

Toward the end of the nineteenth century, courses of study began to appear in the larger cities and some of the states. Most of the early issues were prepared by the superintendent himself or by members of his staff under his immediate direction. Gradually, small committees composed of selected subject specialists,

---

[2] An account of these developments may be found in the Twenty-third *Yearbook* of the National Society for the Study of Education, Part I—"The Education of Gifted Children" (Chicago: The Society, 1924).

supervisory and administrative staff, and a few teachers became the channels for producing and altering courses of study.

The 1890s saw the beginnings of what has since been described as a "generation of curriculum making by national committees." Diversity had become a characteristic of America's schools and the first efforts were directed at bringing about greater order and uniformity. The Committee of Ten (on secondary education) and the Committee of Fifteen (on elementary education) in 1893 were among the first of the national committees to exert considerable influence—directly and indirectly—on the development of school curricula. The committee members, primarily college professors and school superintendents, made rather specific recommendations for the content and organization of elementary and secondary curricula in terms of the subjects to be taught and studied. The pattern which grew out of the national committee reports was the revision of courses of study and the publication of new or revised textbooks to fit the pronouncements.

The national committees were probably the dominant influence, but other streams of activities affected program development. Laboratory schools at the University of Chicago and Columbia University's Teachers College were but two of the important centers for experimentation with new teaching approaches and instructional materials. By 1910 research methods were being applied by psychologists and psychometricians to the study of grade placement of content; to the development of tests for student evaluation; and to the topical arrangement of textbooks. The school survey, an external appraisal of a local or state program, had become a popular procedure widely used by large-city school systems.

Until the close of World War I, the major influences on curriculum-making were largely outside the local school system. The national committees, the textbook writers, the college professors and university researchers, the school survey and laboratory school personnel—all made recommendations which determined, to a greater or lesser extent, local practice. At the local level, the courses of study were prepared by a select few central office administrators or heads of departments; they decided which subjects were to be added or modified and which textbooks would be adopted and used in the classroom. In a few exceptional systems instructional committees did include classroom teachers who were either subject specialists or persons who might facilitate the use of a committee's finished product. In most instances, a product of some kind—syllabus, guide, book, report, test—was seen as the end goal of curriculum activity.

These early efforts and the practices which developed at the time were not without effect. In fact, some practices laid the groundwork for the modern curriculum movement in which the local school system plays the lead role. Supervisory practices were evolving which resulted in this function becoming increasingly important in program development. The supervisor's duties evolved slowly from assisting the superintendent discharge his responsibilities to stimulating new trends in instructional improvement. Supervisors tended to be head teachers who, relieved of classroom responsibilities, assisted in program development in their particular areas of subject specialization. As the supervisory organization unfolded, various devices were introduced to improve instruction. After brief outlines of content came pamphlets detailing a variety of suggested activities and resources. Some of these substantial outlines were distributed widely to other school systems and a few were even published commercially. The role of the supervisor, still formative, varied from school to school. Supervisors inspected classes and rated teacher performance, gave demonstration lessons in the classroom, conducted teacher meetings to discuss techniques and materials, selected textbooks and other resources, and prepared or directed the preparation of courses of study and syllabi.

The courses of study were seen as the prime means by which the classroom performance of the teacher could be guided, the method by which teachers could know what should be taught and how. Faith in the written word was strong. In some instances, either directly or through supervisors, suggestions were solicited from teachers concerning the value of the materials included in the courses of study and these were made the basis for further revision. Through better prepared courses of study, it was expected that better instruction would result.

Until the close of World War I, classroom activities mirrored the courses of study that blocked out subjects with little or no consideration of the broad curriculum. The courses of study, together with the graded textbook—both influenced by national committee reports—set the general pattern as well as the day-by-day activities. As teacher education improved, some of the better classroom teachers were called in to advise the supervisory or administrative committees preparing courses of study. Eventually, the classroom teachers changed from advisers to writers. Curriculum improvement was viewed as the development of better outlines and courses of study to guide the teaching of each subject.

INITIATION OF COMPREHENSIVE PROGRAMS

There is seldom a point at which there is a sharp break with educational practices of the past. The close of World War I can, however, be marked as the time when modern curriculum development programs began. A number of factors combined to fashion a new approach to curriculum problems. The school as a whole and as a social force was being considered. For example, the statement in 1918 of the so-called "Cardinal Principles of Secondary Education" redefined the primary objectives of education in functional areas of health, family life, vocational preparation, leisure, citizenship, and ethical character. In this report, the relationship between school and society was explored, the traditional subject curriculum questioned, and the need for extensive revisions stated. Developments in educational psychology and in learning theory underscored the need for relating educational ends to educational means. As the nation, emerging from a war and embarking on a new era of industrial growth and societal change, took stock of its resources, so did educators reevaluate their tools and stock. Work on the entire curriculum was encouraged by these developments around 1920. Supervisors and administrators found that the courses of study were used neither extensively nor effectively by the classroom teachers. Old practices of curriculum construction were not suddenly discarded, of course, but different ones were initiated. Courses of study were still produced but there were changes in purpose and practice in their preparation. National committees continued to flourish and various philanthropic foundations (for example, the Commonwealth Fund, the Carnegie Corporation, the General Education Board) underwrote studies and investigations.

The Los Angeles program launched in 1922 was one of the first systemwide programs in which the entire curriculum was examined as a prelude to developing a comprehensive plan aimed at achieving a common, consistent direction. Denver and St. Louis initiated curriculum programs at this same time and, as in Los Angeles, used four significant practices: a large number of classroom teachers participated in the curriculum study; varied committees were used extensively; a director responsible for curriculum development was provided; and a curriculum specialist served as general consultant. Between 1922–1924, the Board of Education of the state of Connecticut made provision for a statewide curriculum development effort and the state of Virginia began work on major program revisions which involved thousands of teachers.

The currriculum movement spread rapidly and within the next decade curriculum construction and revision had become an accepted undertaking in all major school systems. The various programs differed in the procedures used and in the effectiveness of changes made, but some of their common characteristics branched away from earlier programs. Among these features were the following:

1. *A comprehensive approach to curriculum making.* Piecemeal revision, narrow and spasmodic, gave way to serious efforts to define over-all curriculum objectives and to integrate the various subjects. Assuring consistency of objectives, creating and stabilizing desirable interrelationships among and within separate aspects of pupil experiences, reinforcing learning through cumulative and unified activities—these problems required study of the educational program as a whole. They raised further questions concerning basic, continuing curriculum problems whose persistence still underscores the need for comprehensive efforts: determination of general and specific objectives, scope, and sequence; of appropriate learning activities; and of effective instructional materials. The concern for the total program as well as related parts has marked many twentieth-century curriculum building efforts.

2. *Extensive classroom teacher participation.* The recognition that courses of study and syllabi, prepared by administrators and supervisors for the most part, were not used effectively by teachers led to the inclusion of teacher representatives in course-of-study preparation and revision as a means of attracting other teachers

to the finished publication. Committee work grew into extensive involvement of teachers beyond the preparation of courses of study. In some of the earliest citywide programs, teachers were released from classroom duties to participate on long-term work committees. Whenever revised courses of study proved inadequate as a means of changing teaching practice, other avenues of curriculum improvement opened up. However, the importance of broadly based, intensive teacher participation was clearly and firmly established. In some of the first statewide programs, thousands of teachers engaged in committee work or in experimental use of developed materials.

3. *Wide and varied use of committee and group work.* The shift from production of courses of study by a small central office staff to widespread teacher activity led to the organization of committees. In many of the early programs, a series of committees were each assigned a specific task: steering or coordinating the over-all activities; relating possible contributions of the subject areas to the general objectives; producing instructional materials, applying them and evaluating their effectiveness. Curriculum-making acquired a somewhat rigid organization as schools followed the formula developed in the earliest of the modern program developments.

4. *Instructional materials diversified.* The limited effectiveness of the course of study; the improved preparation of teachers and their more widespread inclusion in curriculum-making activities; and the acquisition of insights into change itself gradually modified the nature and purpose of instructional materials. Although there was no reduction in the quantity of publications from the city and state school systems (these continued to run into the thousands annually), the role altered. Gradually, the courses of study came to be viewed as source materials for teachers— guides, not prescriptions. Resource units, curriculum bulletins, and supplementary materials of many kinds replaced or expanded the rigid courses of study.

5. *Leadership and responsibility specifically assigned.* The early citywide programs usually assigned responsibility for the direction and coordination of curriculum building to a member of the central office administrative staff. Outside specialists were employed as consultants. The curriculum theorist, the individual concerned with the theory of program design, worked hand in

hand with the school practitioner, the person responsible for the day-to-day activities at the local level. Some specialists provided guidance with the general plans, procedures, and organization of the curriculum program while others advised on some specific aspect of basic curriculum development or in a particular subject area. This welding of theory and practice extended the insights of all concerned.

6. *Curriculum change on a "broken front."* In some of the first comprehensive programs, it was assumed that change would take place simultaneously throughout the system once a new or revised course of study had been approved and published. There was far greater emphasis and reliance on production than on installation of new practices. This concept of the "uniform front," the expectation that all schools and all teachers would initiate a curriculum change at the same time, was soon modified and the concept of a "broken front" approach was introduced. The recognition that curriculum modifications have small beginnings and that change emerges as a jagged line of response to new ideas and needs taught curriculum makers to turn their attention to the process of curriculum making.

Some elements of the earlier curriculum programs have been altered as insights and experiences have multiplied. Although the modern curriculum development movement spread rapidly, its acceptance was by no means general. Nor did the growing organization of curriculum development programs wipe out the older institutions for revisions. Some critics viewed the curriculum-making efforts as "amateurish, trifling and a sheer waste of time—nay, worse than that, an injection of pernicious confusion into what should be orderly progress." [3] Some educators, viewing experimentation as futile do-it-yourself efforts, argued for the trained specialist to assume greater responsibility and more active leadership. Other critics ridiculed the ideas that a curriculum expert merited status or that study of the curriculum was legitimate, maintaining that only the subject specialists were qualified for curriculum construction. From weighing the relative importance of content and process in instruction, the debates continued into the area of curriculum development as well.

[3] Guy M. Whipple, "What Price Curriculum Making?" *School and Society,* Vol. 31 (March 15, 1930), p. 368.

The period at the close of World War I marked a time of major changes in the purposes and structure of American education. Clearly, a fundamental overhaul was called for and local school systems took increasing initiative in appraising and improving their educational programs. Certainly there were—and still are—waste, inefficiency, meaningless activity, and pointless change in local curriculum making. However, by and large, the responsibility for organized curriculum improvement programs has become accepted by most good school systems.

Characteristics common to the early programs of curriculum improvement represent foundation stones for current programs. One alteration has been the way local systems overshadow the influence of external forces. National committees, textbook writers, supervisors, and other curriculum-making instruments now play supporting, not lead roles, in local revision efforts. How to exhaust the possibilities of the varied resources is a continuing problem. Curriculum improvement today, as yesterday, is a complex task requiring steady and coordinated efforts at many different levels.

THE PROCESS OF CURRICULUM MAKING

The changes in the early curriculum programs seldom attained the quality their planners had sought. The administrative arrangements were carefully made, frequently with committee patterns elaborated from the central office. Typically, the superintendent appointed a steering committee of supervisors, administrators, and teachers to formulate general plans and coordinate activities. The steering committee selected personnel for other working committees. A philosophy committee, for example, determined the overall goals. These were then detailed by an objectives committee, which analyzed the purposes in terms of specific contributions from the various subject areas. Production committees then worked out new materials, courses of study, and resource guides, which were submitted to the steering committee for approval. Installation committees were supposed to familiarize teachers and principals with the nature and contents of new materials and to ensure their classroom use. Evaluation committees assessed the new manuals or aids and recommended revisions, alterations, or new areas for study.

These procedures, sometimes called "an administrative approach to curriculum building," yielded many publications, since this was the focus of committee efforts. They did not always bring about the desired changes in the classroom experiences of children and youth. This may have been because the bulk of teachers failed to obtain the experiences which could have extended their instructional competence. Paper changes did not necessarily change behavior. Where the administrative approach to curriculum change foundered was in failure to understand and apply sound learning principles affecting staff development. Some phases of school programs are altered with relative ease: a schedule, printed materials, new personnel, a testing program. More basic and elusive are fundamental changes in people and in the school as a social institution. Teachers tend to do what they consider best and what they know how to do best. Schools are organized in ways which the professional staff believes will lead to optimum learning. Far-reaching changes in curriculum require training in new techniques and attitudes if staff are to alter present behavior and move out into unsure ways of doing things.

Curriculum improvement has been described in many ways: as a social process; as the basic reeducation and reorientation of teachers; as the induction and control of changes in human relationships; as social or educational engineering; and as a redesign of the school as a social institution.[4] Common to all these contemporary analyses is the key position of the classroom teacher in effecting the kind and quality of learning experiences. The first corollary is the need for arrangements designed to induce change in the insights, understandings, attitudes, and relationships of the teacher.

Once curriculum workers had accepted the view that little real curriculum improvement occurs without continuous professional and personal growth of teachers, concern shifted from administrative structure to include the complexities of educating the professional staff. Research and experience in group dynamics, in leadership training, in social psychology, in learning theory, and

[4] For discussions of these views, see Alice M. Miel, *Changing the Curriculum* (New York: Appleton-Century-Crofts, 1946); Kenneth D. Benne and Bozidar Muntyan, *Human Relations in Curriculum Change* (New York: Dryden Press, 1951); B. Othanel Smith, William O. Stanley, and J. Harlan Shores, *Fundamentals of Curriculum Development* (Yonkers-on-Hudson, N.Y.: World Book Company, 1957).

in institutional change have been studied carefully for leads to upgrading curriculum. The process as well as the product has been studied. Process and product—means and ends—are intertwined in curriculum making as are content, method, and goals in all teaching and learning.

In this broadened conception, it is the teachers and students who, in the last analysis, determine what the curriculum actually is. Despite the host of factors and forces influencing the quality of learning, curriculum design draws its vitality from the insights, understandings, attitudes, perceptions, and skills of the teacher as a professional worker and as an individual. Guides, syllabi, and resource bulletins may be built, refined, and revised; but the degree to which their use corresponds to the purposes of the preparers depends on the understandings, enthusiasms, and skills of the classroom teacher. It is the spread of this point of view—that the curriculum can be changed only as the teacher himself changes—which has stirred interest in the process of curriculum improvement.

The parallels between the process of curriculum improvement and pupils' learning are provocative: process changes involve the acquisition of new perceptions, goals and aspirations, skills and understandings as much for the professional worker as for the student. Similarly, the environment for learning—the climate, setting, concerns, and pressures—affects curriculum improvement as it does student learning. In short, curriculum improvement is not a set of autonomous activities, compartmentalized and carried on in the abstract apart from the school program, aimed at improving the teaching-learning process from a distance. Rather, the process of curriculum development is an integral part of the educational program and closely tied to day-to-day instruction as well as long-range planning.

GENERAL CONSIDERATIONS IN CURRICULUM MAKING

The shift in emphasis from changes on paper to changes in people and the setting in which they function as the focus of curriculum making enlarges the dimensions of the problems. The cultural tone of a community, as well as opportunities for social service, may affect the personal and the professional growth of the teacher. When curriculum development encompasses all efforts and activities that enrich student learning experiences the field of program improvement obviously can be broad. The curriculum development programs of public schools, however, deal with those activities which are sponsored in some way and under the guidance of the school system—the regular and systematic activities as contrasted with the incidental and the haphazard. A great deal of professional growth takes place apart from the organized programs of instructional improvement of the school system and it is difficult to synchronize all the avenues and activities which have as their goal the building of better educational programs. However, it is the systematic activities initiated, sponsored, and directed by school authorities which are the main avenue to instructional improvement.

Organizational structure, personnel, techniques, procedures, leadership, and resources differ from system to system. However original the resulting patterns, some strands seem to be constant and common to the diverse improvement programs and practices of public school systems. These are discussed below.

Many schemes are employed for instructional improvement rather than a single crystallized approach. Variety in programs and activities indicates the multiple purposes sought. The immediate goal may range from preparing new publications to evaluating present instructional practices to testing new program proposals. Yet these ends are seen as means for changing the skills, values, relationships, and understandings of the staff—the key to improving the quality of learning experiences for students.

Although some aspects of program development are routine and recurring, others are unique. Textbook adoption or selection of films for the audio-visual library may be a periodic activity. An *ad hoc* committee is the probable channel to explore instructional possibilities of new communication media. Their work may open countless areas of study before decisions are reached on new policies and practices. Program evaluation may stem from a specific instructional problem or it may be a fixture in the year's schedule. Because education is a complicated, multidimensional process, curriculum development cannot be reduced to a simple, routinized procedure. The somewhat rigid committee structure of some earlier programs is too narrow a framework for all essential instructional improvement activities.

Although the end purposes are basically similar for different programs—i.e., improvement of educational experiences as a consequence of professional growth and system change—the spectrum of activities is broad. For example, the focus of a specific activity may be:

Task centered. A group may be assigned a specific, clearly defined task: prepare a science-teaching-materials exhibition; evaluate filmstrips for purchase; compile a report for the board of education. The source of origin of the task will vary and the work of the group will be directed toward completion of the assignment.

Problem or research centered. Using the methodology of identifying, sharpening, and probing to solve problems in an area, a group focuses on studying the education offerings for the gifted students; the effectiveness of arithmetic teaching in the intermediate grades; or the citizenship attitudes of students. While the area of study may be clearly delineated, the specific task is not and the group sets its own limits and duties.

Idea or policy centered. A group may evolve the statement of a philosophical position, a body of ideas, a policy, or clarified concepts. Agreeing on objectives for an elementary science program or preparing guidelines to the use of community resource personnel may lead to task-centered activities or to research: initially the focus is on thinking through ideas and formulating policies as guides to actions.

Skill centered. A group may work on the acquisition of skills required for teaching or other professional activity. Members may practice the skills under real or simulated conditions in order to attain competence and facility. Acquiring new techniques for teaching reading, presenting science demonstrations, or using art media—any of these may focus the group's operations.

General education centered. A group may aim to broaden the participants' cultural understandings or insights into critical issues or appreciation of aesthetics. Extending insights, understandings, and appreciations as part of the general educational development of the individual is a means for simultaneously enhancing his professional competence.[5]

[5] Adapted from Matthew B. Miles and A. Harry Passow, "Training in the Skills Needed for In-Service Programs," *In-Service Education for Teachers, Supervisors, and Administrators.* Fifty-sixth Yearbook of the National Society for the Study of Education, Part I (Chicago: The University of Chicago Press, 1957), p. 353.

In actual practice, of course, these foci are seldom so clear or discrete. Here, they clarify the varied purposes which call for varied approaches. Flexibility in program planning and employing personnel resources is essential.

The techniques and procedures used in curriculum development suit the different purposes or ends to be attained. The nature of activities aimed at improving the curriculum has altered considerably since the early days of the teachers' institutes and reading circles. Courses of many kinds—regular and summer school, extension, correspondence—continue to offer opportunities for teachers to extend their knowledge and competence. Some colleges and universities provide instruction for a particular school system or county group in response to specific requests from a teacher or administrative group. Modern workshops, first fashioned in their present form in the mid-1930s, have proved their value through frequent testing. Other procedures—clinics, conferences, research projects, study groups, seminars—have likewise proved their worth. Properly organized and staffed, each technique or procedure can contribute to suitable goals.

Many considerations enter into the selection of appropriate, individualized techniques and procedures for curriculum improvement. The specific ends to be attained, the foci of curriculum activity, the personnel to be involved, the leadership and resources available, and the potential influence of a particular procedure—all weigh upon the choice. Some procedures are most promising for skill development while others are more likely to yield a product of some kind.

Individual teachers contrast strongly in backgrounds, competencies, personalities, and many other factors. These individual differences—personal and professional—underlie the choice and outcomes of procedures for curriculum improvement. Because curriculum building is basically a learning process, the choice of effective tools for the process is no less critical here than in the classroom.

The spectrum of varied approaches to curriculum progress is examined in Chapter 4, as are some criteria for selection. No single procedure in a continuous program of curriculum improvement will fit all situations and attain all ends. The same procedure will have shadings and modifications to suit separate programs. Participants frequently will need training in the skills required to adapt and use effectively a generalized procedure. Careful selection of procedures and techniques is critical in any organized program for curriculum improvement if end results are to warrant effort and expenditure.

Organizational patterns for curriculum development are aimed at facilitating the work of various personnel and at integrating diverse efforts. To a large extent, early curriculum making emanated from the central office. The organization tended to concentrate initiative and direction in the central office staff. To insure that isolated curriculum-building activities are coordinated and directed into some meaningful pattern, there still must be systematic planning and integration of efforts. But the administrative problem is two-pronged: so organizing curriculum-improvement activities as to yield interrelated and cumulative opportunities for learning while, at the same time, nourishing individual initiative at the classroom level. The balance between systemwide and single school approaches is a major consideration for program planners.

Although present patterns tend to avoid the neat boxes and hierarchies of committees which stamped the first programs, there is usually a framework on which to hang the curriculum building. In some school systems, committees and personnel are fitted into or arranged as part of a pattern devised by the central administration. In other systems, the pattern emerges from the particular tasks or functions to be performed. Preplanned or evolving guidelines are essential to insure optimum conditions for creative work.

Organization patterns can be classified into three general categories—centralized, decentralized, or centrally coordinated—depending on the roles assigned the individual school unit and the central office staff. In many systems, each school building has become the operational and planning unit for curriculum activities. The growing trend toward assigning chief responsibility to the building unit reflects recognition of the belief that continuity, unity, and balance are best achieved when the staff focus their efforts on behalf of their own pupils. It is within a particular school that curriculum plans must be translated into instructional practice. It is at this level that planning seems most meaningful to teachers.

The three patterns of organization for curriculum work reflect different responses to questions about effectiveness at the one school level.[6]

Centralized approach. This pattern represents a belief that curriculum development should be initiated, directed, and co-ordinated by central office personnel and that chief responsibility for providing leadership for curriculum work is also centered there. Under this approach, stimulation for curriculum activity, arrangements for committee work, selection of procedures, and coordination of efforts are central office responsibilities.

Decentralized approach. This pattern represents a belief that the wellspring for initiating and carrying out curriculum planning is primarily the responsibility of individual schools. Under this approach, the determination of which curriculum problems are to be studied, which procedures and which personnel and resources to employ are the concern of the individual school staff. The central office staff may recommend or consult but the role is essentially an advisory one.

Centrally coordinated. This pattern attempts to combine the strengths of the centralized and decentralized patterns while avoiding some of the weaknesses of each. Here the individual school is still the basic planning unit and the source for initiating improvement in its own problem areas. However, the central office coordinates activities of the several buildings and proposes joint criteria for studies to deal with problems common to several schools. In addition, the central office initiates projects whose implications are systemwide.

Although it is not always necessary to classify organizational patterns, these groupings do help to clarify the functions and responsibilities of central office and school staffs. The channels for initiation, communication, and coordination must be clearly drawn and understood if each unit is to help build a unified, comprehensive program. Although responsibilities differ in each of the three approaches, success is directly related to the nature of the administrative provisions for activities. Administrative arrangements may either facilitate or hamstring curriculum change. While it is relatively simple to become bogged down in administrative

[6] These three patterns of organization for curriculum building are discussed in Ronald C. Doll, A. Harry Passow, and Stephen M. Corey, *Organizing for Curriculum Improvement* (New York: Bureau of Publications, Teachers College, Columbia University, 1953).

details, failure to define working arrangements may hamper effective planning. The centrally coordinated pattern has gained favor because it tends to open channels for optimum use of personnel and resources. The lines of communication, from the individual school to the system as a whole and back to the individual school, tend to operate rather better than the more traditional route from the central office to the buildings.

Committees and groups are the most commonly used vehicle for curriculum improvement activities. Committees have been operating on the curriculum for many years, but increased insights into the dynamics of learning and the psychology of change have affected the character of committees. While committee membership must change, group support may facilitate and expedite change. In groups, it is possible to create an atmosphere which stimulates growth toward mutually accepted goals. Together, people can work out definitions of instructional problems, spot needed changes, prescribe skill training and share in planning procedures to be tried and tested.

Merely collecting individuals and assigning them to a committee do not, of course, add up to a mature, working unit. At their best, groups give their members clear, meaningful objectives, along with that sense of cohesiveness and belongingness which encourages exploration of new ways; in short, a climate friendly to the testing of ideas and procedures. A good group—good in the sense of having established desirable standards for its members and effective methods for decision-making—furnishes opportunities combining members' insights and resources in resolving curriculum problems. Groups facilitate change in the individual by creating an environment and atmosphere in which individual problems are recognized and accepted, explored and studied, and possible solutions proposed and tested. From a practical as well as a psychological point of view, meaningful group operations are influential for curriculum development.[7]

Because groups can be decisive in curriculum building, atten-

[7] See, for example, Matthew B. Miles, *Learning to Work in Groups* (New York: Bureau of Publications, Teachers College, Columbia University, 1959); Herbert A. Thelen, *The Dynamics of Groups at Work* (Chicago: University of Chicago Press, 1954); Kenneth D. Benne and Bozidar Muntyan (eds.), *Human Relations in Curriculum Change* (New York: Dryden Press, 1951); Association for Supervision and Curriculum Development, *Group Processes in Supervision* (Washington, D.C.: National Education Association, 1948).

tion must be given to their structure and membership, to their operations and processes, to their leadership and communication. Cooperative curriculum planning has become an important phase of instructional improvement. Teachers and other professional staff members may need to improve their own skills in working, as participants and as leaders of groups. Training in the abilities valuable for curriculum work is essential if groups are to produce. The functions, responsibilities, purposes, and operations of groups vary considerably and must be planned if the promises of cooperative curriculum efforts are to materialize. The limits must be set clearly—the area of operation, the nature of the assignment, the time for working, and the relationships with the total program must be understood by all concerned. The availability of resources—leadership, consultative, personnel, and material—should be clarified. The potential for curriculum development through group efforts is strong if proper conditions are nurtured.

Committee and group activities fan out from the purposes listed earlier—study of curriculum problems, materials production, research, or skill development. Committees may steer, coordinate, plan, produce, or evaluate other committees. They may meet regularly or irregularly and may set a date for terminating activities or not. Membership may be open or restricted, voluntary or appointed. The methods and the times for communicating to other groups will vary. If committee and group work are to advance systemwide curriculum improvement, the conditions for operation must be blueprinted precisely.

Within a school system, committees may be organized vertically or horizontally, depending on goals and purposes. For example, some of the variations may include:

Grade-level committees: organized by single grades either within a single school or from several schools.

Unit-level committees: organized by primary, intermediate, junior high or senior high school units.

Departmental committees: organized by subject areas in either a single school or from several schools.

Systemwide committees: organized by representatives from various levels and areas in the school system (for example, Kindergarten–Grade 12 Committee on Mathematics; or Junior–Senior High School Committee on Articulation; or Committee on Cumulative Records).

Geographical area or regional committees: organized by geographical sections in larger school systems.

Special committees: organized for special purposes with personnel who have appropriate competencies or status positions.

In addition to the committees found within the school system, teachers and other professional workers may participate in the improvement projects of other organizations. These may include state, regional, or national professional bodies; university- or college-sponsored school study councils; state departments of education curriculum studies; educational foundation projects; and nonprofessional organizations at the local, state, regional, and national level.

The use of committees and groups has not always been aided by clear conceptions of how best to arrange and coordinate proper activities. Committee work sometimes has become busy work, without direction or accepted purpose, isolated from the ongoing program and unrelated to instructional improvement. Where committee participation is tied to a salary schedule, the financial gain has at times overshadowed the educational gain. Positive directives can seek to accomplish the following:

1. Define sharply the task or purpose.

2. Select the committee membership so that participants represent a balance of competencies, interests, and viewpoints.

3. Indicate the lifespan of the committee.

4. Establish the relationship of the committee's work to the total curriculum program.

5. Clear the avenues of communication.

6. Allot time and resources so that members can mesh committee functions with other responsibilities.

Committees and groups are widely employed in curriculum activities of many kinds. It is important that conditions are arranged for efficient operation, for continuous appraisal of activities, and for coordination of efforts.

Supervisors and other central office personnel render a variety of services aimed at improving the quality of instruction. Whatever other responsibilities are assigned to them, these officials personify leadership and service for curriculum development. From the central staff, supervisory personnel are well placed to stimulate and sustain both long-term, systemwide program planning and the classroom teacher's day-to-day work. The immediate demands of maintaining a school program may sometimes shrink perspective on the total educational needs of a community. It is the supervisory staff which can energize a balanced, comprehensive program, its continuing appraisal, and regular analysis of curriculum problems. The diverse activities which all this entails must be meshed and coordinated by skilled, versatile central office personnel.

Because theirs is an enveloping responsibility, supervisors can gain a communitywide view of educational needs. Sensitive people can spot problem areas and find significant curriculum concerns for intensive study. In many systems, the supervisor's role has shifted radically. Once it was to determine a particular program and gauge its effectiveness by inspecting classrooms. Now the role is much more complex, calling on the supervisor to stimulate creative teaching and locate necessary resources. Thus, the responsibility of many supervisory staffs today is to help teachers acquire the abilities and understandings which will lead to richer teaching and learning. This trend in supervision is reflected sometimes in the assignment of a title such as "resource person," "area consultant," or simply, "coordinator," "helping teacher." However, the real change has not been in the new title but rather in the altered conception of the purpose and nature of supervision.

Specific duties of supervisory and other central office personnel vary from system to system, according to the administrative setup and its underlying concepts. Among the services rendered by supervisors in connection with curriculum improvement, the following are common:

Identifying and pinpointing instructional problems. Spending time in classes, in faculty meetings, in educational groups of many kinds, supervisors are able to identify significant, recurring problems. Alertness and sensitivity can pave the way for broad perspective and leadership in coping with obstacles.

Making arrangements for in-service curriculum activities. Work groups, committees, workshops, and other activities necessitate meeting facilities and arrangements. Supervisors usually are in a better position than classroom teachers to arrange the time, place, and tools for in-service work.

Coordinating the curriculum improvement efforts and activities of individuals and groups. The separate rivulets of diverse efforts must be channeled and coordinated into a purposeful stream.

Supervisors, as members of a central staff determined to improve instruction, often can see the total picture better than others and can coordinate the elements of personnel, purpose, activities, meeting times, resource use, reports.

Communicating and sharing ideas among various individuals, from one building to others, from one work group to another. Cross-fertilization is ideally the function of supervisors who watch the growth of ideas and can communicate the findings and developments to and among various working groups.

Securing consultants and resource specialists. Most groups require persons with special and unusual competencies from time to time to supplement the regulars in tackling problems. Supervisors can help in locating specialists at a point when they can most usefully advance the group's project. Consultants of many kinds are essential in developing educational programs.

Working as part of a supervisory team with an individual school or teacher group. Many curriculum problems, particularly those which affect the building of a unified educational program, are best attacked by a team combination of backgrounds and skills. Some training is often needed to ensure efficient operation as a team but the results will repay the extra effort.

Locating and providing instructional materials. In modern educational programs, a variety of curriculum materials are needed by teachers and students. The supervisor-leader is constantly on the lookout for materials which might strengthen a teacher's planning and instruction. The rich and extensive reservoir of curriculum materials is arid unless the classroom teacher can tap it at need. Supervisors feed materials to teachers on request and without being asked—hoping the teacher will find that an unsolicited discovery is, in fact, a useful gem.

Counseling with individual teachers. Supervisory conferences with teachers are times for talking over instructional problems, examining ideas and suggestions for improving instruction, and making requests for assistance. Supervisory conferences may be formal or informal, regular or irregular, with initiative coming either from the teacher or the supervisor. They are the means by which the supervisor provides direct assistance to the individual teacher or simply lends a sympathetic ear. If timely and purposeful, the conference can be an aid to program evolution.

Supervisory and other central office personnel fill important leadership roles by setting the tone and creating an environment by which they initiate, encourage, facilitate, and coordinate activities for improving instruction.

Resource persons and consultants are engaged to assist school personnel in a variety of aspects of curriculum work. The complexities of curriculum building—content, method, and process—frequently call for specialized competencies beyond those possessed by the participants of the immediate planning group. Increasingly, school systems appoint individuals with special competence to advise curriculum groups. Supervisory and other central office personnel frequently serve as resource persons but consultants may come from many other sources as well. Within a school staff, there are often teachers and others who are expert in a needed area—some phase of curriculum building or teaching. Professional educators outside the school system—college and university, state department and county office, regional and national professional association personnel—are sources from which school systems draw outside consultants. Publishing houses and school-supply firms furnish persons to demonstrate instructional materials and to work with in-service groups. Many regional and national organizations, service and philanthropic, offer competent specialists to planning groups. Finally, there are many citizens in the community—parents and other lay persons—who possess talents valuable in curriculum work groups. The scientist, the mathematician, the artist, the dramatist, the author—all have found a place in some schools, working with the teacher and the student.

The kind of help provided by resource persons and consultants in improving instruction varies considerably. Effective use of consultants and resource persons, however, requires skills and understandings which curriculum committees must often develop while working.[8] In some instances, resource persons may work directly with students: instructing individuals, small groups, or whole classes in cooperation with the regular teacher. Here the resource person supplements the classroom teacher's work in upgrading the quality of instruction.

The consultant is used most frequently in some phase of the in-

[8] An analysis of factors affecting success of consultants is found in Marcella R. Lawler, *Curriculum Consultants at Work* (New York: Bureau of Publications, Teachers College, Columbia University, 1959).

service program working with the professional staff. The tasks and roles of the educational consultant vary according to the needs of the group he is working with and may range widely: selecting and organizing areas for curriculum improvement; programing in-service activities; providing scholarly insights into a specific problem area; extending the professional staff's understandings of human relations; training groups in techniques for problem solving; lecturing; introducing materials and resources; assisting in the development of program plans; and helping to plan new facilities. In brief, the consultant may serve on many levels to promote educational change.

Whether the consultant helps a group depends on the extent to which (1) he has the essential knowledge, skills, insights, or understandings which that group requires; (2) he is able to work skillfully and sympathetically with the group; (3) he and the group are able to communicate effectively what the latter wants and the former is able to provide; and (4) he is able to work within the framework of the institutional structure. The method by which the consultant is selected may affect his potential for helping the group. If the group perceives that the consultant has the competencies they require to move toward their goal, his work is likely to bear fruit. Wise selection of consultants and clarification of the tasks or roles expected of them are important first steps in a productive working relationship. Although the consultant may reject the "oracle complex" of some groups, he will indeed be expected to answer practically the specific problems raised, ranging from instructional problems to those involving human relationships.

Because consultants are still novel to many curriculum groups, such groups must often acquire the skills needed for exploiting this resource. Similarly, the techniques and procedures which consultants use in their normal work may not be appropriate to service as resource persons. The potential for enhancing curriculum improvement efforts through harnessing expertness is only now beginning to be realized. Systematic studies and reports of ways of working with resource persons are yielding leads to assist other curriculum groups to better results. As the consultant multiplies experience with what various groups expect of him, he will develop the fitting skills and insights for each kind of situation.

The recognition of the classroom teacher's primacy in improving instruction led to his being assigned a central place in curriculum activities. However, few teacher groups have all the necessary competencies with which to surmount their varied curriculum problems. One of the significant departures of the city systems which pioneered in comprehensive curriculum programs in the 1920s was to name specialists as consultants. This welding of outside and local practitioners has been a notable development in curriculum building. Its present maturation promises steady progress. With experience, school personnel learn how to select and work with resource persons, and consultants enhance their skill in sharing their special competencies. This is especially true in school groups which not only seek outside assistance but search out the resources within their own school system and community as well.

Time and facilities are provided for curriculum improvement activities.   Faced with the normal teaching load, the demands of day-to-day classroom instruction limit the creative efforts possible and necessary to progress in curriculum development. Some curriculum work can be carried on only through the sustained efforts of individuals and groups, intensively concentrating for long stretches. Administrators who think of curriculum improvement as an integral part of the classroom teacher's responsibilities adjust schedules and allot appropriate time and facilities for effective planning operations.

The time provisions made for curriculum work vary with local conditions. Such items as the nature of the problems surveyed, the personnel and financial resources available, the in-service techniques and procedures employed, and the philosophical principles guiding the instructional improvement efforts—all influence a system's policies regarding time allocated for program development.

The time provisions are also affected by the accepted definition of the school day and of the professional work day. Where the two coincide, little or no time remains for curriculum activities unless prearrangements release the teacher from the classroom. However, where the professional day takes into account the need for planning, both daily and long-range, and is longer than the actual teaching span, in-service activities can be scheduled regularly. Program development is then viewed as part of the total professional responsibility and not as an optional luxury. This distinction between the teaching day and the professional day is too substantial to neglect, though often it is not recognized. By various means, school systems block out the time for curriculum activity. Five such adaptations are:

Released time for curriculum work. Early dismissal, closing school for whole or part days, or the assignment of substitute teachers to the classroom permit regular teachers to attend meetings or engage in other curriculum work. In some instances, teachers are released for a period of days or even weeks to complete a particular assignment or engage in a specific activity. In some schools, the youngsters are brought together for special large-group instruction while the teachers meet in groups. By including planning in the school timetable, some principals free teachers periodically for curriculum work.

Reduced instructional load for program planning. The teaching assignments of some instructors may be reduced slightly or substantially. For example, a teacher may be given a half or two-thirds normal teaching load in order to use the remainder of his time for a specific in-service assignment. Or, a teacher may count on an afternoon a week to participate in an in-service program or on a committee.

Extension of school year for planning time. In some school systems, the school year has been extended for a period ranging from a few days to a few weeks before or after the normal school calendar. For this additional time in which planning fills the hours without the additional demands of classroom teaching, teachers are paid regular salaries. Schools which regularly have had teachers report a few days early and stay on a few days after the close of the school year have found it relatively easy to extend the time for curriculum planning.

Extension of the professional day. Faculty groups and total staffs have found time to work on curriculum planning by meeting either before the opening of the school day, at its close, or even during the lunch period. If a system's leaders recognize the integral nature of in-service activity and program planning, some teachers prefer a regular planning period at the start or close of the school day to released time during instructional hours.

Additional employment for curriculum planning. School systems sometimes employ teachers during the summer vacation period to work on a particular curriculum assignment. Bulletins, guides, and instructional materials have been developed by teachers hired for an additional period of time to undertake or to complete some curriculum assignment.

Against the advantages of special times for planning, there are a number of administrative problems. One is that of striking a desirable balance between time for appropriate curriculum activities and time for the teacher's central responsibility to instruct and counsel. Another is that, although curriculum improvement is the means of upgrading instruction, activities sometimes become an end in themselves, engrossing teachers to the point of becoming divorced from classroom realities. Steadying the focus on the means-ends relationship is an important responsibility for curriculum leadership.

Some teachers balk at released time for curriculum work, resenting the interruption. If they can learn to relate to instructional improvement, resistance may abate. Here, again, responsible leadership ensures that program planning is meaningful and thereby helps avoid drains on the classroom teacher's time and energies.

Mounting details of a curriculum improvement program require careful scheduling and coordination lest the pressures on participants increase with bunched-up demands. Some teachers tend to get themselves heavily committed to program planning and need a shield against the tensions of overenthusiasm. A coordinated calendar in which certain days or periods are reserved for specific kinds of meetings—faculty, in-service courses, standing committees—can reduce conflict and frustration.

The facilities provided for curriculum-planning sessions can influence the quality of the work which emerges. Experiences with group dynamics and research into the factors affecting change as a process have molded insights that in turn influence the setting for curriculum planning. The nature of the meeting place—the kind of room, its size, the furnishings, the equipment, even the decorations—affects attitude and, eventually, the quality of the work. The comfort of the work space, the flexibility of arrangements, the relative accessibility of resources, the ease of reaching the meeting place—all make a difference in how well the group functions. Some school systems maintain a professional center in which the facilities and the resources are keyed to staff activities for in-service growth and curriculum planning. Here, a curriculum library may contain instructional materials of all kinds collected and supervised by a trained librarian. Conference rooms may be designed with the equipment and facilities most likely to be needed for the particular kinds of in-service activities commonly used. However, other schools, without funds to build and maintain a professional center still have equipped such facilities as are available, perhaps as simple as serving coffee on comfortable seats in the home economics room of a school.

Leadership roles are filled by many different members of the professional staff. Since curriculum improvement is a human process carried on, to a large extent, in groups of various kinds, there are many different leadership functions to be performed. One of the significant departures in the early programs for curriculum development was the delegation of responsibility for instructional improvement to an individual. Director of instruction, assistant superintendent for instructional services, or similar title indicated an assignment for initiating and coordinating organized efforts for curriculum revision. Leadership for instructional improvement was vested in an administrator who parceled out responsibilities to members of his staff and others in the central office.

Over the years the experience gained from shaping and altering educational programs has resulted in tapping new veins of leadership. Leadership for curriculum improvement now comes from many directions, beginning with the status person, the administrator or supervisor assigned specific curriculum duties. These may involve coordination of individual and group activities, allotment of necessary resources, communication of data, stimulation of planning groups, and evaluation of work. Leadership in this sense —providing the means a group needs for effective functioning— goes beyond administrative domination and direction. Leadership on the part of successful modern administrators and supervisors really boils down to helping the classroom teacher do a better job.

As the individual school has become the basic unit of participation in curriculum building, the leadership role of the principal has necessarily been redefined. It is the building principal, particularly at the elementary level, who has had to function as instructional leader as well as administrative manager. The building principal is the one who arranges the conditions for involving faculty in program planning, for encouraging continuous study and experimentation, and for maintaining constant appraisal of the educational program. These demands for instructional leadership have placed new requirements on principals for developing the skills and techniques in personnel management and group work required for stimulating and coordinating staff efforts at program improvement.

Functional leadership also emerges from teachers and other professional personnel, particularly in connection with on-going group operations. Teachers fill many leadership roles serving as group chairmen, providing specialized competencies, facilitating all aspects of in-service activities. Lay citizens in many places have contributed fundamental ideas and service to their schools. The sources of leadership have multiplied as the circles of participation in regular efforts toward curriculum improvement have widened.

Some school systems have excelled in identifying leadership (potential and active) and providing training to fill gaps in skills, insights, and attitudes. Studies of the process of curriculum improvement have pinpointed the need for supplying adequate leadership for work groups with good internal resources found within the group itself. Probably no aspect of curriculum building is as crucial as the quality of leadership available.

CONCLUSION

Ceaseless pressures on schools necessitate constant study, appraisal, and revision of educational programs. To meet the demands of curriculum building, organized programs have evolved as continuous, cooperative enterprises integrating teachers, supervisors, administrators, lay citizens, and students.

Because they most directly affect the quality of education, teachers occupy a key position in any program of curriculum improvement. As the instructor acquires deeper insights and surer skills, as he modifies his values and attitudes, he alters the conditions for teaching and learning. It is this concept of behavioral change which guides modern curriculum improvement programs. Techniques and procedures are selected which may encourage teachers to participate in the solution of real and bothersome curriculum problems. As individuals and as members of groups, teachers identify and seek to improve various weak points in the instructional program. Attention is given to building an atmosphere conducive to professional study, to critical appraisal, to experimentation with new ideas, resources, and methods. Time, facilities, and resources—personnel and material—are made available to help foster professional growth.

Over the years, activities which once were separate have merged gradually. In-service education, supervision, administration, and similar activities have blended into organisms directed toward improved instruction. By thoughtful approaches, school systems across the nation have sought to accommodate individual differences among students, teachers, schools, and communities in curriculum programs. The ultimate goal has been to apply the resources in school and community to problems whose solution could result in a richer educational program.

SELECTED READINGS

ASSOCIATION FOR SUPERVISION AND CURRICULUM DEVELOPMENT, *Action for Curriculum Improvement*. Washington, D.C.: The Association, NEA, 1951.

BENNE, KENNETH D. and MUNTYAN, BOSIDAR, *Human Relations in Curriculum Change*. New York: Dryden Press, 1953.

MACKENZIE, GORDON N., COREY, STEPHEN M. and ASSOCIATES, *Instructional Leadership*. New York: Bureau of Publications, Teachers College, Columbia University, 1954.

MIEL, ALICE M., *Changing the Curriculum—A Social Process*. New York: Appleton-Century-Crofts, 1946.

NATIONAL SOCIETY FOR THE STUDY OF EDUCATION, *Inservice Education for Teachers, Supervisors and Administrators*, Fifty-sixth Yearbook, Part I. Chicago: University of Chicago Press, 1957.

SAYLOR, J. GALEN and ALEXANDER, WILLIAM M., *Curriculum Planning for Better Teaching and Learning*. New York: Rinehart and Company, 1954.

SHARP, GEORGE, *Curriculum Development as Re-education of the Teacher*. New York: Bureau of Publications, Teachers College, Columbia University, 1951.

SMITH, B. O., STANLEY, W. O., and SHORES, J. H., *Fundamentals of Curriculum Development* (rev. ed.). Yonkers-on-Hudson, New York: World Book Company, 1957.

STRATEMEYER, FLORENCE B., FORKNER, HAMDEN L., MCKIM, MARGARET, and PASSOW, A. HARRY, *Developing a Curriculum for Modern Living* (2d ed., rev.). New York: Bureau of Publications, Teachers College, Columbia University, 1957.

3

ADMINISTERING AND ORGANIZING
THE CURRICULUM
IMPROVEMENT PROGRAM

IMPROVING the quality of instruction is a continuing, complex undertaking. A school staff working on program development too often engages in a bewildering and uncoordinated array of endeavors, all ostensibly aimed at instructional improvement. Teachers participate in meetings: they may discuss "Great Books"; attend an intensive child study program, perhaps for college credit; or analyze data collected in their classrooms for a research project. They may staff committees of a professional association or engage in in-service activities of other kinds. Because so many aspects and persons within the educational process directly affect quality, the success of program planning may hinge on the kinds of administrative provisions made for facilitating and coordinating such work. Administrative arrangements can either encourage or impede curriculum change.

Obviously, not all instructional planning is done within the framework of organized curriculum development programs. However, it is the systematic, coordinated efforts which are most likely to produce effective, balanced educational programs. These are, therefore, the focal concern of school personnel—whatever their title and status may be—for studying and improving program quality.

How are program improvement activities organized? How are curriculum improvement activities initiated? How are problem areas selected for study? How are teachers and other personnel interested and involved in curriculum study? How are various activities coordinated? What procedures and techniques are used? How is communication maintained among the individuals and groups working on curriculum development? How are program planning activities evaluated? These are some of the concerns of individuals with leadership responsibility for improving the quality of instruction.

On what bases can decisions be made about problems of curriculum improvement programs? Unfortunately, no research base exists to guide planning, organization, and procedure. Studies of specific aspects of curriculum work—such as the effectiveness of certain group procedures, the nature of instructional leadership, the value of a particular workshop experience—have yielded many hypotheses which require testing in school situations.[1] The need for evaluation of school programs and practices in order to build a comprehensive guide for organizing and planning curriculum work is evident.

ADMINISTERING THE CURRICULUM IMPROVEMENT PROGRAM

Administration of curriculum improvement programs has changed in the past generation. The organization and administration of such programs depend on the conception of curriculum held by those responsible for its operation. The administration of curriculum programs may be looked at from a number of different but related vantage points: those of the roles of central office personnel, building principals, supervisory personnel, and the lay public.

[1] G. N. Mackenzie and C. Bebell, "Curriculum Development," *Review of Educational Research*, Vol. 21 (June 1951), pp. 227–37; A. H. Passow, "Organization and Procedures for Curriculum Improvement," *Review of Educational Research*, Vol. 24 (June 1954), pp. 221–36; and H. M. Evans, "Organization for Curriculum Development," *Review of Educational Research*, Vol. 27 (June 1957), pp. 287–94. All three reviews stress the need for testing hypotheses which have emerged from existing research.

Central Office Personnel

It is sometimes assumed that the concept of the curriculum as guided experiences with consequent implications for diffusion of responsibility and participation in curriculum development and revision somehow also implies appreciably less leadership in curriculum matters on the part of the administration. What is necessary is not less but rather a different type of leadership which is, in many respects, more demanding than is restricted centralized direction.

Katz has proposed that there are three orders of skills operative in the administrative process: technical skills, human skills, and conceptual skills.[2] By conceptual skill, Katz refers to the ability to comprehend the relationship of the parts to the whole, to see "the big picture," to marshal the relevant data and arrive at a balanced judgment as to the best course of action to be taken. The higher one goes in an administrative hierarchy, the greater is the premium placed on conceptual skills and the emphasis on technical skills is proportionately reduced. This notion seems to describe well the function of the central office in the curriculum development program. The central office is responsible for seeing "the big picture" of the school district and of the community which is its immediate setting.

Such skill is also called for in conceiving an organization and procedure for appraising the educational program, and for identifying and analyzing improvement needs. Central office personnel alone do not decide the curriculum needs to be met nor the activities to be undertaken but rather provide leadership in helping staff members to become aware of and to clarify needed improvements.

Conceptual skill is called upon also in the coordination of broad-based programs. Careful curriculum coordination is necessary to avoid its having any disintegrating effects on the teacher. This could occur, for example, if two groups were independently to develop conflicting proposals for the intermediate-grades program. It can also happen in cases where the authority and respon-

[2] Robert L. Katz, "Skills of an Effective Administrator," *Harvard Business Review*, Vol. 33 (January-February 1955), pp. 33–42.

sibility of some personnel (such as supervisors and principals) are not specified clearly.

The task of the central office, then, is one of wide-visioned, over-arching, creative leadership. The central office group provide leadership which helps the general staff to identify needs, to pioneer new ideas, and to work together as a team in the improvement of the learning experiences of the children in the classrooms. In order to achieve this, Caswell proposed in an earlier volume that the functional administrative leadership for curriculum and instruction be assigned to a single person.[3] In a modern program, responsibility for curriculum and for instruction can hardly be separated. Such unified responsibility is well illustrated in the programs described later.

The Building Principal

Throughout the accounts of curriculum development programs perhaps one of the most persistent themes is the degree of responsibility reposed in the building principal. Policies, objectives, framework and the like may be determined by persons other than the local building personnel, but, in the last analysis, the staff that works directly with the children determines the children's learning experiences. This is true under any type of curriculum or curriculum organization.

The building principalship has become a critically important position in determining program quality. The type of instructional leadership exercised by the principal will significantly influence the quality of the educational program. Consequently the selection and appointment of principals should be done with exceptional care. Once appointed to the position, the principal should be given responsibility and commensurate authority for his school's instructional program. He should be responsible directly to the individual in charge of the system's program of curriculum and instruction and his authority and responsibility should not be infringed upon by supervisory or other consultative personnel. He should be provided with those conditions which will enable him

[3] Hollis L. Caswell and associates, *Curriculum Improvement Programs in Public School Systems* (New York: Bureau of Publications, Teachers College, Columbia University, 1950), pp. 80–81.

to exercise positive instructional leadership. There is evidence that the teaching principalship (in which the principal spends a half or more of the day in the classroom) is already obsolescent.[4] However, a 1958 survey of the principalship indicated that 32 per cent of elementary school principals with six or more teachers are still without secretarial help.[5] Principals need the assistance and conditions which enable them to devote the major part of their attention and energies to their most important task: the coordination and constant improvement of the learning program. Able leadership on the part of the building principals of a school system will go far to insure the curriculum program's success. Without the cooperation and leadership of principals, no curriculum program can be effective.

Supervisory Personnel

In most school systems today, supervisors are considered primarily as curriculum development personnel contributing to program modification and upgrading. With teachers, principals and other members of the staff, supervisors help identify needs, plan, and put into operation proposals in individual schools and classrooms. In doing so, they generally act as specialized staff personnel and not in a line capacity. When they are working in school buildings, they serve within the jurisdiction of the building principal. Such understanding avoids conflicts in authority and duplications of responsibility which all too often have confused teachers and adversely affected morale. In some systems, the term *consultant* is being substituted for *supervisor*, in order to indicate the relationship more clearly. This relationship is evident in the curriculum accounts in Chapters 5 through 11.

University Staff Personnel

The resources available in university and college staffs for work on various aspects of the educational program are many. The

[4] Department of Elementary School Principals, *The Elementary School Principalship: A Research Study,* Thirty-seventh Yearbook (Washington, D.C.: National Education Association, 1958), pp. 223–25.

[5] *Ibid.,* p. 72.

schism between the professors of education and the professors of liberal arts has had particularly serious consequences in situations where necessary and available competencies have been ignored in curriculum work. Encouraging signs have appeared that schools are learning how to use university specialists more effectively. The interest of the university professor in the curriculum problems of the elementary and secondary schools, if approached and used intelligently, can open up to the program developer a reservoir of resources inadequately tapped in the past.

Lay Citizens

The same may be said with respect to using specialists in the community. In seminars, in in-service programs, in materials development groups, specialists from the community—artists, writers, scientists, engineers, historians, and others—are being used as consultants in curriculum improvement efforts of many kinds.

The period following World War II has seen a tremendous increase in the degree of popular interest in education. Even though some of it has been adversely critical, schoolmen have applauded this interest and have been in the forefront in advocating lay participation in school affairs. However, considerable confusion concerning the proper role of laymen in educational affairs has resulted. There are those who maintain that educators have permitted laymen to exercise too much of a voice in decisions which properly should be made by professionals.[6] The laymen of a community already have a part in school policy and program decisions through their duly constituted board of education. This is the only lay group in the community which has official standing in the making of school system decisions. It is their function to deal with the broad questions and problems of schoolwide policy and program, and to pass upon professional proposals made by the superintendent and his staff.[7]

[6] See, for example, Myron Lieberman, *Education as a Profession* (Englewood Cliffs, N.J.: Prentice-Hall, Inc., 1956).

[7] American Association of School Administrators, *School Boards in Action,* Twenty-fourth Yearbook (Washington, D.C.: National Education Association, 1946), and *School Board-Superintendent Relationships,* Thirty-fourth Yearbook (Washington, D.C.: National Education Association, 1956); Daniel R. Davies and Fred W. Hosler, *The Challenge of School Board Membership* (New York: Chartwell House, Inc., 1949).

There is much to be gained for education in the cooperation of lay and professional personnel. In many communities much good has come from the functioning of lay advisory committees which serve at the behest of the board of education to marshal information and assist the board in specified respects. Parent-teacher organizations also serve in this manner. In addition, curriculum workers call upon community members in a consultative capacity because of their specialized backgrounds or abilities. The participation of laymen with special contributions to make in the instructional program can be most helpful and conducive to good school-community relations. In curriculum development and modification, however, the laymen's role is primarily advisory in nature. With rare exceptions, laymen are not qualified to serve on working committees whose tasks involve the improvement of the teaching of reading, or the revision of the junior high school mathematics program, or the development of teaching methods to challenge gifted children. Curriculum development is a professional responsibility for professional personnel and difficulties have arisen when the laymen's role has not been made clear.

Administration and Marshaling of Resources

The many roles which must be filled in program improvement efforts suggest that the chief functions of administration are (1) marshaling personnel resources for work on program development; and (2) creating the conditions which facilitate effective operation and utilization of those resources. In the final analysis, everything that is done in the school system affects the curriculum and the quality of instruction in some way. At times, these relationships seem peripheral and even remote; nevertheless, they are real and must be dealt with in planning and administering a program aimed at optimum curriculum development.

ORGANIZING FOR CURRICULUM WORK

Curriculum planning takes place at many different levels—classroom, building, system, county, state, regional, and national—and under diverse auspices. Consequently, the varied organizational patterns for curriculum planning reflect the particular setting in which the work is to take place. Ultimately, planning must improve the quality of learning if it is to have value and, therefore, must affect the classroom teacher and the conditions of his instruction. At whatever level the planning occurs, the organization must take into account factors which affect the participation of key personnel in ways which will improve program quality. The purpose of any organization pattern should be to help marshal resources in a particular school situation in the most efficient and effective way to work on instructional problems. Although no single pattern can meet the varied conditions found in the diverse settings in which program planning is carried on, certain conditions must be considered in organizing for curriculum work at any level.

Assigning Leadership Responsibility

Assignment of leadership responsibility for curriculum development to a central office individual or department is a practice widely used in school systems today. The specific title given varies with the relationship of the individual or position to the central office and general administrative organization. *Director* or *coordinator of instruction, assistant superintendent, general supervisor, curriculum coordinator,* and *director of instructional services* are some of the titles assigned to persons with responsibilities for program development. How clearly defined the assignment is varies with school systems, ranging from a concise job specification to an informal, implied area of responsibility. The latter is particularly true in smaller school systems where individuals with curriculum improvement responsibilities frequently carry other assignments as well.[8]

Providing Coordination

In larger school systems, steering committees (central curriculum councils, curriculum coordinating committees, or instructional councils are other names used for groups performing these func-

[8] See, for example, G. N. Mackenzie (ed.), *The Work of the Curriculum Coordinator in Selected New Jersey Schools* (New York: Bureau of Publications, Teachers College, Columbia University, 1955), for a report of the varied nature of these positions.

tions) play an important role in curriculum improvement work. Generally, the coordinating committee has either administrative or advisory responsibility for initiating, directing, and coordinating the varied planning efforts throughout the school system. This group provides the overview for curriculum work, weaving the diverse activities undertaken into some meaningful pattern.

In brief, the coordinating committee is the group through which many important aspects of instructional leadership function. The key to the effectiveness of such leadership depends on the committee's membership, the conditions under which it operates, and the perceptions of its operations held by the professional staff. Therefore, the establishment of a coordinating committee and the selection of its members require careful consideration of a number of factors.

Functions. The specific functions of curriculum steering committees can be spelled out in detail and made part of official school policy. Some school systems indicate the responsibilities of the committee in terms of areas of responsibility or tasks to be accomplished. Other school systems are less specific. They assign to the committee responsibility for initiating and coordinating curriculum development, leaving to the members the task of determining how to work and in what areas to function. In some instances, the specificity of role and responsibility impedes committee operations while in other cases it facilitates work by making explicit to the group and the rest of the professional staff what tasks are to be done. The committee's functions may include:

1. Surveying the curriculum needs and instructional problems of individual schools.

2. Arranging necessary work groups and committees for undertaking study of curriculum problems.

3. Sanctioning the activities of various planning groups.

4. Providing for communication among schoolwide and citywide curriculum study groups.

5. Coordinating the efforts of work groups studying different aspects of common problems.

6. Providing consultants and resource persons as required by work groups.

7. Arranging for in-service activities as required for program planning.

8. Providing liaison with curriculum planning groups outside the school system itself (i.e., county, state, regional, or national groups).

9. Evaluating instructional planning activities.

Membership. The membership of a steering committee is critical since the effectiveness of the group's work is determined by its composition. Steering committee members may be appointed or elected, or even chosen from volunteers. Representation is sometimes by educational level (primary, intermediate, junior high or senior high); by type of position (teacher, supervisor, administrator, special services personnel); by department affiliation or subject specialization; by geographic area (where schools are grouped this way administratively); by committee assignment (representing an operating committee); or by some combination thereof. In some instances, membership is determined on the basis of individual capabilities without regard to representation of any group. University and other professional workers, as well as lay persons, may be included on a coordinating committee. The members may serve for a fixed or indefinite term. The basis for membership should, of course, be determined by the kind of personnel resources needed for the leadership responsibilities assigned to, or assumed by, the steering committee.

Size. Steering committees range in size from six or seven members to sixty or seventy, depending on the criteria for membership. In addition, the ability of a group to function adequately must be considered. When a committee is too large, communication and group-process problems become almost insurmountable, necessitating subdivisions for most work. When the group is too small, adequate representation may be impossible and members may be unable to handle all the tasks with which they are confronted because of manpower shortages. A steering committee of between 20 to 30 persons has been suggested as an optimum-size group because face-to-face operations are still possible while adequate representation can be arranged.

Time. Coordinating committee work is generally time-consuming if it is done well. Representatives on such coordinating groups are sometimes released from normal responsibilities for a certain portion of their time in order to participate in committee work. Released time may be provided by reducing the teaching load during the period the teacher serves on the committee or by assigning substitute teachers during meeting times. In some instances, extra compensation is provided for the additional work involved.

In smaller school systems, steering committees are much less formally organized, with less attention to structure and more to considerations which will facilitate the work of the group. Even in larger school systems, each of the building units may have a coordinating committee to direct and harmonize the planning efforts at the local level and to serve as a liaison group with the systemwide steering group.

Flexibility of the Organization

Committee and group work, in-service programs, and other professional activities follow many different organizational patterns. In some school systems, the coordinating committee and central curriculum office have established fixed or standing work groups responsible for initiating and directing program planning in specific study areas. A "Senior High Committee on Instruction" or a Kindergarten–Grade 12 Mathematics Committee" or a "Central Articulation Committee" are examples of continuing groups which serve as both steering and work units, generating curriculum planning and study activities which may be carried out by subgroups or by additional committees especially established for a specific task. A chart of curriculum committees in such school systems would indicate a number of fixed, continuing committees as well as some which are created for a specific task and remain in existence only until a job has been finished.

Some school systems have no logical organization pattern but simply provide a structure for committee work as indicated by the needs of the time. Committees are launched as required for a given task with groups so formed recognized by the central office. Generally, few schools have a rigid framework for curriculum planning although many have a scheme for an evolving organizational pattern determined by the particular work under way. Some machinery is provided for initiating, recognizing, and helping groups undertake curriculum study. It is such flexibility which makes the roles of the central curriculum office and the steering committee particularly important in guiding and harmonizing the multiple efforts for instructional improvement. Flexibility is essential if the organizational pattern is not to become so crystallized that its rigidity hampers, rather than facilitates, curriculum development.

Clarifying Roles of Participants

The organizational pattern should help make clear the particular roles of participating individuals, groups, and units. The relationships between the single building and the systemwide planning groups as well as the responsibilities of individuals, committee, and central office personnel can be made explicit by the expression of working arrangements in an organization scheme. For example, the particular aspects of curriculum development which should be studied at the building level, those which are to be examined by a group of schools, and those to be subjected to systemwide attack can be made clear through the organization for program improvement. Such an approach encourages sound working relationships and implementation of program planning while minimizing the dangers of pattern crystallization.

Establishing Evaluation Procedures

No single scheme will stimulate and expedite effective program planning in all school situations. The following criteria may suggest guides to evolving and evaluating an appropriate organization for curriculum improvement.[9] The organization pattern should:

1. Reflect the purposes and goals of the school by creating the kinds of conditions for program planning which the school is aiming at in instruction.

2. Facilitate a variety of approaches to, and activities in, curriculum improvement.

3. Support and facilitate individuals and groups at each planning level so that they contribute effectively to the improvement of the total program.

[9] Adapted from F. B. Stratemeyer, H. L. Forkner, M. G. McKim, and A. H. Passow, *Developing a Curriculum for Modern Living* (2d ed. rev.) (New York: Bureau of Publications, Teachers College, Columbia University, 1957), pp. 671–81.

4. Enhance communication among the various individuals and groups working at program development.

5. Facilitate effective use of personnel and material resources in the school and the community or otherwise available for upgrading teaching and learning.

6. Provide for involvement of lay persons, including parents and students, in the processes of curriculum development where they can contribute their special competencies.

7. Provide for the development of skills necessary for undertaking curriculum improvement activities.

8. Facilitate the emergence of leadership at all levels of planning.

9. Assure the coordination of diverse activities by planning groups attacking many different kinds of curriculum problems.

The organization for improving the quality of education must constantly be appraised to ascertain the ways in which it facilitates or impedes work. Criteria such as these—or others locally developed—can guide this essential reexamination.

INITIATING CURRICULUM PLANNING ACTIVITIES

Seemingly, the initiation of work on instructional improvement would simply involve deciding which problem areas need study and what procedures will be used. However, the task is usually far more complex. Teachers and professional staff members are not equally interested in, or stimulated by, curriculum improvement activities. Nor do teachers have equal competence in the skills required for certain kinds of in-service activities. There are many different causes for staff resistance to participation in curriculum planning, such as failure to recognize the need for improvement; fear of experimentation; unwillingness to give the necessary time; disillusion or frustration with past experiences.

Identifying Significant Problem Areas

It has been frequently stated that teachers participate most willingly and most effectively when engaged in solving instructional problems which have personal significance for them. While this is not the only condition to be met in initiating curriculum work, the identification of problem areas which are meaningful and significant is an important step in initiating curriculum work. The very way in which problems are identified can affect curriculum work. That is, the procedures used in identifying problem areas can also generate work on curriculum development. Consequently, the lines are not always clear between procedures for identifying problem areas and those for refining particular areas in the process of solution.

Included among the variety of procedures which schools use for initiating curriculum studies and in-service programs are the following:

Problem census. This technique in a variety of forms is used to determine the areas with which the instructional staff is dissatisfied or would like help. In some instances, a list of pressing problems is prepared by a committee, and teachers are asked to react to the items in terms of personal importance. The teacher reactions to the checklist are then used by a planning committee to launch work on the problems identified. Sometimes, completely open-ended techniques are used to identify problem areas: "What are the most pressing instructional problems you face?" "What kinds of difficulties are most persistent in your teaching of reading?" "What kind of an in-service workshop do you want this fall?" Or, the faculty may be divided into small work groups to ascertain members' perceptions of problems. These listings are then reported to the total group, problems pooled, and plans made to attack those which seem most significant or pressing.

Surveys. A school survey can pinpoint areas of dissatisfaction or weakness which need study. As an appraisal technique, a survey can stimulate interest and activity by involving individuals who can affect program quality. There are many different kinds of surveys: some, internal or self-surveys; others, external. An individual or agency (e.g., an accreditation team or a university survey committee) may be invited or employed to survey a program generally or some specific aspects of it. Self-surveys by professional staffs of program quality or of particular facets using available guides (e.g., Cooperative Study of Secondary School Standards Committee's Evaluation Criteria) or homemade instruments can suggest program inadequacies. Schoolwide or systemwide testing programs, such as the Denver public schools' triennial surveys which measure school achievement and mental health (see

p. 210), indicate deficiencies which can be worked on. The Denver *Points of Emphasis* statements which guide that system's curriculum activity stem, in part, from the results of the triennial testing survey. Surveys may be undertaken in conjunction with a student evaluation or pupil-needs study. Parents and other citizens may be surveyed to ascertain their judgments about educational goals or quality of program. The Illinois Curriculum Program's Local Area Consensus Studies (see p. 122) "afford procedures whereby professional educators and lay citizens may come together to study and to make recommendations for the solution of specific problems or to bring about improvements in some portion of the total school program." [10] The Opinion Surveys conducted triennially by the Denver public schools (see p. 215) aim at gathering citizen judgments about the quality of learning in the public schools as well as their views about values in education besides subject matter.[11]

Studies and appraisals. Having valid data available for study and interpretation may provide the stimulus for program development. An analysis of the school population can suggest areas needing further study or educational services which must be added.[12] Systematic testing and inventory programs—achievement, interests, pupil needs, special aptitudes—can yield useful information for planning program modifications. Studies of students who leave school early, or of graduates, or of aspects of the program such as hidden tuition costs, extra class activities, guidance services, or provisions for the gifted, may indicate needed curriculum modifications. The case conferences used in Lewis County (see p. 181), each focusing on an intensive study of a single child, point up facets of the program which need study as well as ways of providing help for the student. The University of Maryland's Institute for Child Study programs illustrate a way of working designed to help teachers understand important child-

---

[10] H. C. Hand, *How to Conduct the Local Area Consensus Studies*, Illinois Curriculum Program Bulletin No. 25 (Springfield: Superintendent of Public Instruction, State of Illinois, October 1956), p. 2.

[11] *Denver Looks at Its Schools 1959* (Denver, Colorado: Denver Public Schools, 1959).

[12] See, for example, the manual prepared for the Illinois Curriculum Program: P. H. Bowman, *How to Study Your School Population*, Illinois Curriculum Program Bulletin No. 26 (Springfield: Superintendent of Public Instruction, State of Illinois, June 1957).

developmental processes in a cultural and social setting. Child study group activities provide important leads for modifying educational provisions. Exploration through study and data gathering can help staff members see the dimensions of a particular educational problem and understand its significance.

Conferences and meetings. Identification of significant problem areas and stimulation for curriculum development may also emerge from staff meetings in which teachers and administrators share new insights acquired at professional conferences, university or college courses, workshops, or other sources. Classroom-initiated projects may be demonstrated in faculty meetings and serve to stimulate further study. Discussions of teaching problems in regular faculty meetings—raising and exploring difficulties and instructional needs without attempting to propose solutions—can pave the way for action by study groups.

Conferences in which teachers and a supervisor or supervisory team meet to discuss program, materials, instructional techniques, and other class-centered problems can often lead to more intensive work. Spending considerable time observing classroom practices, supervisors are able to provide an overview and broad perspective for classroom teachers and to help arrange in-service and other curriculum activities.

Attendance at state and national conventions by classroom teachers as well as administrators can lead to ideas for planning and testing. Some school systems make provisions for staff members to report to their own faculties on return from such conference participation, sharing new insights and demonstrating materials rather than reporting on arrangements and schedule.

The teacher institutes, teacher association meetings, and similar one- or two-day conferences now serve primarily an inspirational or stimulating function. Focusing on a specific theme and organized for appropriate total-group and small-group activities, such meetings can direct staff exploration of an idea in such a way as to lead to the launching of in-service activities in the local situation more suitable to problem study. Shifting the purposes of these short meetings to instructional, exploratory, and stimulating ends has resulted in more realistic planning. Follow-through, in terms of developing appropriate professional in-service activities, is now seen as an integral part of the planning.

The White House Conferences held regularly on the national level have stimulated "Little White House Conferences" at the local, system, county, and state levels to focus on educational problems. Some school systems have such meetings annually for the specific purpose of bringing together lay and professional people to identify program strengths and weaknesses.

Research, experimentation, and pilot programs. Opportunities to participate in experimental programs or tryouts of new materials have involved teachers in curriculum planning activities. The cooperative research undertakings of the Horace Mann–Lincoln Institute of School Experimentation have frequently involved individuals and groups of teachers in active research studies.[13] Similarly, the Illinois Curriculum Program has included teachers in pilot programs, extending the work to larger numbers of teachers as the studies continued. Participation in the work of a school study council may trigger planning activities in the back-home situation. Council activities have also involved local studies for gathering information about programs and practices or for testing out new materials. Materials or programs prepared at summer workshops, for example, may be formally tested in pilot classes during the school year.

The programs of many national professional associations and foundation fund-supported groups have served to spur local curriculum activities. Teachers have participated in the development or testing of new materials or programs. The Physical Science Study Committee and the University of Illinois Committee on School Mathematics,[14] for example, developed materials in science and mathematics which have been introduced in teacher workshops and tested in classes.

The National Education Association's Project on the Academi-

---

[13] See, for example, S. M. Corey, *Action Research to Improve School Practices* (New York: Bureau of Publications, Teachers College, Columbia University, 1953); R. Cunningham and associates, *Understanding Group Behavior of Boys and Girls* (New York: Bureau of Publications, Teachers College, Columbia University, 1951); and A. W. Foshay and K. D. Wann and associates, *Children's Social Values* (New York: Bureau of Publications, Teachers College, Columbia University, 1954).

[14] See Physical Science Study Committee, *First Annual Report* (Cambridge, Massachusetts: The Committee, 1958); and University of Illinois Committee on School Mathematics, "The University of Illinois School Mathematics Program" (Urbana, Illinois: The Committee, 1957; mimeographed).

cally Talented Student has invigorated professional efforts at national and local levels through a series of publications and meetings, each with suggestions for local action. The North Central Association of Colleges and Secondary Schools' Superior and Talented Student Project has involved "a significant group of principals, teachers, and counselors (in some hundred selected schools) in an intensive study, adaptation, and evaluation of procedures for identifying, guiding, and motivating superior and talented students." [15] Similarly, the Citizenship Education Project aimed at stimulating the participation of teachers, administrators, pupils, and the general public—both in planning and carrying out the program.[16]

The initiation of such plans as the Advanced Placement Program [17] has required teacher study and instructional modifications. Three-day work conferences are held annually for school and college teachers and administrators. Development of new instructional aids (such as television, language laboratories, self-teaching machines) necessitate teacher study and planning.

The few projects and programs mentioned above simply illustrate the nationwide variety of sources at work on particular aspects of the school program. To these could be added numerous professional association activities at state and national levels. Although usually aimed at improving program quality directly, these groups simultaneously stimulate planning locally by involving individuals in ways which can facilitate further dissemination to colleagues.

Other sources for initiating curriculum work. In addition to some of the ways listed above, the stimulus for program study may come from many other sources. A professional or lay advisory committee, the curriculum coordinating council, or a central administrative group may suggest in-service activities; journal articles, books, speakers, and courses may provide ideas for cur-

[15] North Central Association of Colleges and Secondary Schools, Superior and Talented Student Project, *A Prospectus* (Chicago: The Association, 1958), p. 3.

[16] W. S. Vincent, and others, *Building Better Programs in Citizenship* (New York: Citizenship Education Project, Teachers College, Columbia University, 1958).

[17] College Entrance Examination Board, *Advanced Placement Program* (New York: The Board, 1956).

riculum study. Committees engaged in one activity (for example, a textbook or film selection group or a report-card work party) may see other problems which require study and planning.

Selecting and Refining Problems and Areas

Since almost every facet of the educational program and every aspect of teaching can be studied, the selection and refinement of curriculum problems are critically important. Poor problem definition can result in frustration and unproductive results, in the dilution of staff efforts, and in discouragement of professional enthusiasm. Interesting the teacher in work on improving the quality of education is but one part of the leadership problem; another is to insure that such interest will not be dissipated through poor planning efforts.

Significance. A test of significance should be applied to problems being examined. Problem significance should be judged in terms of (1) its potential for involving individuals both intellectually and emotionally; (2) its meaningful relationship to classroom activities and to teaching tasks; and (3) its possibilities for being resolved. Creating the conditions whereby real concerns are proposed instead of "safe and legitimate" ones, is a major leadership problem. In addition, opening new vistas for staff members so that significance can be seen is an important leadership responsibility. Curriculum workers may begin with somewhat limited and restricted understandings and these must be recognized, accepted, and broadened.

Involvement. Individuals who are to be involved in the solution of a problem should participate in its definition. Is the problem area one in which individuals may be involved meaningfully? The degrees of participation may vary so that not all individuals are concerned in all steps of problem determination. However, it is important that all persons concerned be involved at the point where goals are being formulated and plans made for working toward their attainment.

Scope and time. Problems must be so refined that they are of manageable size in terms of the personnel resources available and so that there is promise of tangible results with a reasonable expenditure of time and effort. Considerable work may be required to cut global problems down to size or to define problems which can be attacked by smaller groups.

The suggested ways for stimulating professional interest in identifying problem areas and carrying on curriculum studies are, of course, illustrative only. There are obviously many different ways of identifying instructional problems and initiating curriculum activities. Listing some twenty "psychological levers" used by schools, an early publication of the Illinois Curriculum Program advised readers to pick one and get started:

> These levers include carrying on such activities as studies, visits, readings, and self-surveys by local faculties, and then using the resultant data as a basis for arousing discontent with the existing program and encouraging a desire to do something constructive by way of change.[18]

Criteria for Initiating Curriculum Change

There are many means for stimulating professional and lay persons to cast aside present practices and to work on important educational problems. The involvement of key individuals in work on curriculum problems which have meaning and significance is a critical function for instructional leadership. Simply to announce that workshops are to be started and courses are to be taught, inviting all who would like to participate is usually not enough. Effective machinery for initiating curriculum improvement activities should include provisions for:

1. Regular discussions for sharing common concerns to make significant problems visible and for exchanging ideas.

2. Development of channels for communicating instructional problems to a central planning and coordinating group.

3. New materials to be sent to individuals and groups, keeping them abreast of new developments.

4. Opportunities for individuals and groups to have contact with new ideas and practices through conferences, meetings, and school visitations.

---

[18] V. M. Houston, C. W. Sanford, and J. L. Trump, *Guide to the Study of the Secondary Schools of Illinois*, Curriculum Bulletin No. 1 (Springfield: Superintendent of Public Instruction, State of Illinois, 1948), p. 25.

5. Study of practices and procedures to gather pertinent information about the educational program.

6. Encouragement and support of experimentation and research in the classroom by furnishing necessary aid (e.g., consultants, materials, and skill training).

7. Periodic evaluation of learning and teaching, and analysis of results for leads to improving program quality.

Central office personnel at the systemwide level and the principal or coordinator in school buildings have responsibilities for initiating curriculum improvement activities although teachers and others may share these charges. Exercising these functions requires conditions whereby staff members feel free to ask questions about the school's program and practices and to inquire into the possible value of new developments and proposals in education. At the same time, the staff can acquire the skills needed to deal responsibly with the pressures from local sources as well as the challenges from the national level. Awareness and ability critically to appraise curriculum issues is an important part of the process of upgrading program quality.

SELECTED READINGS

American Association of School Administrators, *American School Curriculum*, Thirty-first Yearbook. Washington, D.C.: National Education Association, 1953.

Anderson, Vernon E., *Principles and Procedures of Curriculum Improvement*. New York: Ronald Press, 1956.

Association for Supervision and Curriculum Development, *Group Processes in Supervision*. Washington, D.C.: The Association, NEA, 1948.

——, *Leadership and the Improvement of Instruction*. Washington, D.C.: The Association, NEA, 1960.

——, *Leadership Through Supervision*. Washington, D.C.: The Association, NEA, 1946.

——, *Time and Funds for Curriculum Development*. Washington, D.C.: The Association, NEA, 1951.

Caswell, Hollis L. and Associates, *Curriculum Improvement in Public School Systems*. New York: Bureau of Publications, Teachers College, Columbia University, 1950.

Crosby, Muriel, *Supervision as Cooperative Action*. New York: Appleton-Century-Crofts, 1957.

Doll, Ronald, Passow, A. Harry, and Corey, Stephen M., *Organ-*

izing for Curriculum Improvement. New York: Bureau of Publications, Teachers College, Columbia University, 1953.

GRIFFITHS, DANIEL E., *Human Relations in School Administration.* New York: Appleton-Century-Crofts, 1956.

KRUG, EDWARD, BABCOCK, CHESTER D., FOWLKES, JOHN GUY, and JAMES, H. T., *Administering Curriculum Planning.* New York: Harper and Brothers, 1956.

MITCHUM, PAUL M., *The High School Principal and Staff Plan for Program Improvement.* New York: Bureau of Publications, Teachers College, Columbia University, 1958.

SAYLOR, J. GALEN and ALEXANDER, WILLIAM M., *Curriculum Planning for Better Teaching and Learning.* New York: Rinehart and Company, 1954.

SPEARS, HAROLD, *Curriculum Planning through In-service Programs.* Englewood Cliffs, N.J.: Prentice-Hall, 1957.

STRATEMEYER, FLORENCE B., FORKNER, HAMDEN L., McKIM, MARGARET, and PASSOW, A. HARRY, *Developing a Curriculum for Modern Living* (2d ed. rev.). New York: Bureau of Publications, Teachers College, Columbia University, 1957.

4

PROCEDURES FOR WORKING ON
PROGRAM IMPROVEMENT

THE NOTIONS about how curriculum improvement takes place have very obviously influenced the spread of group procedures for program planning. For example, the annual production of curriculum guides in one form or another increases steadily with a continuing emphasis on cooperative production. In one survey, four-fifths of the curriculum guides examined were produced by groups of teachers and administrators working together.[1] Committees and work groups are seen in most schools as one of the essential conditions for effective development. Most of the techniques and procedures currently employed in program development are basically methods for forming groups and for facilitating their operations. This does not mean that individual study and work are not provided for. Rather, the same attention is given to the creation of optimum group-work conditions as is necessary for building an effective classroom environment for the individual learner.

As pointed out in Chapter 2, there are many different foci of attention for curriculum activities. Many of the procedures by

[1] E. Merritt and H. Harap, *Trends in the Production of Curriculum Guides* (Nashville, Tennessee: George Peabody College for Teachers, 1955), p. 40.

which staff personnel analyze and evaluate educational programs, identify instructional problems, and initiate studies are essentially the same as those used to work on curriculum improvement. By the kinds of conditions created, the personnel involved, and the resources made available, some procedures have greater inherent promise for facilitating certain kinds of tasks than do others. A workshop, for example, can contribute far more to skill development than a two-day teachers' institute. The former focuses on problem solution while the latter tends to be primarily inspirational and informative. In either case, the procedures are the vehicles for working on curriculum problems, not the ends.

Terminology by which various procedures are labeled has become cloudy and confused. The distinction between curriculum improvement programs and in-service education has disappeared as activities under both classifications aim at improving the quality of education. The *Dictionary of Education,* for example, defines in-service education as "all efforts of administrative and supervisory officials to promote by appropriate means the professional growth and development of educational workers: illustrative are curriculum study, classroom visitation and supervisory assistance." Many diverse activities from a one-day meeting to a six-week program are now designated as workshops or conferences. Labels are not important, of course, and insistence on more rigorous use of terms would probably not affect the use of these procedures. However, the use of certain designations could affect individual and group perceptions of their tasks and assignments.

THE FACILITATION OF WORK

The procedures and techniques described below may be called by other names in a particular school system's program. Here they are described briefly in terms of facilitating work on particular kinds of curriculum improvement tasks. Since the relationship between procedures for involving personnel and providing optimum conditions for their working on instructional problems is an integral one, the same procedure may serve both functions.

Another problem in terminology is the lack of distinction between the use of the terms "technique" and "procedure." The difficulties arise because the ways of working on curriculum programs are of many orders or levels of complexity and comprehensiveness. Research methods may be used by a number of different groups as they work on curriculum problems; a research project may be the means by which change is brought about. Role playing may be employed in various procedures—workshop or clinic. Skill practice sessions may be used to improve instruction. The rubrics are unimportant, but the clarity of purpose or goal, the kinds of arrangements to be made, the resources to be provided, and the end product expected are crucial.

Committees and Work Groups

A widely used procedure or vehicle for curriculum development is the committee or work group. Such groups may have a rather specific assignment or a broad charge, for example, the preparation of a bulletin for parents on the teaching of reading, or proposals for a policy on promotion practices. Committees may meet regularly or only as required. With broad responsibilities for fostering program development, work groups may use any technique or procedure which will facilitate professional change. Because of broad flexibility in function and ways of operating, the committee or work group is sometimes viewed more as a method of organization than a specific procedure as such. However, through study, discussion, preparation of materials, fostering experimentation, and evaluation, the working committees constitute one of the most important instructional improvement arrangements.

For example, a Steering Committee or Instructional Council may appoint a Committee on the Gifted to study the problems involved in providing an adequate educational program for intellectually able children. The Committee on the Gifted may have several meetings during which time it explores effective ways of fulfilling its assignment, namely, to prepare recommendations for policies, program, and practices for identifying and educating gifted children. Following exploratory study and discussion during which time committee members may bring in information gathered from their colleagues or from study of research reports and descriptions of other programs, the group may then determine how it can best attack the general problem through its component parts. With members of the parent Committee on the Gifted as a nucleus for subgroups, working committees may then be set up to deal with specific problem areas, such as Identification, Instructional and Administrative Modifications, Methods and Materials, Guidance and Counseling, Working with Parents, Using Community Resources, Program Articulation, Evaluation and Research. The Committee on the Gifted then becomes, in effect, a steering committee which coordinates and guides the working groups, with its members active participants in the subcommittee operations. The parent committee meets regularly to receive and discuss reports, to appraise and judge action proposals, to coordinate the complementary studies under way, and to communicate with the systemwide Steering Committee or Instructional Council. Eventually seeing the program through to implementation and evaluation in the classrooms may be the end task of this group.

Each subcommittee will plan its own approach to its particular problems. The subcommittee on Identification of the Gifted may begin with a thorough search of the literature to see what research findings and the experiences of other schools have to suggest for identifying such children. The subcommittee may survey schools in the system to ascertain what procedures are presently used and what problems are encountered in employing them. Teachers may be interviewed to learn what kinds of help they feel they need. The committee may prepare a guide for administrators, counselors, and teachers. The guide may then be taken back to a few staffs or selected individuals for study, discussion, possible try-out, and revision suggestions. The guide may then be revised and tested in a few pilot situations. The subcommittee may sponsor afternoon meetings at which the guide is discussed with a larger number of teachers. The guide may then be ready to pass on to the parent Committee on the Gifted and then to the Instructional Council for systemwide distribution. Faculty meetings may be held for the purpose of explaining the use of the guide and even demonstrating some of the techniques suggested. The subcommittee may make recommendations for evaluating the procedures outlined for effectively identifying gifted children. This evaluation may be carried out by the subcommittee with the assistance of the Evaluation and Research subgroup or the latter may undertake this appraisal.

The Instructional and Administrative Modifications subgroup

may operate in a similar fashion. It may explore the administrative arrangements which seem to block current instructional practices and study the kinds of modifications needed to facilitate teaching of the gifted. Here, again, there is a wealth of research and reported experiences indicating other possibilities. The subcommittee may study various alternatives to discover which have most promise in terms of the educational goals of the school system. Members may interview teachers individually or in groups to determine what the staff perceptions are as to difficulties encountered in teaching the gifted. As a result of its studies, the subcommittee may recommend that a workshop be held to probe classroom problems. Or, a series of in-service courses may be arranged for on a systemwide basis. Pilot studies may be initiated in a few schools. Eventually, the subcommittee will be ready to suggest a basic design to be adopted as part of the systemwide policy. This design would be subjected to testing and evaluation.

Each of the other committees would, in similar fashion, use whatever techniques seemed most feasible to move ahead its study of a particular aspect of the general problem of improving the quality of education for the gifted. The Methods and Materials subcommittee, for example, may develop bulletins suggesting ways for teachers to differentiate assignments, materials, and other aspects of instruction. Or, self-teaching materials for students and guides for directing independent study may be prepared and tested by the subcommittee. Each of the subcommittees may undertake whatever studies and activities seem most likely to yield positive results. The Committee on the Gifted, as coordinating group, secures the necessary consultant and other resources, appraises subcommittee progress, and provides balanced perspective to the various activities. In turn, the systemwide Instructional Council keeps check on developments and provides the necessary balance of activities and program development.

Flexibility in organization and in procedures employed in attacking problems is characteristic of committee work on program improvement. In general, the quality of the improvements which result depends on the skills and competencies of the committee members, the cohesive nature and maturity of the group, the leadership provided and emergent, the resources made available, the conditions under which activities take place, and the ability to keep the purposes closely related, at the practical level, to instruction.

Study Groups

Closely related to the work committees as a procedure for curriculum improvement are the many kinds of study groups. Probably the most widely used focus for such groups is child study. Teachers are helped with techniques for studying children and develop understandings which are basic to effective teaching and guidance. The child study programs (such as those under the guidance of the University of Maryland Institute for Child Study) usually extend over a period of several years. They are designed to help teachers understand the important developmental processes and the environmental influences on the child as he grows up. Systematically, within a guiding framework, the teacher is helped to acquire the techniques and skills for studying children. Through observations and anecdotal records, the teacher undertakes an intensive study of the behavior of a single child, analyzes the data in relation to known norms and behavior scales, examines changes in terms of predictions made, and evaluates the educational program's effectiveness as judged by what is known about the child. Studies of children can provide leads to curriculum inadequacies through pointing up the gap between the child's development and the kinds of educational experiences he is having. Specialists are generally available to guide the teachers to an understanding of the psychological, cultural, and social settings that affect child behavior. Acquisition of the necessary insights and skills for observing and studying child behavior is a competence developed in such study programs.[2]

The case conference technique involves a group of teachers and other staff members in an intensive study of an individual child—

[2] American Council on Education, *Helping Teachers Understand Children* (Washington, D.C.: The Council, 1945); M. Almy, *Ways of Studying Children* (New York: Bureau of Publications, Teachers College, Columbia University, 1959); G. P. Driscoll, *How to Study the Behavior of Children* (New York: Bureau of Publications, Teachers College, Columbia University, 1941); V. White, *Studying the Individual Pupil* (New York: Harper and Brothers, 1958); D. Prescott, *The Child and the Educative Process* (New York: McGraw-Hill Book Company, 1957).

either an "average" child or one having difficulties—in an attempt to marshal insights to appraise curriculum implications from data presented.[3]

Study programs can focus on areas other than child study. Community studies by faculty staffs can serve the functions of locating instructional resources, extending teacher insights into forces affecting student learning, and generally broadening professional competence. Sociology, architecture, population growth, public services, governmental structure, geographical and ecological setting—these are but a few aspects of the community which can be studied by staffs for curriculum implications. A human resources file—a complete listing of individuals in the community who could bring some special competency or service to the classroom or to the staff—has emerged from some such studies; a series of guides to the existence and use of community resources from others. Bulletins for teachers and students describing in detail geological structure, native flora and fauna, historical documents and buildings, and similar instructional materials have also been produced.

Professional and lay groups have studied the goals of the public school and the success with which the goals are being attained. Such studies have been concerned with total school programs and have extended over a period of time. In other instances, a more circumscribed area has been examined, for example, special services, youth recreation, teaching of the basic skills.

Workshops and Work Conferences

Many different types of meetings and conferences are called workshops. The essential characteristic of a workshop is the opportunity provided for participants to study and act upon problems which they have identified as significant. The workshop activities, the schedule, and all other arrangements are based on the problems, needs, and interests of the members. Some other features of a workshop are:

1. A steering or planning committee has responsibility for pre-workshop problem census and for preparing work arrangements.

[3] Details of the use of such conferences are found in G. Morris, *The High School Principal and Staff Study Youth* (New York: Bureau of Publications, Teachers College, Columbia University, 1958).

2. Provisions are made in preplanning and early workshop sessions for members to participate in identifying and refining the problems on which they will work.

3. At work sessions individuals and small groups are arranged in terms of the nature of the problems, with flexible patterns of organization and ways of working.

4. General sessions feature activities (e.g., a speaker, a panel discussion, a demonstration, an audio-visual presentation) which deal with common concerns or one of the problem areas are planned.

5. Consultants and other resource specialists are available as needed to assist individuals and groups.

6. Library and other instructional materials are on hand for use by participants as required.

7. The schedule is flexible, adjusted to the functions to be performed, and constantly examined by the planning committee.

8. Provisions are made for training in the skills required for effective participation, such as those needed for leadership roles, for using consultants, for group functioning.

9. Evaluation of workshop procedures and products is planned for from the beginning.

10. Common social and recreational activities are provided for participants.

The primary differences between the workshop and the work conference tend to be in the length of the program and the amount of prestructure. Since work conferences are of much shorter duration (ranging from three or four days to two or three weeks), the schedule may be more fully preplanned. Workshops are usually four weeks or longer in length although the time arrangements may vary from a six- or eight-week summer session to a single day weekly over the academic year.[4]

In addition to stimulating involvement in curriculum activities, workshops and work conferences may have one or more of the following purposes:

[4] A detailed description of a university-centered afternoon-evening workshop is found in E. C. Kelley, *The Workshop Way of Learning* (New York: Harper and Brothers, 1951). An account of how a school system organized and conducted a workshop over a two-year period is contained in "Report of the Washington School District Inservice Workshop" (West Sacramento, California: Washington School District, 1956; mimeographed).

Increasing insights and understandings through study of some aspect of classroom instruction to deepen knowledge and extend perception. A workshop may focus on such broad problem areas as the teaching of superior readers or integrating music, art, and social studies, or enriching mathematics learning in the intermediate grades. Or, the focus may be more specific, such as studying a foreign language or music appreciation in order to enrich the elementary school program.

Familiarizing teachers with new developments through systematic opportunities to become acquainted with new knowledge, methods, materials, or concepts. A workshop may focus on discussion of knowledge emerging from the International Geophysical Year and implications for educational programs. Opportunities to familiarize themselves with methods and materials of new programs in mathematics, science, language arts or other areas may be provided.

Developing teaching skills by extending the teacher's understanding of, and familiarity with, various instructional techniques and procedures. A workshop may provide opportunities for teachers to discuss and practice skills involved in differentiating instruction with small groups or using various art media or employing new devices in language instruction. In studying ways of reporting to parents, staff members may increase their skills in parent-teacher conferences through role-playing experiences. Teachers may develop their skills in observing child behavior through workshop experiences.

Producing instructional and other educational materials either as a specific end or in connection with other workshop activities. A workshop may focus on the preparation of resource units, curriculum bulletins, or similar instructional aids for teachers or the production of self-teaching units for students. A workshop group may develop a portable science laboratory for the primary grades or a language arts library kit or a filmstrip or a motion picture. A new cumulative record form or an evaluation guide may emerge from a workshop.

Resolving common instructional problems by careful analysis of concerns which cut across departmental, administrative, or unit levels. A workshop may attack problems of scope and sequence in a particular subject area in order to build a unified program or may develop a consistent policy on promotion and reporting to parents or may develop guides for dealing with discipline problems in a systematic fashion.

A single faculty may organize a workshop, or teachers from all over the country may meet to work on problems (such as those connected with a particular syllabus or examination in the Advanced Placement Program). A number of states have sponsored countywide and statewide workshops to develop new and improved methods and materials, to stimulate curriculum projects, to research programs, to examine basic issues and problems, or otherwise to initiate studies. Professional associations, regional, and national groups have used workshops to work on curriculum problems.[5] Together with courses at colleges or universities, workshops are one of the most widely used forms of in-service education.[6]

University and College In-service Programs

The institutions of higher education—universities, colleges, departments of education—have always played important roles in in-service education. University staff members have served as speakers or consultants in planning meetings. College courses, summer sessions, extension classes, and other class programs have been modified somewhat to meet the special needs of teachers in service. Increasingly, institutions of higher education have broadened the kinds of services provided for school personnel and, as a consequence, have developed close working relations with school staffs on improving the quality of education. Some of the ways in which university personnel and programs contribute to curriculum improvement are:

Classes, courses, and institutes arranged in response to a specific request from a school system and usually conducted in one of the local buildings. Although the course may be conducted in a fash-

---

[5] A survey of such programs may be found in K. J. Rehage and G. W. Denemark, "Area, State, Regional, and National In-service Education Programs," in *In-Service Education for Teachers, Supervisors, and Administrators,* Fifty-sixth Yearbook, Part 1, National Society for the Study of Education (Chicago: The University of Chicago Press, 1957), pp. 224–63.

[6] K. E. Anderson and H. A. Smith, "Preservice and In-service Education of Elementary- and Secondary-School Teachers," *Review of Educational Research,* Vol. 35 (June 1955), p. 221.

ion similar to an on-campus class, it is usually designed to meet special needs of the local staff. Short-term refresher and intensive preschool and postschool courses have been arranged to meet teacher needs for specific knowledge or skills.

Seminars, practicums, and continuing conferences in which school staffs and university consultants work on a specific instructional problem over a school year or longer.[7] College personnel may demonstrate certain teaching procedures or materials in school classrooms with staff members as observers. Discussions of the class observations follow. Local instructional leaders may receive help in skill development by participating in continuing conferences at the university, bringing to the regular sessions problems which have emerged in the interim period. Or, in connection with in-service curriculum activities, problems emerge which are discussed at sessions in which direct help is provided.[8]

Conferences, workshops, and institutes of short duration to which school staffs, selected teams, or individual members are invited. The conferences and meetings can deal with specific topics, such as "Remedial reading in the junior high school" or with broader areas such as "Improving teaching of reading." Such conferences may be devoted to skill training wherein participants are provided with opportunities to discuss, to see demonstrations, and to practice a specific skill such as the preparation of a filmstrip or the use of a tachistoscope.

Cooperative projects and studies in which school and university personnel engage in joint field studies. The college personnel may undertake a cooperative survey, or initiate a research project or design an experimental program together with school staff members.[9] With teachers as co-investigators and the research focusing

[7] W. M. Alexander, R. S. Fleming, and others, "Working on Curriculum Problems Through University Seminars," *Educational Leadership*, Vol. 10 (May 1955), p. 467.

[8] A continuing conference to stimulate cooperative research is described in A. H. Passow, M. B. Miles, S. M. Corey, and D. C. Draper, *Training Curriculum Leaders for Cooperative Research* (New York: Bureau of Publications, Teachers College, Columbia University, 1955).

[9] Some of the ways in which universities initiate studies with schools is described in Chapter 5 in which the work of the Illinois Curriculum Program is reported. Many of the field projects of the Horace Mann-Lincoln Institute of School Experimentation of Teachers College, Columbia University, are cooperative research studies. A pamphlet describing this Institute, its ways of working and its publications is available on request from the Executive Director.

on improving classroom practices, university personnel are functioning both as researchers and research consultants.

School study councils designed to facilitate exchange of practices, to initiate studies, and to pool resources. In a relatively short
period of time, the school study council has spread to universities
and colleges across the country. The school study council is a
cooperative arrangement involving a number of systems and one
or more universities and colleges. The institution of higher education usually furnishes an executive director, secretarial services, a
central office, a core of its staff as a pool from which to draw consultants and resource specialists, and meeting space as required.
Some of the kinds of activities undertaken by study councils include conferences for the exchange of ideas, practices, teaching
techniques and materials; collecting and publishing "promising
practices" in instruction, administration, and guidance; initiating
and coordinating surveys, studies, and research; arranging for
sharing of services and personnel among school systems; stimulating utilization of council activities at the local level; and publishing materials for use by school staffs.[10]

Service projects in which resources and materials, consultants,
and planning meetings are organized under the direction of a
university or college staff. The Citizenship Education Project is
an illustration of a college-based project which aimed at improving citizenship education by providing planning services of
many kinds to schools.[11] Another kind of university service project
has expanded rapidly with the renewed concern for educational
provisions for intellectually able children and youth. Here universities have cooperated with schools in developing instructional
programs for both students and teachers. The "Wide Horizons
Program" of the University of Rochester, for example, brings together a teacher, one or more gifted students from his school, and
university professors in monthly seminar meetings wherein the

[10] A description of the operations and impact of one council is found in
"A Progress Report of the Metropolitan School Study Council," *Teachers
College Record*, Vol. 50 (October 1948), pp. 1–59. A detailed report of the
functioning of one group in a council is available in P. Carter, D. Nesbitt,
and M. Harden, "Co-operative Action Research of the Metropolitan Detroit
Bureau of Co-operative School Studies," in *A Look at Co-operative Research
in Michigan* (Lansing: Michigan Education Association, 1954), pp. 51–69.

[11] W. S. Vincent, and Others, *Building Better Programs in Citizenship* (New
York: Citizenship Education Project, Teachers College, Columbia University,
1958).

professor presents a statement on some "great idea of mankind" and then leads a discussion on the relationships of the idea to the life of man. Universities have initiated or cooperated in developing courses, seminars, lecture series, and similar arrangements for gifted students and staff members as well as providing opportunities for such students to work as "apprentices" to researchers.

Institutions of higher education have developed active and significant roles in improving the quality of education. In addition to organized courses, both on and off campus, and modified to meet the needs of participants, universities have developed many other avenues through which to aid schools attack problems of program quality directly.

Clinics make available expert assistance in the diagnosis of an instructional problem and in the development of suggestions for possible solutions. In a clinic, help may be provided in problem analysis, in suggesting alternative solutions, or in examining implications of practices. For instance, teachers have an all-day meeting in which they bring in the problems encountered in providing remedial reading instruction in the regular classroom or they analyze the persistent blocks that are present in teaching a particular mathematical process. Specialist help is provided in studying the problems and working out techniques and procedures to be tested in the classroom.

A demonstration clinic is one in which new materials, methods, techniques, and practices are demonstrated by a specialist or group of experts. Participants then have an opportunity to explore, discuss, and possibly test the presentation materials or practices. Included in this category of procedures are some of the training sessions used to improve the skills involved in working on curriculum improvement. For example, group chairmen may meet to examine the problems they are facing in their discussion groups. Under the direction of a consultant or trainer, the chairmen may test various techniques for handling the specific problems, appraising the effectiveness, and enhancing their skills in the use of the techniques.[12]

[12] For a report of one such session, including a script for a training tape employed, see S. M. Corey, P. M. Halverson, and E. Lowe, *Teachers Prepare for Discussion Group Leadership* (New York: Bureau of Publications, Teachers College, Columbia University, 1953). Other training activities in a clinic-type program are reported in A. H. Passow, M. B. Miles, S. M. Corey, and D. C. Draper, *op. cit.*, pp. 61–73.

Research, experimentation, and evaluation are used by school systems in improving the quality of education. Some curriculum specialists have seen classroom research and experimentation as "inextricably related to effective curriculum planning." [13] Still, curriculum research activities as carried on by school systems tend to be relatively scarce and of varied quality. Such procedures, however, are being used increasingly as school personnel grasp the potential values of a research approach to curriculum building, as they increase their skills in the methods and techniques of research, and as research consultants are available.

Research is a process, a method of study or investigation, an orderly approach to problem solving. The aim of research may be the deepening of insights into the nature or dimensions of a problem; the exploring or establishing of relationships between causes and effects; the collecting of evidence to judge the effectiveness of an idea or practice; or the acquiring of leads for new ideas or practices which can then be tested. Experimentation is one form of research: the systematic testing of an idea, a program, a practice, or some material. Basic to good-quality experimentation is the gathering of data on which to judge effectiveness and not simply the maintenance of tentativeness of judgment with respect to the tryout. Evaluation and appraisal are techniques for assessing the attainment of specified objectives.

In terms of curriculum planning, the most significant development has been the growing stress laid upon involving teachers in the research process as a means of improving the quality of education. Action and cooperative curriculum research are the two most common labels attached to undertakings in which teachers, as individuals or in groups, use research processes in studying their own practices. As described by Corey in an analysis of the meaning of this approach for curriculum development, action research "is conducted by teachers or supervisors or administrators in order that they may know, on the basis of relatively objective evidence, whether or not they are accomplishing the things they hope to acomplish." [14] The focus of action research has been on

[13] J. G. Saylor and W. M. Alexander, *Curriculum Planning* (New York: Rinehart and Company, 1954), p. 503.

[14] S. M. Corey, *Action Research to Improve School Practices* (New York: Bureau of Publications, Teachers College, Columbia University, 1953), p. 143.

the direct improvement of instruction and, as a consequence, the involvement of teachers and the development of their research skills and understandings have been two major concerns.[15]

The Horace Mann–Lincoln Institute of School Experimentation has published a number of reports of research studies undertaken in cooperation with public schools. These describe a variety of studies in which teachers and administrators participated in action research projects affecting instructional programs.[16] Other reports have added to available descriptions of action research and cooperative research programs.[17] Evaluation of experimental projects and research have contributed to insights about learning and teaching as well as to the general effectiveness of programs.[18]

Considerable discussion appears in the literature about the value and the validity of action research. Fortunately, comparisons between action and other types of research which commended or depreciated one or another have begun to dwindle. Whatever the resulting contribution to general theory of educa-

[15] An excellent discussion and description of research and curriculum planning is found in the 1957 yearbook of the Association for Supervision and Curriculum Development, *Research for Curriculum Improvement* (Washington, D.C.: The Association, 1957). Included as an appendix is a description of a one-week training institute designed "to strengthen participants' competencies in conducting and helping others conduct cooperative research."

[16] These studies include R. Cunningham and associates, *Understanding the Group Behavior of Boys and Girls* (New York: Bureau of Publications, Teachers College, Columbia University, 1951); S. M. Corey, *op. cit.;* H. M. Evans (ed.), *Cooperative Research and Curriculum Improvement* (New York: Bureau of Publications, Teachers College, Columbia University, 1950); A. W. Foshay and K. Wann, *Children's Social Values* (New York: Bureau of Publications, Teachers College, Columbia University, 1954); G. N. Mackenzie, S. M. Corey, and associates, *Instructional Leadership* (New York: Bureau of Publications, Teachers College, Columbia University, 1954).

[17] See, for example, M. Hughes and others, "Iron County Teachers Study Their Problems Scientifically," *Educational Leadership*, Vol. 12 (May 1955), pp. 489–95; E. H. Johnson, C. W. Sanford, and H. C. Hand, "The Research Program of the Illinois Curriculum Program," *Journal of Educational Research*, Vol. 47 (January 1954), pp. 367–73.

[18] Illustrations may be found in reports of research connected with the development of programs for children with exceptional endowments, as for example, Portland Public Schools, *The Gifted Child Project* (Portland, Oregon: The Public Schools, 1959); Dade County Public Schools, *Teaching the Talented* (Miami, Florida: The Public Schools, 1955); M. Goldberg and associates, "A Three-Year Experimental Program at DeWitt Clinton High School to Help Bright Underachievers," *High Points*, Vol. 61 (January 1959), pp. 5–35.

tion, there is little doubt that action research can make a contribution as an in-service procedure for curriculum improvement. Sober analyses have pinpointed the limitations and difficulties of teacher-conducted research and have indicated training needs if the quality of research is to improve. The continuing trend in curriculum research which emerged from a recent survey, emphasizes research for school improvement.[19]

Short-term meetings are used to contribute to professional growth of staff and improvement of educational quality. The after-school faculty meeting is probably the most commonly used procedure in terms of frequency. Discussions, demonstrations, role-playing, and skill practice sessions, lectures, and similar techniques are employed during these meetings. A newer development has been the Business–Education, Labor–Education, and Community–Education Days when business, labor, or community leaders exchange visits with teachers. In studying and discussing new developments in the community, the teachers can extend their insights into program possibilities. Some school systems now provide for planning sessions for as much as one or two weeks prior to the opening and/or the closing of school. Regular times—a whole day or a part thereof monthly or bimonthly—are made available in some schools for staff planning. Attendance at teachers' association and other professional meetings—system, district, county and state—is provided for by releasing teachers and thus enabling exchanges of ideas and programs.

Supervision through individual and group conferences and other supervisory techniques aims at improving the quality of instruction. The prime function of supervision in most school systems across the country is to extend and enrich the classroom teachers' competencies and resources. In this respect, the supervisor is "resource person, coordinator, service agent and consultant." [20] In performing these many roles, the supervisor may:

1. Secure desired instructional materials or introduce teachers to new materials.

[19] R. S. Fleming, "Research and Evaluation in Curriculum Planning," *Review of Educational Research*, Vol. 27 (June 1957), pp. 295–303.

[20] W. M. Alexander and D. S. Patterson, "Developing Leadership," in *Action for Curriculum Improvement* (Washington, D.C.: Association for Supervision and Curriculum Development, 1951), p. 164.

2. Observe and discuss classroom activities, demonstrating teaching techniques when appropriate.

3. Arrange for, and participate in, conducting case studies.

4. Lead or sponsor study groups designed to extend teacher insights and competencies.

5. Counsel and confer with teachers on their professional problems in individual or group conferences.

6. Encourage the "cross-fertilization of ideas" and practices.

7. Assist in making arrangements for in-service and curriculum planning activities.

8. Arrange for consultants and resource persons as needed.

9. Participate in evaluations of program.

10. Provide opportunities for sharing experiences among teachers in one or more schools.

11. Contribute to the development of group process skills.

Few other leadership roles have undergone such major redefinition in the past few decades as that of the supervisor. It was in 1928 that Courtis expressed as a hope the belief that "tomorrow the goal of supervision will be the facilitation of the natural process of growth of personality in teachers, a process which yields inevitably the important concomitants, sympathy with children and teaching power." [21] Whatever other responsibilities may be assigned the supervisor of today, in most school systems his primary function has become one of assisting the professional staff to grow in ability to study and to solve instructional problems and to upgrade the quality of instruction.[22]

School visits are used to encourage and stimulate teacher growth. Many school systems provide regular opportunities for teachers, as individuals or as members of a team, to visit classes in other schools either within or outside the system. Some systems also provide for intervisitation within the building itself. The

[21] S. A. Courtis, "A Philosophy of Supervision," in *Educational Supervision* (New York: Bureau of Publications, Teachers College, Columbia University, 1928), p. 251.

[22] See, for example, W. S. Elsbree and H. J. McNally, *Elementary-School Administration and Supervision* (New York: American Book Company, rev. ed., 1959); H. Spears, *Improving the Supervision of Instruction* (New York: Prentice-Hall, Inc., 1953); S. H. Moorer, *Supervision: the Keystone to Educational Progress* (Tallahassee: Florida State Department of Education, 1952); M. Crosby, *Supervision as Co-operative Action* (New York: Appleton-Century-Crofts, Inc., 1957).

purposes of such visits are many. In some instances, opportunities are provided for teachers to see how others teach and to observe classes of special interest. Where a teacher or a school is testing out a new program or some new materials, teachers may visit to become acquainted with the development or to see how it works in action. There are many other possibilities for visitation through which teachers may get help on a special problem or acquire new insights about a practice or simply see how another colleague handles a similar situation.

In general, the value of such professional visitation depends on the care with which the arrangements have been made, the exactness of the preplanning that takes place, and the nature of the opportunities for observing and analyzing the situation. Good results from school visits do not occur from simply releasing teachers from classroom responsibilities and permitting them to go where they will. Careful selection of places to be visited must be made within some meaningful framework and preplanning must help teachers clarify the purpose of the visit. In some instances, training in the skills needed for effective observation and analysis may be required. Arrangements must include preparation not only for the teacher who is visiting but for the staff of the school being visited as well. Few school systems have begun to realize the potentialities of school visitation for professional growth although more and more systems are using this procedure as an integral part of their curriculum improvement efforts.

In this general area of activity, teacher exchanges are being made in increasing numbers. Sometimes the exchange is with a person from another country and the teachers trade positions for an academic year or so. This period of time is sufficiently long for the exchangee to get some insights into the educational processes and problems, the cultural setting, and the way of life of the community in which he is temporarily living. He sees how another culture deals with some of the same problems he faces. In addition to exchanges, more and more teachers are touring the United States and other lands to broaden their own general education and thus increase their professional competencies by deeper insights into other lands and people.

Curriculum libraries and professional centers are used by schools to improve the quality of education by providing a central laboratory for planning and study. Such libraries make possible a center in which curriculum work groups and individual teachers have an up-to-date, compact collection of available teaching and learning materials as well as a place in which to use them. Instructional materials of all kinds—curriculum bulletins and guides, journals, books, and other publications, audio-visual materials and other teaching equipment—are gathered and arranged to make them readily available for persons planning programs or working on some aspect of curriculum improvement. In larger school systems, a staff is provided to insure that the materials are kept current and usable in the most efficient manner. The staff orders new materials, catalogs it upon arrival, calls new items to the attention of potential users, and otherwise services the center to make curriculum-planning tools useful and available. The resources with which to attack instructional problems are thus accessible to groups and individuals as needed.

Other techniques and procedures are used in program improvement efforts to get a specific task done or a particular product developed and made available. For example, some school systems employ teachers during the summer vacation or other time during the school year either to prepare materials to be used by work committees or to report on materials which have emerged as a result of the planning of such groups. For example, an individual or small group may be assigned responsibility for preparing a summary of research findings, assembling a collection of materials, or preparing a policy paper which will serve as the basis for deliberations or study for a planning group. Similarly, an assignment may involve the preparation of a report or a curriculum guide or a bulletin for student use, the product having emerged from the work of a committee. This use of the individual or small group for a specific assignment may represent the most efficient use of personnel by a larger group at a particular point in its work.

Individuals and teacher teams may participate in the work of curriculum planning groups initiated or sponsored by groups other than the school building or system. State departments of education, for example, are increasing their efforts in instructional improvement by initiating and coordinating studies of many kinds. School systems send teachers and other professional staff to work on these programs. Regional groups, such as the North Central

Association of Colleges and Secondary Schools have provided leadership in improving the quality of education in planning programs involving several school systems.[23] In addition, professional associations at the state, regional, and national level are involving teachers, supervisors, and administrators in many kinds of curriculum planning activities. For example, the National Education Association's Project on the Academically Talented Student, together with other departments of the NEA, has convened a number of meetings in which conferees study particular aspects of problems of improving programs for these students.[24] These efforts all represent ways in which school systems contribute to curriculum planning efforts outside their boundaries, anticipating that instructional improvement will result—directly through teacher growth and indirectly through the products of the work.

Criteria for Selection of Techniques and Procedures

The descriptions of the many procedures used by school systems in their work on improving instruction reflect the marked changes that have occurred since the time when preparation of courses of study was viewed as the major and practically sole method of program development. The selection and use of appropriate procedures for working on program problems are crucial. Some criteria which may serve as guides in the selection of procedures for program planning follow. The procedures and techniques should be such that:

1. The particular needs of a situation are met through their

[23] North Central Association of Colleges and Secondary Schools, Superior and Talented Student Project, *A Prospectus* (Chicago: The Association, 1958), describes one such project. The Southern States Work Conference on Educational Problems is another example of such an activity; school staff members, university professors, and state departments of education personnel engage in a regional program of in-service education.

[24] J. H. Hlavaty (ed.), *Mathematics for the Academically Talented Student in the Secondary School* (Washington, D.C.: National Education Association, 1959); R. R. Donaldson (ed.), *Science for the Academically Talented Student in the Secondary School* (Washington, D.C.: National Education Association, 1959); and Invitational Conference on the Academically Talented Student in Secondary School, *The Identification and Education of the Academically Talented Student in the American Secondary School* (Washington, D.C.: National Education Association, 1958) are reports which have emerged from such conferences.

contribution to desired growth of staff and by the facilitation of work on specific kinds of curriculum improvement tasks or foci of attention.

2. Individual differences in needs, resources, and ways of working among professional staff and school faculties can be taken into account and appropriate provisions made.

3. Necessary resources, both personnel and material, are either already available or can be obtained.

4. The skills, competencies, and knowledge required for effective participation and leadership are studied and, where necessary, training sessions are provided for extending these.

5. Coordination is readily possible so that separate strands of curriculum work can be interrelated for building a consistent, comprehensive educational program.

6. Effective communication among individuals and groups involved in planning, as well as others who are concerned, is strengthened by systematic efforts to inform while work is in process as well as at its completion.

7. Implementation possibilities of program planning are kept visible throughout and the relation between curriculum development and changes in classroom instruction is constantly in focus.

8. Evaluation of both process and product—the procedure and the program change intended—is made an integral part of the undertaking.

Procedures and techniques aimed at bringing about changes in classroom teaching are simply means for making planning and learning possible. Consequently, the procedure or technique can only facilitate or impede program development by affecting the conditions under which curriculum improvement groups operate. On the one hand, the procedure or technique may be a mechanical device by which individuals are enmeshed in an activity with the outcomes vague or nonexistent. On the other hand, the staff can become involved in meaningful, goal-oriented processes. It is frequently distressing and disheartening to appraise the changes in instruction which have resulted when these are examined in terms of the expenditure of staff time and effort. Selection of inappropriate methods for working on curriculum problems or mechanical use of a particular procedure may yield considerable activity but little change.

PARTICIPATION IN CURRICULUM PLANNING

The question of who should participate in curriculum planning is as important as how such persons should be involved in the work. In discussing participation, the issue of what is the most effective unit for curriculum improvement is also raised. Certainly over the years, the individual school has either been assigned or has assumed a more central role in educational planning. And, at the same time, a partnership relationship has grown among the individual buildings in a school system and between the system and other educational units—the state department of education, universities and colleges, and regional associations. Questions of participation have been answered, in part, by the nature of the organization and the procedures used in program planning and by the problem focus.

Proposals for Participation

Opinions concerning responsibility for curriculum development range from a belief that participation in planning should be on as broad a basis as possible and should include students and lay persons as well as classroom teachers to a conviction that such activities can only be carried on by skilled experts and trained scholars.[25] A number of proposals have been advanced for establishing a national curriculum laboratory or planning board which would assign to specialists the responsibility for developing directive principles and teaching-learning units based on objectives derived from a nationwide hierarchy of lay committees.[26] The National Citizens Commission for the Public Schools spurred the organization of numerous local and state groups and provided working guides for lay groups to work for betterment of schools. Its emphasis, however, was on local effort: "With renewed faith

[25] See, for example, L. T. Hopkins, *Interaction: the Democratic Process* (Boston: D. C. Heath and Company, 1941); and A. E. Bestor, *The Restoration of Learning* (New York: Alfred A. Knopf, 1955) for two divergent proposals.

[26] T. H. Briggs, "The Secondary School Curriculum: Yesterday, Today and Tomorrow," *Teachers College Record*, Vol. 52 (April 1951), pp. 399–448; and P. R. Hanna, "Design for a National Curriculum," *The Nation's Schools*. Vol. 42 (September 1958), pp. 43–45.

in the democratic tradition, the lay citizens and the school men and women of each community must find their answers." [27]

Some of the confusion in defining roles and responsibilities for curriculum planning stems from failure to clarify the dimensions of program development and the varied kinds of participation possible and necessary at different levels. Involvement can be examined and appraised in terms of the roles of specific types of individuals—students, parents, lay citizens, teachers, administrators, supervisors, special service persons (i.e., counsellors, psychologists, school nurses), state department staff, regional and national association personnel, and nonprofessional agencies staff. Or, involvement can be studied in terms of the unit at which planning takes place—building, system, county, state, regional or national. Or, participation can be reviewed in terms of the focus of the curriculum problem—policy evolvement, program guidance, practice suggestion, or materials production. Some illustrations of the kind of planning involvement possible in terms of types of individuals follow.

Pupil Participation

In the classroom, pupils can plan cooperatively with the teacher in the selection, development, and evaluation of learning experiences.[28] Such pupil-teacher planning may be officially recognized as part of a school's program development and provisions made for ways to increase the skill with which it is done. In some systems, students are involved in gathering data about concerns, needs, and resources to be used in program planning. At this level, then, learners participate rather directly in the day-to-day development of the program and in the creation of better conditions for learning. Such participation, however, is far different from

---

[27] D. B. Drieman, *How to Get Better Schools: a Tested Program* (New York: Harper and Brothers, 1956), p. 254. The experiences of lay groups in five communities are reported, the story of the National Citizens Commission recounted, and tools for citizen participation in improving public education presented.

[28] A compilation of practices, together with a presentation of the underlying basis for pupil-teacher planning, is found in A. M. Miel and associates, *Cooperative Procedures in Learning* (New York: Bureau of Publications, Teachers College, Columbia University, 1952).

the preparation of a course of study to be issued by the state department of education or the publication of a guide to the teaching of mathematics.

Parent and Other Lay Participation

Lay persons are involved in curriculum planning in diverse ways, which include participation in a general advisory committee or on a committee studying a specific area. Individuals may serve as resource persons advising curriculum work groups as special consultants on problems to which they can bring an expertness—science, mathematics, citizenship, art, or almost any other area of the school program. Individuals and groups of lay persons may cooperate with teachers to extend the learning opportunities for students—serving on seminar staffs, providing informal apprenticeship experiences, lecturing on and discussing key issues.[29]

Teacher Participation

Every teacher, simply by virtue of his own instructional responsibilities, is involved in curriculum planning. Since the key to the quality of instruction is the classroom teacher, curriculum improvement activities must facilitate his working directly on those factors affecting instruction—including those which influence his behavior as a person and as a professional. The teacher plays a role in many different kinds of curriculum planning, and in-service education aimed at professional growth of school personnel has come to be widely accepted by school systems of all types and sizes.[30] The varied procedures and techniques employed reflect efforts to obtain effective involvement. In the groups and teams

[29] A study of the extent and ways of lay participation in Kansas is reported in F. C. Scritchfield and O. C. Jones, "The Use of Lay Personnel to Improve Instruction," *University of Kansas Bulletin of Education*, Vol. 9 (November 1954), pp. 23–29. For a comprehensive review, see National Society for the Study of Education, *Citizen Co-operation for Better Public Schools*, Fifty-third Yearbook, Part I (Chicago: University of Chicago Press, 1954).

[30] The current extent of in-service education programs is noted in C. G. Hass, "In-service Education Today," in *In-Service Education for Teachers, Supervisors, and Administrators, op. cit.*, pp. 13–34.

studying and revising the curriculum, teachers increasingly exercise leadership responsibilities.

Central Office Participation

Curriculum making by the superintendent and some of the central office staff gave way long ago to more general involvement of teachers in the improvement process. However, central office staff participate in upgrading the quality of education through a variety of leadership roles in initiating studies and providing the means for working on them. Instructional leadership is the most important function of central office personnel for, in the final analysis, arranging optimum conditions of teaching and learning is the basis for supervision and administration.

The staffs of state departments of education, universities and colleges of education, professional associations, regional and national groups—all participate in curriculum development, performing a variety of leadership and service functions. Some of these activities are fixed by regulation and law; some emerge from interpretation of responsibility; some from the initiative of individuals to attain some desired objectives. In some instances, resources for planning are provided to the work group with little direct participation on the part of the agency itself.

Criteria for Determining Participation

There are many different kinds and levels of curriculum planning—individuals and groups attacking instructional problems and difficulties affecting the quality of education and of varying degrees of complexity and comprehensiveness. In determining who should be involved in curriculum planning, the following guides can be applied.

Participation in various aspects of program development should include those individuals who will be affected by the policy or action decisions which may emerge from the work of the group; by those who have a competency or resource which is, or will be, required for effective functioning and goal attainment by the group; by those who will function more effectively in the total educational program as a consequence of involvement; and by those who can fill leadership roles essential for optimum group operation.

There are other questions which school systems need to consider in determining participation of professional staff in in-service programs and other planning activities. These questions have to do with whether such involvement should be voluntary or required; whether all professional personnel should participate or only selected individuals; and whether participation should be related to salary or merit-rating schemes. These problems are essentially parts of the same general issue of who should be involved and the same criteria apply in resolving them.

Problems of involvement are not simply questions of who and how. Diversity and balance are needed to provide for individual differences among participants in a total curriculum improvement program. In addition, attention must be given to the development of the varied skills needed for all kinds of effective participation. Many of these skills are those involved in effective group operation (e.g., agenda-building, goal-setting, group problem-solving, decision-making and follow-through), those of conducting research and inquiry, and others related to carrying on specific curriculum procedures and techniques (e.g., using consultants and resource specialists, role-playing and demonstrating methods, communicating to other groups).[31]

EVALUATION OF CURRICULUM
DEVELOPMENT PROGRAMS

Evaluation of curriculum development programs can have two foci, one of process and one of product. The ultimate criterion of all program planning—the *raison d'être* for initiating and organizing curriculum programs—is the improvement of the quality of education. Providing better learning experiences for students is the end product or goal of all programs of instructional improvement. Establishing a cause-and-effect relationship between a particular in-service education activity or curriculum planning

[31] This point of view is developed in detail in M. B. Miles and A. H. Passow, "Training in the Skills Needed for In-service Education Programs," in *In-Service Education for Teachers, Supervisors, and Administrators, op. cit.,* pp. 339–67. Specific suggestions for organization and activities for such training are presented in M. B. Miles, *Learning to Work in Groups* (New York: Bureau of Publications, Teachers College, Columbia University, 1959).

procedure and the improvement of learning experiences can be a difficult and complex evaluation problem. It calls for appraising student attainments of well-defined goals both before and after curriculum development activities and the gathering of data to relate any changes to these procedures. The center of such evaluation efforts is the student, and the techniques and procedures used are those which will provide data on his growth and achievement.[32]

The term *evaluation,* as distinguished from *measurement,* grew out of the Eight-Year Study of the Progressive Education Association in which the staff developed methods for gathering data about pupil growth in a wide variety of areas, many of which were considered intangibles. A comprehensive appraisal of attainments in ten goal areas related student accomplishment to a particular kind of school program.[33] The Pennsylvania study attempted to relate program to achievement.[34] However, both of these imaginative and complex studies attempted to measure the effects of existing programs and not to appraise the results of work efforts to improve the quality of education. Evaluations of change in total programs involve the identification of important educational objectives, the development and application of techniques to observe and record practices over a period of time, the examination and assessment of changes as indicated in the comparisons, and the making of plans to initiate and test further changes.[35]

[32] A number of useful books are available with specific and practical suggestions for pupil evaluation. See, for example, G. S. Adams and T. L. Torgerson, *Measurement and Evaluation for the Secondary School Teacher* (New York: The Dryden Press, 1956); H. Greene, A. Jorgensen, and J. R. Gerberich, *Measurement and Evaluation in the Elementary School* (New York: Longmans, Green and Company, 1953); H. Greene, A. Jorgensen, and J. R. Gerberich, *Measurement and Evaluation in the Secondary School* (New York: Longmans, Green and Company, 1954); R. L. Thorndike and E. Hagen, *Measurement and Evaluation in Psychology and Education* (New York: John Wiley and Sons, 1955); T. Torgerson and G. S. Adams, *Measurement and Evaluation for the Elementary-School Teacher* (New York: The Dryden Press, 1954); and J. W. Wrightstone, J. Justman, and I. Robbins, *Evaluation in Modern Education* (New York: American Book Company, 1956).

[33] E. R. Smith, R. W. Tyler and the Evaluation Staff, *Appraising and Recording Student Progress* (New York: Harper and Brothers, 1942).

[34] W. S. Learned and B. D. Wood, *The Student and His Knowledge* (New York: Carnegie Foundation for the Advancement of Teaching, 1938).

[35] V. E. Herrick, "The Evaluation of Change in Programs of In-service Education," in *In-Service Education for Teachers, Supervisors, and Administrators, op. cit.,* pp. 311–38.

The second aspect of evaluation is the appraisal of the effectiveness of the program itself—the organizational pattern, the procedures and techniques, the resources used in working on curriculum improvement. However desirable it may be, it is difficult to appraise a total organization for curriculum development. The difficulties may account for the lack of comprehensive evaluation programs. It is somewhat easier to get evaluative data on the effects of a particular procedure—a workshop, a teachers' institute, an in-service committee. The focus here is usually an assessment of the nature and quality of change in people as individuals and as professionals with data gathered through such procedures as questionnaires, inventories, interviews, and observations.[36] The emphasis is on collecting evidence of growth in competence of the professional worker.

Evaluation of curriculum improvement programs must be built in as an integral part of planning. Provisions must be made for appraisal of the selection of the problem area, the organizational pattern, the techniques and procedures used, and the arrangements made to see how all these contribute to growth in professional competence in such a way that sound educational programs and practices emerge. A checklist to guide evaluation of the process of curriculum improvement appears in Chapter 12.

The establishment of an organizational pattern and the selection of procedures in most school systems are based on certain assumptions about how program change takes place. The basic assumption—that changing the behavior of teachers as persons will ultimately be reflected in improvement in the classroom—is still exactly that a hypothesis, derived from a sound theoretical base with research, is still needed to "pinpoint what specific aspects of organization and which particular procedures actually contribute to change learning experiences for the better." It is here that well-conceived and competently designed evaluations of specific programs can contribute.

[36] See A. H. Passow, M. B. Miles, S. M. Corey, and D. C. Draper, *op. cit.*, and M. B. Miles and S. M. Corey, "The First Cooperative Curriculum Research Institute," in *Research for Curriculum Improvement, op. cit.*, pp. 305–48, for descriptions of two training institutes and the methods used to evaluate their effectiveness. See also M. B. Miles, *Learning to Work in Groups, op. cit.*, pp. 223–52, for suggestions on data-collecting techniques for evaluating professional and committee growth and change.

CONCLUDING STATEMENT

This chapter has been devoted to reporting some of the kinds of procedures used by school systems to work on the improvement of the quality of education. The inherent problem in compiling such descriptions is that the essence of the human relationships—the social structure in the school and community, the situational factors which affect the nature, direction and amount of change—are not recaptured and are lost.

Improvement of instruction is not a mechanical process. No organization, and certainly no procedure, is foolproof in bringing about change that will upgrade instructional quality. The participants in curriculum development programs are individuals whose behavioral changes are determined by a great many factors including their perceptions of themselves as persons and as professionals, the structure of interrelationships among them, the guiding conceptions of their varied roles and the total framework within which they operate. These are all factors which must be considered in the initiation and maintenance of activities for curriculum development. Finally, those responsible for leadership in curriculum improvement must guard against the perpetual danger that they and the work groups will become so enamored with the procedures and the processes that the end goal—the betterment of learning and the upgrading of an educational program—is forgotten and bypassed.

School systems have gone all out involving individuals in various aspects of program planning. Many activities have been routine, haphazard, and aimless with the considerable expenditure of time and effort yielding little or no change in the learning experiences of the students. Understanding of the comprehensive nature of curriculum planning and of the forces affecting change can help in the selection of procedures and the evolvement of an organizational pattern which will be meaningful and purposeful.

SELECTED READINGS

ANDERSON, VERNON E., *Principles and Procedures of Curriculum Improvement*. New York: Ronald Press, 1956.

ASSOCIATION FOR SUPERVISION AND CURRICULUM DEVELOPMENT, *Research for Curriculum Improvement*. Washington, D.C.: The Association, NEA, 1957.

BEAUCHAMP, GEORGE A., *Planning the Elementary School Curriculum*. Englewood Cliffs, N.J.: Allyn and Bacon, 1956.

COREY, STEPHEN M., *Action Research to Improve School Practices*. New York: Bureau of Publications, Teachers College, Columbia University, 1953.

KRUG, EDWARD A., *Curriculum Planning*. New York: Harper and Brothers, 1957.

MENGE, J. WILMER and FAUNCE, ROLAND C., *Working Together for Better Schools*. New York: American Book Company, 1953.

MORRIS, GLYN, *The High School Principal and Staff Study Youth*. New York: Bureau of Publications, Teachers College, Columbia University, 1958.

NATIONAL SOCIETY FOR THE STUDY OF EDUCATION, *Citizen Cooperation for Better Public Schools*, Fifty-third Yearbook, Part I. Chicago: University of Chicago Press, 1954.

————, *Inservice Education for Teachers, Supervisors and Administrators*, Fifty-sixth Yearbook, Part I. Chicago: University of Chicago Press, 1957.

SAYLOR, J. GALEN and ALEXANDER, WILLIAM M., *Curriculum Planning for Better Teaching and Learning*. New York: Rinehart and Company, 1954.

SPEARS, HAROLD, *Improving the Supervision of Instruction*. Englewood Cliffs, N.J.: Prentice-Hall, Inc., 1953.

STRATEMEYER, FLORENCE B., FORKNER, HAMDEN L., McKIM, MARGARET, and PASSOW, A. HARRY, *Developing a Curriculum for Modern Living* (2d ed. rev.). New York: Bureau of Publications, Teachers College, Columbia University, 1957.

REPORTS OF
CURRICULUM PROGRAMS

5

THE ILLINOIS
CURRICULUM PROGRAM *

In America, public education is a function of the states, but the actual schooling is carried on in local school districts. While the state departments of education have general responsibility for the maintenance and improvement of the schools, local initiative provides the dynamic force that leads to improvement. The relationship of the state office to the local school district is essentially of an advisory nature. In matters of program, the state office may advise generously and valiantly, but if the people in local schools do not feel a need for the counsel, little accomplishment is likely.

THE SETTING OF THE ILLINOIS CURRICULUM PROGRAM

This is a short account of how one state has gone about the job of helping the people in 9,715 local school administrative units work toward the betterment of their schools. Or, more accurately expressed, this is how one state has tried to give voice

* This chapter was written by Fred P. Barnes, Professor of Education, University of Illinois; formerly Director of Illinois Curriculum Program.

to the many excellent ideas on education that otherwise might have been obscured in almost 10,000 separate subdivisions.

The Illinois Curriculum Program was launched in 1947 as a branch of the Office of the Superintendent of Public Instruction to find ways of coordinating the numerous efforts of school people and citizens to improve their schools. But the Illinois Curriculum Program (hereinafter, ICP) was intended to be a unique approach to the job of school improvement in a large state.

Voluntary Groups and Interests

Because the Superintendent's professional staff of more than 30 assistant superintendents and special-subject supervisors was necessarily occupied with legal and operational duties, *voluntary* projects on school improvement in Illinois communities could not be given sustained attention. It seemed obvious that voluntary associations and informal groups represented one of the richest resources for curriculum improvement. Voluntary groups—like the professional education organizations (more than fifty in the state), the Illinois Congress of Parents and Teachers (more teachers belong to this than to any other single professional organization in the state), business groups, labor organizations, school study councils, and many others—were conferring about the problems of education and making their influence felt, here and there. To realize the wealth of this resource, the ICP was intended as a reagent to precipitate the study, experimentation, and influences of voluntary groups and organizations in local communities.

The ICP itself is the result of a voluntary professional group. It came about mainly through the efforts of the Illinois Association of Secondary School Principals. In cooperation with Vernon L. Nickell, Superintendent of Public Instruction, the IASSP convinced the Illinois General Assembly that such an agency was needed. The legislature responded through granting a budget to the Illinois Secondary School Curriculum Program. Five years later the decision was made to change the name to the Illinois Curriculum Program, and officially recognize what had been happening, inevitably, for some time: other levels of the public schools could not be kept out.

Autonomy in Policy-Making and Decision-Making

To permit the ICP (which is more a vehicle for other organizations than a well-defined organization in its own right) sufficient leeway and flexibility to match the constantly emerging voluntary interests of school people and laymen, it was given a considerable degree of autonomy in decision-making and policy-making. It operates under policies and direction determined by a large steering committee made up of representatives of lay and professional voluntary associations. The ICP staff is not drawn from the regular staff of the Superintendent of Public Instruction, which has its office in Springfield. Mainly, they are "borrowed" from the state universities and have office space at the University of Illinois in Urbana.

Small Staff and Limited Budget

The state's approach to local curriculum improvement is indicated by the small professional staff and obviously limited budget of the ICP. There are four people, all part-time, on the staff, which consists of a Director, an Associate Director, a Research Assistant, and an Administrative Assistant. These four people equal 2.8 full-time staff equivalents. One and three-fourths' time stenographers handle the office work. The program operates on a budget granted by the Illinois General Assembly. It also has the benefit of a small amount of money provided by the University of Illinois. The University does not charge for office space or facilities. All traveling expenses, materials, and salaries are paid for from the two budgets, which total approximately $3,000 per month. Publications are financed through the printing budget of the Office of the Superintendent of Public Instruction.

The central staff and its budget represent the smallest of the ICP's resources for curriculum work. Without the voluntary efforts of numerous school and community people throughout the state, and the financial support of school districts and institutions of higher education, the Program could not long exist. But the limited resources are more an advantage than a handicap. Were the Program to have a large full-time staff coupled with a large budget, it would run the very real danger of doing curriculum work *for* the schools instead of working *with* them and encouraging them to work with each other.

Of course, a small staff and a small budget cause some inconvenience in terms of the sheer size of the undertaking. Illinois is one of the country's larger states. In geographical area it is twenty-fourth but ranks fourth among the states in population. It is an extremely long state, reaching approximately one-third of the distance from the Canadian border to the Gulf of Mexico. The east-west borders are about 200 miles apart at the greatest width. There are almost 60,000 certified persons employed in Illinois school districts with more than 1,500,000 children enrolled in them.

To complete the picture, however, it must be pointed out that on several occasions grants of money have been given the ICP by foundations and funds for specific purposes. At such times, temporary personnel have been added to the staff.

Objectives

Six general objectives have served to guide the work of the ICP almost from its inception. These objectives are not "paper aims," since they are used to plan and evaluate each year's activities. These broad objectives clearly describe the boundaries and directions of the program:

1. To encourage statewide, continuing concern with curriculum improvement.

2. To provide materials for local curriculum studies.

3. To initiate experimental projects in local school systems that will explore improvement in teaching and services.

4. To conduct workshops that will bring school and lay people together for work on school problems.

5. To prepare and distribute publications.

6. To assist other organizations and agencies without duplicating their efforts.

Organizational Structure

The ICP staff members have absolutely no administrative authority over any persons employed in Illinois school districts.

Whatever status the staff does enjoy is derived from the opinions of volunteer persons engaged in volunteer projects. Work situations with face-to-face groups are the stock-in-trade of the ICP (workshops, clinics, talks to teachers, demonstrations) and informality is prized. The ICP has come to be known as a force that sanctions experimentation and change. It promotes group freedom and ability to make decisions.

The characteristics of the ICP are almost impossible to express in the usual chart of personnel relationships. If one remembers that the lines do not signify a hierarchy of authority, but lines of communication, such a chart (Figure 1) may be useful as a summary of the foregoing description. (See p. 119.)

Other reports on the ICP have appeared in the educational literature [1] and may be consulted for additional background data.

THE ICP IN ACTION

Although no two successive years are exactly alike, the six major objectives of the ICP serve to promote continuity from one year to the next. Some selected ventures of the ICP which have characterized the past few years are reported in terms of the six general objectives and can be used to present a cross-sectional picture of the program in operation.

1. STATEWIDE CONCERN WITH CURRICULUM IMPROVEMENT

Numerous organizations and individuals in the State of Illinois are vitally concerned with the conduct of public schools. These civic and educational groups present recommendations and useful information intended to influence or assist the schools in their constant task of curriculum improvement. Such activities and efforts form a sizable and valuable resource for educational good.

Steering Committee

The ICP maintains contact with state-level interests through its Steering Committee. Ordinarily, this committee meets twice a

---

[1] One such report, which cites several earlier accounts, may be found in Kenneth J. Rehage and George W. Denemark, "Area, State, Regional, and National In-service Education Programs," *In-service Education*, Fifty-sixth Yearbook, National Society for the Study of Education, Part I (Chicago: The University of Chicago Press, 1957).

year. Sometimes it meets in Chicago and at other times in Springfield. One Chicago meeting dealt with procedures for expanding Steering Committee membership, ICP publications, proposals for new workshop themes, and further expansion of workshop participation.

At one Springfield meeting the Steering Committee evaluated past concerns of the ICP and recommended steps to be taken in the future. Seven major emphases for future operation saw the ICP:

1. Concentrating more on work at the local school level.
2. Encouraging increased involvement of lay people in school concerns.
3. Securing increased involvement of teachers at all levels.
4. Giving far more attention to teacher research.
5. Developing a clear definition of boundaries for the work of the ICP.
6. Widening the scope of publications and making more of them available.
7. Planning for new publications to be distributed through instructional clinics for teachers.

The Steering Committee appointed an *ad hoc* committee to develop operational plans for the implementation of the proposed program. In particular, the committee was to make recommendations relative to budget and personnel requirements.

Citizens' Education Councils

Of major importance to the ICP is the work of the Illinois Citizens' Education Committee, a citizens' group organized for the purpose of continuing the studies and recommendations which began with the Illinois "Little White House" Conference in 1955. The ICP has unusual interest in the work of this influential group. The ICP Director serves as a consultant for this Committee's Workgroup on Planning Educational Programs.

Over the state an increasingly large number of citizens' education councils are being set up in local school districts. These councils generally act in an advisory capacity to boards of education. Staff members of the ICP meet with several such councils

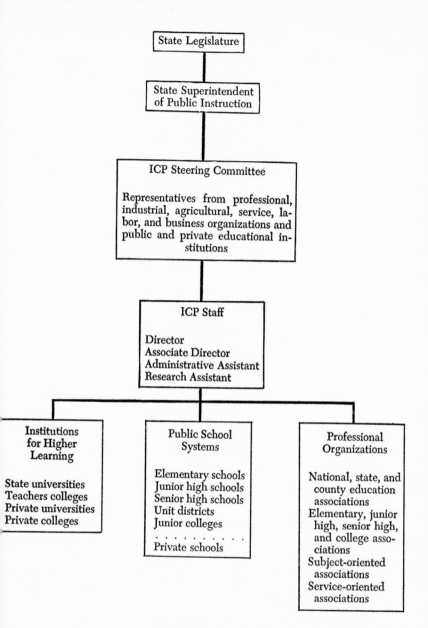

FIGURE 1

COMMUNICATION LINES OF ILLINOIS CURRICULUM PROGRAM

and are available to lend encouragement and consultation when desired.

Education, to be fully effective, must have the broad-based support of the community. This is as true on the state as it is on the local level. Consequently, the ICP seeks to further the work of citizen as well as professional groups.

Allerton House Conference

The Allerton House Conference on Education was organized in 1953 and terminated in the spring of 1958. The organization of a conference to study the controversy between "scholars" and "schoolmen" was sparked by the upsurge of criticism of the public schools beginning about 1951. Some of the criticisms were identified with specific faculty members of the University of Illinois, while others were supported by some "scholars" in almost every institution of higher learning in the state.

The Conference was organized around twelve study groups, each examining a major area of study important to the controversy. Each study group had one or more representatives from the institutions of higher learning in Illinois, the public school teachers and administrators, the Illinois Congress of Parents and Teachers, the Illinois Association of School Boards, and the Office of the Superintendent of Public Instruction. The study groups focused their attention on some of the most common subjects taught in the public schools, following the teaching of these subjects from the primary grades through college.

The ICP, in cooperation with the Office of the Superintendent of Public Instruction and the University of Illinois, shared in bearing the major costs of the enterprise, other than expenses of representatives. In most cases, these expenses were paid by the organization or institution represented. In addition, the ICP assisted in caring for the detailed operations of the conference meetings.

The Allerton House Conference reflected a timely statewide interest in problems of the school. Because of this, the ICP participated actively in the work of the organization.

The ICP financed and distributed two of the seven publications released by Conference study groups. The others were published by the Office of the Superintendent of Public Instruction, the University of Illinois, Illinois State Normal University, and Southern Illinois University. Another publication of the Office of the Superintendent of Public Instruction, the *Educational Press Bulletin* (February 1957), carried a complete account of the Conference up to that date.

2. MATERIALS FOR LOCAL STUDIES

During the period immediately following the organization of the ICP, an attempt was made to provide specialist consultants to schools participating in local curriculum study. Teams of consultants were drawn from the Office of the Superintendent of Public Instruction, from the public and private institutions of higher learning, and from the schools. These consultant teams were made available, on call, to schools that had identified specific curriculum study projects. During the ICP's first eight years, more than 500 different consultants worked with Illinois schools. This approach was successful. As a matter of fact, it was too successful for continued operation.

By 1955 it had become apparent that the constantly growing requests from Illinois schools would soon exceed the total number of consultants available or potentially available. The shortage of consultant help, coupled with a growing effort to free time for consultants from their regular positions, resulted in a sharp curtailment of this type of assistance. Since then, an effort has been made to offer consultant services of a different nature. Rather than attempt to send individuals or teams of consultants to schools engaged in local studies, assistance has been prepared, in printed form, and made available to schools.

"How-to-do-it" Bulletins

One of the first of these was prepared by Paul Bowman.[2] Another bulletin, now in an experimental stage, is being readied for production. The trial edition [3] is described as follows:

[2] Paul Bowman, *How to Study Your School Population,* Circular Series A, Number 51, Illinois Curriculum Program Bulletin No. 26 (Springfield, Illinois: Office of the Superintendent of Public Instruction, June 1957).

[3] Fred P. Barnes, *Practical Research Processes: A Guidebook in Research Methods for Practitioners in Education* (Springfield, Illinois: Office of the Superintendent of Public Instruction, August 1958).

A bulletin intended to present useful research procedures for studies in local communities. The procedures are applicable to a wide range of investigations. The bulletin deals with the similarities between teaching and researching, a description of setting up a research seminar based on the "dry-run" idea, a chapter on research design, another one on quantitative measures, and a final one on qualitative measures.

"Fugitive" Materials

Another kind of material has been developed and made available to schools for use in their own local studies. This kind of material is developed through ICP workshops and study groups. Workshop participants and others may have these materials furnished on request. The following three examples of workshop materials are illustrative.

The ICP has been active in developing a rating scale (see p. 129) for the evaluation of workshops and other meetings. This rating scale is based on the so-called Likert technique and is useful in obtaining participants' reactions to meetings.

The ICP has also made available, on request, copies of tape recordings of addresses and discussions from workshop meetings. In this manner, consultants who are unable to meet with numerous local systems can still make available their ideas on specific topics.

During ICP workshops, members of study-discussion groups may have their contributions mimeographed for the use of all participants. These materials are sent to local schools in cases where the materials might be relevant to studies under way.

Current ICP Publications

The ICP constantly makes "consultant services in print" available through the distribution of its current publications. These publications include "how-to-do-it" studies on such topics as hidden tuition costs, participation in extraclass activities, guidance services, student follow-up, and the series of Local Area Consensus Studies.

The Local Area Consensus Studies were designed as opinion surveys for use in school-community curriculum planning sessions. In relation to a particular subject or problem, students, teachers, and parents respond to the inventories and then use summary information to compare attitudes. Fourteen of these studies have now been prepared. Four are concerned with secondary school studies in extraclass activities, family living, guidance, and mathematics. The other ten deal with art education, health, library services, music, safety, citizenship, physical education, and parent-teacher cooperation.

The ICP has constantly experimented with ways to make available "consultant help in print." This is a large and challenging task and much remains to be learned.

3. EXPERIMENTAL PROJECTS

Research is of great importance to a profession. Through an attitude of responsible skepticism and a disposition to seek proof for beliefs, practice is improved. Without constant research-oriented questioning, practice quickly becomes stereotyped or accepted on the basis of prescription. The question has been asked as to whether teachers can become good researchers. This is important and has concerned the ICP for some time.

Research Training Seminars

Recently, the ICP began investigating whether teachers were ready to do home-grown research projects on their own local school problems. The Program began trying to find whether teachers could be researchers—beginning right at the creative level of original problem definition. An analysis of the research process and of problem definition seemed to suggest that well-trained teachers already have been largely trained as researchers. The training still needed included information and practice in research techniques and operations. The problem then was raised as to whether there was some economical and efficient way by which teachers could learn these necessary techniques and operations. There was apparently no precedent or body of literature which offered leads on how an in-service training program in research might be devised.

However, a training device from the armed forces offered a

possible answer to the problem. During the war, the services operated a so-called "dry-run" for training military men in battle operations, where the dangers of getting shot and the hazards of real shooting were eliminated. Adapting this idea, a "dry-run" training device in research practices was developed, consisting of small groups of teachers and administrators organized into conference teams to perform "thimble-size" research projects.[4] The participants use themselves as a research population and employ synthetic, but real enough, research problems which interest them. Such projects contain all necessary research steps but are performed in a threat-free environment where mistakes are harmless. This idea was first tested at a research training seminar in February 1956. A follow-up seminar was held a year later.

Between the two seminars, ICP staff members were invited to demonstrate the idea at seven out-of-state conventions and school systems. In the same period, two Illinois school systems used the training device for their teachers and classroom research projects actually under way.

The evidence gathered on practitioner research indicated that teachers can learn necessary research techniques and put them to good use in a surprisingly short period of time.

Reassured by the initial experimental trials with the "dry-run" device the ICP planned and conducted a series of three state-wide research seminars held at Père Marquette State Park Lodge to gather better evidence on the feasibility of training in research methods for all teachers, and to encourage a broader acquaintance with research-oriented approaches to curriculum development. All school systems in Illinois were invited to send not less than two or more than four participants to any one seminar. A "first come, first served" principle was observed and 253 applications were accepted from a total of more than 400 submitted. The maximum number of participants that could be accommodated at any one seminar was limited to approximately eighty due to space and staffing restrictions. However, it was encouraging to note that when Illinois school people were extended an

---

[4] A rationale for this approach is presented in Fred P. Barnes and Eric H. Johnson, "The Teacher as a Researcher," *Educational Leadership*, Vol. 14 (April 1957), pp. 445–47.

invitation to attend a research-training seminar more than 400 voluntarily responded with applications for acceptance. Costs for each participant amounted to $29, not including travel expenses. In practically all cases local school boards and higher institutions of learning paid the costs for their representatives.

The distribution of participants listed by professional positions is indicated in Table 1.

TABLE 1

POSITIONS HELD BY PARTICIPANTS IN THREE RESEARCH SEMINARS

Type of Position	Seminar			Total
	November	January	February	
Superintendent and assistant super-				
intendent	9	7	3	19
Principal and assistant principal	22	37	22	81
Curriculum coordinator and instruc-				
tional supervisor	4	2	3	9
Teacher	15	16	26	57
School board member	2	1	3	6
County administrator	2	1	0	3
Foreign observer (from the National				
Office of Education, Ankara, Turkey)	6	0	0	6
Member of leadership team	12	12	12	36
ICP staff; guest speaker	7	6	7	20
Participant (personal information forms				
not returned)	4	6	6	16
Total	83	88	82	253

The seminar participants were divided into four "research team" groups of seventeen plus three staff members each. The "dry-run" idea was used, with each of the four groups identifying and completing two research projects of its own. Each project started with the locating of a "researchable" problem, selecting a design fitted to the problem, gathering relevant data, analyzing the data through inferential statistical tests, selecting a level of acceptable significance, and deciding upon the findings. Typical "dry-run" problems were as follows: (1) the effect of persuasive arguments on attitudes; (2) the effect upon retention of different means of communication or instruction; (3) the difference between teachers and administrators with respect to such attitudes as those toward released time for faculty meetings, merit rating, job satisfactions, and ability grouping; and (4) the relationship of teaching experience to attitudes toward ability grouping and the like.

The tests of statistical inference were all taken from non-parametric statistics which allow research studies on very small groups, are distribution-free, and are much simpler to apply and understand than are the usual parametric tests. The tests employed were the Mann-Whitney U Test, the Sign Test, the Spearman Rank Correlation Coefficient Test, and the Chi-Square Test of Significance. With the help of the three staff members assigned to each group, participants who completely lacked any previous training and experience with research and statistics were using and understanding one or more of the inferential tests in less than one day's time. Information on these tests and research methods was made available through mailing to each participant a copy of *Practical Research Processes* [5] for use before and during the seminars.

The way that the various sessions were planned and timed is explained in Figure 2 which shows the "Map of Seminar Sessions" for one of the three research seminars.

The research seminars were carefully measured. Upon registration for a seminar, and prior to attendance, each participant was mailed test forms designed to measure cognitive knowledge concerning research methodology and attitudes toward the production of research in familiar teaching problems. On the last day of each seminar, after the training sessions, these tests were administered again. The research hypothesis of the ICP trainers was that there would be a significant gain in knowledge of research techniques and a significant change in attitudes in the direction of teacher production as opposed to teacher consumption of research findings. The null hypothesis was that there would be an equal number of gains and losses in scores both on the knowledge tests and the attitude scales. Using a "before-and-after" design with the experimental group only, one of the distribution-free inferential tests used by participants in the seminars was employed to test the significance of the findings. The scores on the pretests and post-tests were paired for each par-

[5] Barnes, *op. cit.*

RESEARCH SEMINAR SESSIONS, ILLINOIS CURRICULUM PROGRAM

Wednesday

A.M.
- 9:00 Staff preseminar planning
- 10:00 Registration begins
- 12:00 Luncheon. Seminar begins

P.M.
- 1:30 GENERAL SESSION
  - (a) Introduction of staff members
  - (b) Orientation to seminar
  - (c) "Research conducted by practitioners" (a sociodrama)
  - (d) Group analysis of roles, discussion
  - (e) Demonstration of a "dry-run" research project *
  - (f) Administrative detail and assignment to research teams
- 6:00 Dinner *
- 7:30 TEAM MEETINGS
  Begin work on first project
- 9:00 Adjournment

Thursday

A.M.
- 8:00 Breakfast
- 9:30 TEAM MEETINGS Continue first projects
- 10:45 Coffee break
- 11:00 Complete first projects *
- 12:00 # Luncheon

P.M.
- 1:30 GENERAL SESSION
  - (a) Group reports and critique on first projects
  - (b) Preparation for second research projects
- 3:15 Coffee break
- 3:30 TEAM MEETINGS Begin and complete second research projects *
- 6:00 # Dinner
- 7:00 GENERAL SESSION Group reports and critique on second projects *
- 8:00 # GENERAL SESSION Presentation, "Portrait of a Research Project," Herbert A. Thelen, University of Chicago *

Friday

A.M.
- 8:00 Breakfast
- 9:30 GENERAL SESSION Evaluation of Research Techniques *
- 10:30 SMALL-GROUP MEETINGS Identification of researchable back-home problems
- 11:00 GENERAL SESSION Field day
  - (a) Specific questions
  - (b) Plans for using research procedures in own schools *
- 12:00 Luncheon

P.M.
- 1:30 Final adjournment

Key to symbols
* P.C.I. rating
# Reports from groups due

FIGURE 2

RESEARCH SEMINAR SESSIONS, ILLINOIS CURRICULUM PROGRAM

127

ticipant in order to determine his gain (+), loss (−), or no change (0). The Sign Test was used to analyze the data and indicated that gains in knowledge were statistically significant at the .01 level. Thus the null hypothesis was rejected and the research hypothesis accepted. The research seminars did, indeed, increase the participants' knowledge of research methodology to a statistically significant degree.

The attitude inventories did not reveal scores that were significant at less than the .25 level. However, the weight of change was in the direction of gain in producer attitudes. The participants who elected to attend the seminars made initially high scores reflecting "producer" attitudes on the pretest forms of the attitude scales. Their post-test scores showed relatively small differences. This might have been due to the self-selection influence of the seminars in attracting people who already wanted to undertake research, or the participants might have started and ended with a scant regard for the use of other people's research findings.

The various seminar sessions were rated by the participants nine separate times during the course of the seminar. The mean score of the ratings for each session was promptly calculated for each team, and for all the teams combined, and "fed-back" for discussion and self-appraisal. A Personal Classification Indicator (PCI) form—as shown in Figure 3—was used for this purpose. The mean summary ratings, from all three seminars, placed the participants' evaluation at a point somewhat more favorable than "quite satisfied."

Additional evaluative procedures could have been used but it was felt that the "before-and-after" measurements and the PCI ratings and comments might approach the limits of participant tolerance for information-giving. The evaluation of experimental meetings like the seminars is difficult and never completely satisfactory. In spite of this realization it was possible to reach some conclusions: (1) many school people in Illinois are interested in experimentally trying training procedures in research; (2) beginning research methods and the application of statistical tests can be learned in a relatively short time through whole-person learning where participants can feel, act, and think the learning experience rather than just listen or talk about what they

Group No. _____

Directions: Do not sign your name. Please indicate your
feelings about the group session, or sessions, being rated.

Very dissatisfied		Quite dissatisfied		So-so	Quite satisfied		Very satisfied	
x	x	x	x	x	x	x	x	x
1	2	3	4	5	6	7	8	9

Draw a circle around the x that most nearly expresses how you feel.

Most important reasons for satisfactions:

Most important reasons for dissatisfactions:

Additional comments:

FIGURE 3

FORM FOR PERSONAL CLASSIFICATION INDICATOR: MEETING EVALUATION SCALE (PCI)

are learning; (3) cognitive knowledge of research can effectively
be increased through the "dry-run" technique; and (4) school people can effectively conceptualize school problems through research and statistical terminology and symbols.

Plans were made for further experimentation with this approach in local school systems. Three school systems volunteered
to serve as pilot centers in the testing of practitioner research
and have tried elementary and secondary school projects under
the direction of the ICP staff. If additional testing indicates that
the approach is practicable, it may not only stimulate experimental projects in Illinois schools but serve as an answer to the
shortage of consultants as well.

Project for the Improvement of Thinking

Another experimental project carried on with the cooperation
of ICP during the past several years is concerned with teaching
practices designed to promote the improvement of thinking.

Dr. B. Othanel Smith (College of Education, University of Illinois) is in charge of this project in which experimental work has been carried on in high school pilot centers. Materials used experimentally have been carefully selected and prepared for publication by the University of Illinois Press. Plans have been made for a study of the logical operations that teachers and students actually carry on. This new study has received a grant from the United States Office of Education. The project, like others, received ICP support until it could become self-sustaining.

4. Workshops

Workshops are important to the activities of the Illinois Curriculum Program. Since the Program was launched in 1947, some 49 three-day workshops have been held for school administrators, teachers, school board members, and interested laymen. In ten years' time these 49 workshops have enrolled approximately 6,000 people. Workshop programs have dealt with such varied topics as the basic subject areas, curriculum organization, supervision, public relations, instructional materials, child psychology, and procedures for curriculum development.

Workshops offer a unique way to make wide use of the consultant services available from the Office of the Superintendent of Public Instruction, from the institutions of higher learning, and from the school by utilizing specialists in leadership teams. In addition, workshops allow school people from different areas within the state to meet and work together. Frequently people from schools working on similar projects can be of unusual help to each other.

Each year workshops are planned by a broadly representative group of school people invited to serve on a planning committee. This group explores pertinent problems in need of study, decides the themes for the workshops to be held, and plans the activities of specific work groups around which workshops are structured.

All ICP workshops are held at Père Marquette State Park. The park has excellent overnight accommodations and food service and can handle 115 people at each meeting. Attendance is voluntary and is based on the principle of "first come, first served." A recurring problem is that for every workshop more applications are submitted than can be accepted.

To give a clear picture, four workshops on the same theme, held between October 1957 and January 1958, are summarized to indicate the size and complexity of operations.

The Program

The four 3-day workshops for 1957–1958 were planned as one, focusing on four different levels of the school program: elementary school (October); senior high school (November); unit district (December); and junior high school (January). The general plan remained constant with variations related to the differences in emphases for each specific level. The four workshops and the five work groups within each were task-oriented. That is, in addition to providing opportunities for sharing ideas and experiences, each workshop was designed to contribute ideas on ways to develop and improve Illinois curricula. A rigorous schedule was maintained. The day's activities commenced at 8 A.M. and continued until 9 P.M.

The general theme for the four workshops was "Practical Problems in Improving Educational Programs." Each of the five work groups within a workshop dealt with one of the following topics important to curriculum making:

1. Administrative and supervisory roles and functions in curriculum development
2. **Human relations in curriculum development**
3. Ways of working in curriculum programs
4. Selection and pacing of curriculum content
5. Research in curriculum development

A successful innovation at this series of workshops was the "feed-back" reports. Immediately after each group meeting, the five recorders turned in their notes to the ICP staff who, after minor editing, mimeographed and distributed the set of reports to all participants. Thus, when the workshop was adjourned, each person took home a cumulative report of the deliberations in all five work groups.

A highlight of the general session on the second evening of each workshop was an address by a distinguished guest from one of the institutions of higher learning in the state. Each speaker built on the discussions in the work groups and related their concerns in curriculum making to similar concerns of people working on curriculum at the college and university level.

Participants

Immediate response to the original invitation to attend resulted in oversubscription of all four workshops. The voluntary registration was restricted only by space limitation and the requirements of good working conditions. The nominal expenses covering food and lodging for the conferees at ICP workshops are normally paid by the institution, organization, or school system represented.

Table 2 (p. 133) summarizes attendance at each workshop and indicates, in general categories, the nature of participants' positions in their home communities. Total participation is shown in Table 3 (p. 133). More than 150 separate communities in Illinois were represented by these 530 participants.

Leadership teams for the five work groups in each workshop were made up of volunteer specialists drawn from public schools, higher institutions of learning, and from county and state supervisory offices. A chairman, recorder, and three coordinators accepted leadership responsibility for the achievement of group goals. Each member of the team was responsible for a specific function as developed in the leadership training session on the morning of the first day.

Geographical Distribution

Participants traveled from all parts of the state to study their curriculum problems at the ICP workshops. Table 4 (p. 134) presents the geographical distribution of participants according to six regional areas of Illinois. In addition, it may be noted that workshoppers came from 61 counties, representing 86 per cent of the total pupil enrollment of the state.

Financial Statement

ICP was able to operate the four workshops only because of the voluntary nature of participation and the support of cooperating institutions and organizations. More than $12,000 was

TABLE 2

SUMMARY OF WORKSHOP PARTICIPATION, 1957–1958 SERIES

Elementary School Workshop, October 21–23, 1957
Administrators and supervisors	143
Teachers	7
College and university personnel	9
School board members and lay persons	2
County superintendents, OSPI [a] and ICP staffs	10
Total	171

Senior High School Workshop, November 13–15, 1957
Administrators and supervisors	64
Teachers	16
College and university personnel	11
School board members and lay persons	4
County superintendents, OSPI [a] and ICP staffs	9
Total	104

Unit District Workshop, December 11–13, 1957
Administrators and supervisors	77
Teachers	7
College and university personnel	15
School board members and lay persons	10
County superintendents, OSPI [a] and ICP staffs	10
Total	119

Junior High School Workshop, January 8–10, 1958
Administrators and supervisors	98
Teachers	9
College and university personnel	13
School board members and lay persons	2
County superintendents, OSPI [a] and ICP staffs	14
Total	136
Total Participation	530

[a] Office of the Superintendent of Public Instruction.

TABLE 3

TOTAL PARTICIPATION IN FOUR WORKSHOPS, 1957–1958 SERIES

Administrators and supervisors	382
Teachers	39
College and university personnel	48
School board members and lay persons	18
County superintendents, OSPI [a] and ICP staffs	43
Total	530

[a] Office of the Superintendent of Public Instruction.

TABLE 4

GEOGRAPHICAL DISTRIBUTION OF PARTICIPANTS IN
FOUR WORKSHOPS, 1957–1958 SERIES

Illinois Area:		
	Northwest	23
	Northeast	158
	West Central	116
	East Central	135
	Southwest	90
	Southeast	8
Total		530

itemized in total expenses but the actual cost of this extensive undertaking to the ICP was less than $1,000.

Workshop Outcomes

The most important and greatest number of results from such a series of workshops are, of course, difficult to describe in quantitative terms. Participants found opportunity for mutual consultation under the guidance of a team of specialists. Thinking together, they were able to identify commonly felt problems and to suggest alternative approaches to solutions. The fresh perceptions acquired are likely to be reflected in improved programs of instruction throughout the state.

There were, however, certain more tangible outcomes. As described on page 137, the four major addresses were printed and released in a publication dated March, 1958. A library of tape recordings of major addresses and of other talks has been collected in the ICP office. These are freely available to interested curriculum workers, as are edited copies of each of the twenty recorders' reports.

Data for a new bulletin, dealing with curriculum building at all grade levels, came directly from material developed in the workshops. In this way participants have made a meaningful and valuable contribution to improved school practice in Illinois.

Evaluation

PCI (Personal Classification Indicator) ratings were given by all participants after every work meeting or general session. After compilation, the summarized evaluations for all four workshops were plotted on a graph. Generally speaking, a most encouraging degree of satisfaction was indicated for all workshops, increasing as the workshops proceeded.

Since the leadership teams had access to the completed PCI sheets after each session they were able to report on the ratings to each group. Positive results were obtained with respect to group synthesis and productivity.

5. PUBLICATIONS

Since 1947, a total of seventy-four publications dealing with various aspects of curriculum development have been published under the imprint of the ICP. These are all available to Illinois schools through the Office of the Superintendent of Public Instruction. Of these seventy-four publications, twenty-five are major bulletins with one of these divided into five complete publications. The remaining publications include inventories, questionnaires, and tests.

The earliest publications of the ICP were not produced under any comprehensive plan that would relate one publication to another. Several dealt with similar areas of concern and, in effect, formed a series even though as a series they were not necessarily related to other ICP publications.

Plan for ICP Publications

In 1955 the Steering Committee approved the adoption of a comprehensive plan for ICP series bulletins. The plan was based on the postulate that information relating to teaching and school operation could be subsumed under seven categories which could apply to elementary schools and high schools alike. Publications could be anticipated in each of the seven categories of information. An outline of this plan follows:

Series	*Suggested Publications*
A. Growth and learning	Child Development Studies Guidance

Series	*Suggested Publications*
B. Techniques and procedures	Curriculum Making in School Systems Developing the Local Curriculum
C. Subject fields	School Begins with Kindergarten [a] Thinking in the Language of Mathematics [a] Children Learn and Grow Through Art Experiences [a] Science Music Social Studies Physical Education Language Arts
D. Special fields	Library Services Exceptional Children
E. Student progress	Evaluation of Student Progress Reporting to Parents
F. Administration and supervision	Faculty Organization Organizing the Citizens' Council
G. Curriculum research	Practical Research Processes [a] Developing Concepts: A Study in the Teaching of History [a] Local School Self-Surveys

[a] Bulletins already completed.

The plan in progress. It is intended for all these bulletins to be produced in cooperation with college and university personnel and public school people who are specialists in the relevant areas. One of the major goals in writing these materials is to make available basic, fresh ideas indigenous to the State of Illinois, using a method of production that will encourage a sense of involvement on the part of the teachers who will use the materials. Each bulletin is prepared by two committees: a small writing committee and a larger advisory committee. The committee members are selected to represent all geographical areas of the state. In this fashion the bulletins attempt to promote for all teachers a feeling of being represented while at the same time the needed competence of the authors is insured.

Additional publications. The ICP plans to produce publications other than series bulletins. These will consist of publications on subjects of unusual interest and timeliness. An example of this type is the booklet, *University Curriculum Making.* The content of this publication consists of the major addresses delivered at the four workshops held between October 1957 and January 1958.[6] All four speakers discussed the same subject, "Problems of Curriculum Making at the University Level." Typescripts of the addresses were taken from tape recordings made at the workshops.

The booklet presents material ordinarily not available in literature used by public school people. It documents the similarities between problems of curriculum making faced by public school people and by college and university people.

6. Cooperation with Other Organizations

The ICP attempts to participate in, and cooperate with, other organizations that voluntarily help Illinois schools. Some illustrations of this cooperation follow.

Economic Education

An example of this can be found in the ICP's collaboration with the Illinois Council on Economic Education. During the past seven years the ICP has helped arrange summer workshops in economic education. These workshops—which draw teachers from elementary and secondary schools, with all expenses paid—are financed through the Illinois Council on Economic Education. Workshop faculties are made up of specialists in economics and school curriculum development. At the workshops, teachers study economic analysis and current problems; administrators' attention is directed to the importance of economic education in public schools.

[6] Published, March 1958. The four speakers, who are also the authors of the publication, are Joseph R. Smiley, Dean, College of Liberal Arts and Sciences, University of Illinois; Francis B. Belshe, Assistant Dean of the Faculty, Illinois State Normal University; Francis H. Horn, Visiting Distinguished Professor of Higher Education, Southern Illinois University; and Quincy Doudna, President, Eastern Illinois University.

Teacher Utilization

Another example of the ICP's assistance to other organizations is found in cooperation given to the project on teacher utilization. Initially, a workshop was conducted at the University of Illinois' Allerton House in November 1957, which the ICP helped plan and arrange. The ICP's experience with workshop evaluation was put to good use. In addition, the ICP made available its findings on practitioner research.

In September 1958, the Commission on the Experimental Study of the Utilization of the Staff in the Secondary School, sponsored by the National Association of Secondary-School Principals, underwrote a statewide project in Illinois. The study is supported by The Fund for the Advancement of Education. The ICP was requested to supervise the project, and promptly renamed it the Illinois Staff Utilization Studies (ISUS). Sixteen schools serve as the experimental locations.

A research consultant was added to ICP's staff to work exclusively with the sixteen high schools involved in the project. Each administrator and teacher in these schools was extended an invitation to participate in two training seminars in research methods and more than forty of them accepted. The seminars were planned along the lines of the "dry-run" training device explained earlier in this chapter, and conducted by the ICP staff. Subsequent written reports on the staff utilization projects exhibited all the characteristics of good research studies and gave ample evidence of having been influenced by the seminars in research training.

Conventions

The ICP assists in planning and conducting the annual conventions held by associations of Illinois school administrators and teachers. This kind of assistance is given to the Illinois Association of Secondary-School Principals, the Illinois Junior High School Principals Association, and the Illinois Association for Supervision and Curriculum Development.

Consultant Service

Still another kind of assistance for other organizations is the provision of consultant services for some of their special interests. For instance, the ICP furnished a consultant for the Research Committee of the Illinois Association for Supervision and Curriculum Development. In connection with this, the original "dry-run" training device in research practices was developed. Thus the ICP not only assists another organization but has the opportunity to gain and perfect ideas that may be useful on a wider scale.

Cooperative Enterprises

Sometimes other organizations are requested to participate in ICP-sponsored activities where there is a mutual interest. Examples may be found in the close collaboration of the Illinois Association for Childhood Education in the production of the bulletin, *School Begins with Kindergarten.* Another instance may be found in the cooperation of the Illinois Council of Teachers of Mathematics in the production of an elementary school mathematics bulletin. Still another cooperative example is the Illinois Art Education Association's production of the elementary school art education bulletin. Finally, the ICP is interested in lending encouragement at all times to other organizations with a wide range of activities. Prominent among these are the Illinois Congress of Parents and Teachers and the Illinois Education Association.

Fifty-four organizations of teachers and laymen directly concerned with schools are listed in the 1958–1959 *Illinois School Directory.* Each one of these groups has special interests in public education. Potentially these organizations can wield a powerful influence on the improvement of Illinois schools. Because of this it is important for the ICP to assist, but not duplicate, good contributions wherever they may be found.

IN CONCLUSION

The basic objective of the ICP is to assist, encourage, and plan with the numerous voluntary groups interested in education in Illinois. If schools are to provide the kind of education that people want for their children, it is essential for citizens to take an active interest in school curricula, buildings, equipment, and teachers. It is also essential for teachers and administrators, through their voluntary organizations, to study constantly the values of educational programs offered to children. In numerous ways, voluntary contributions to education constitute an expression of future ambitions for the schools. More than ever it is true that schools, from elementary grades through college, will seldom be better than people want them to be.

The ICP has been and continues to be a pioneering and cooperative statewide venture in the task of providing improved educational opportunities for children and youth. As a pioneering program it must necessarily concern itself with experimental projects and experimental school programs. Concern for experimentation calls for careful charting of policies to be followed and projects and programs to be undertaken. Whatever success the ICP has achieved has been a result of the careful judgment of those individuals who make up its Steering Committee, composed of lay and professional persons, and especially of the devoted work of those who voluntarily contribute so much to the education of children in the State of Illinois.

6

DADE COUNTY, FLORIDA

CURRICULUM IMPROVEMENT *

IF THERE is such a thing as a one-word description of a school system, the most appropriate one for the Dade County schools is
growth! Within the lifetime of one man, this system has ex-
ploded from a small-town operation with a single high school
to one of the largest school systems in the nation. It now consists
of twenty-six incorporated municipalities, including the cities of
Miami and Miami Beach plus the surrounding rural areas. There
is an annual average upsurge in the pupil population of about
10 per cent. The Dade County Public School System has more
than tripled its size since 1945.

A mild climate—cooled in the summer and warmed in the
winter by the winds from the Gulf Stream—attracts thousands of
tourists who annually help to increase the population of Dade
County. The city of Miami Beach is the foremost example of
this skyrocketing seasonal influx of winter visitors. This city,
which normally has 56,000 permanent residents, leaps in population to about 175,000 during the winter season.

---

* This chapter was written by JEFF WEST, Director of Curriculum and Instructional Services, Dade County Public Schools.

THE CHANGING SCENE

What does this spectacular growth in Dade County mean to the schools? For every single school day of the year, there is pressing need for two more classrooms. Over a thousand new teachers must be employed each year. The need is intensified for supplies and materials, for administrative, supervisory, and operating personnel, for school buses and other equipment, and for funds to supply all of these. A continuous program of in-service training is essential for new principals who must be added to the school system each year.

One solution to the demand for new classrooms has been portable schools. These can be moved rapidly from site to site in the county wherever there is a sudden overflow of pupils, as in the many housing projects that have mushroomed almost overnight. In one 5,000-home development it became necessary to move in a portable school during the Christmas vacation. The pupils attended this school in its old location right up to the last day before the holidays. When the vacation was over, the same buildings were in use at 8:30 A.M. of the first day of school on the new site. This particular school included ten classroom buildings, a cafeteria, an office building, and a building with rest rooms—all moved, complete with furniture, during this short space of time.

A Diverse Student Population

With this phenomenal physical growth has come a parallel expansion in the scope of the curriculum. The diverse pupil population includes, among others, the sons and daughters of business and professional people, migrant workers, Air Force personnel, immigrants, tourists, and farmers. In some of the schools in Dade County, over half of the pupils come from homes in which very little, if any, English is spoken. Many of these pupils enroll in the public schools when they are still unable to speak or understand the English language. Special instructional materials and procedures must be used with these pupils. A flexible curriculum is needed to meet the multiple objectives and interests of the many students in Dade County with their varying backgrounds.

A program of special education is offered for exceptional children. Provisions are made for those who are physically handicapped, homebound, hospitalized, hampered by speech difficulties, deaf and hard of hearing, blind, and mentally exceptional.

There are many gifted students in the Dade County schools who possess outstanding talents and need a differentiated program of instruction. The educational program must provide for early identification of these students and the development of special administrative and instructional provisions which challenge and foster their unusual abilities.

Some students plan to terminate their education at the senior high school level and are interested in developing skills in trades and occupations that will fit them for gainful employment. The goals of these students have made it necessary to design a curriculum which includes a variety of vocational offerings. In addition, a technical program is offered for those students who wish to prepare themselves for college-level engineering work.

Educational opportunities must also be provided for adults in the community. Courses in the adult division range from agriculture through the training of television technicians and aircraft workers. A fifteen-story building serves as the adult school center, as well as the headquarters for many extension courses which operate in the various communities.

Experimentation with Varied Instructional Media

Experimentation is under way to discover effective ways in which to use television. For example, some schools are testing the possibilities of educational television as a means of using large-area spaces as classrooms and still maintaining a sound instructional program for students. A school building's student-population capacity can be increased up to 25 per cent by scheduling the large areas and extending the school day. In some school situations, different groups of students begin and finish their school day at different times.

An illustration of one experimental pattern which is designed to utilize large areas within a school building is the junior high school English and history program. A teacher who gives both English and history courses is scheduled for four classes of English and one period of history. The English classes are normal-size classes with about thirty students in each class. These classes join with several other English classes in the auditorium to form one large history class of about three hundred pupils. A history teacher, assisted by several other teachers and a teacher aide, conducts preliminary learning activities before the showing of a 30-minute televised history lesson. Following the lesson there are coordinated follow-up learning activities in the auditorium. Because the English teachers assist in these history lesson activities, they are able to relate the history learnings to the learning experiences in the normal-size English classes. A careful evaluation of the educational television experiment is in progress, and modifications will be made in the light of the evidence accumulated.

Summer Program

School facilities and personnel are used extensively in a summer program. There is, for example, a camping program for underprivileged boys and girls, operated in cooperation with the Dade County Parks Department and directed by instructional personnel provided by the schools. A recreation program, as well as a summer academic program, is available to the students. Many of these programs are organized in school centers which have complete staffs, including principals. The program is open to those students who wish to take more subjects than would normally be possible during the regular school year as well as those who are interested in bringing their work up to grade-level standards. Full-time music, shop, and recreational programs are operated at all these centers. In addition, a summer educational television program has been inaugurated, designed to broaden interests and to extend learning in selected academic areas.

INITIATION OF THE CURRICULUM
IMPROVEMENT ORGANIZATION

The present systemwide curriculum improvement organization was initiated some time ago by a group of principals working in an in-service training seminar. These principals were dissatisfied with the prevailing organization which centered about school levels and subject areas. They pointed out serious problems of communication concerning instructional matters among elementary, junior, and senior high schools. There was a strong tendency for curriculum groups to concentrate on their particular grade level, school level, or subject area. Not enough emphasis was placed on coordination among school levels, grade levels, and other subject areas and there were often gaps in the program. Problems were also created in overlap and duplication of content, procedures, and instructional materials. On occasion the personnel in the senior high schools would blame their instructional difficulties on the junior high schools and this same problem irritated relations between the junior high and elementary schools. The reverse was also true: some of the elementary personnel felt that the junior and senior high school people did not appreciate or understand their situation. All these difficulties were identified specifically by the principals working in the seminar.

A subcommittee was set up and began work immediately gathering information about curriculum development in other large school systems. Curriculum organizational problems unique to the Dade County schools were also identified. Working through the fall semester, the committee developed a tentative proposal for organization which was presented to the total principals' group. Here the proposal was discussed and many changes were suggested. During the remainder of the school year, the plan was presented to faculty and administrative groups, as well as to PTA groups. Recommendations and criticisms were carefully compiled from all these sessions. Further modifications were made, and finally, the new organization was adopted. A chart of the organization that was developed appears on p. 147. The purposes, operations, and functions were described in the *Administrators' Handbook* and put into effect during the next school year.

Guidelines for Curriculum Improvement

The following general guiding principles serve as the basis for the present systemwide curriculum improvement organization:

1. Because of individual differences, social change, and the nature of the educative process, continuous planning, development, and evaluation of the curriculum are necessary.

2. Curriculum improvement is basically a social change which

results from growth within people who cooperatively participate in the development of the educational program.

3. The participation of the classroom teacher in the curriculum improvement activities is indispensable to the effectiveness of the educational program.

4. A sound program of curriculum improvement provides for the development of understandings and acceptance of changes by pupils, teachers, administrators, and citizens.

5. Curriculum improvement is a multichannel process. The lines of communication should be open at all times to consider proposals and recommendations, wherever they originate.

6. The key to a dynamic program of curriculum improvement is the leadership of the principal. The individual school will not emerge as the basic unit for curriculum improvement, regardless of central office support and coordination, unless the principal assumes active leadership in developing a unique curriculum for the students within the school. Competent leadership works toward making the improvement of the curriculum a cooperative responsibility.

7. The in-service training program should be geared to curriculum needs.

8. The purpose of a systemwide curriculum-improvement organization should be to provide guidance to, and coordination of, the total program. This organization is to be constantly evaluated and improved.

9. All curriculum councils and committees are responsible for giving consideration to the total program, which includes articulation between subject areas, grade levels, and schools.

Council Organization at Three Levels

The membership of the County Curriculum Planning Council is composed of representatives elected by each Area Council, plus the Directors of Curriculum, Guidance, and Special Education and representatives from the elementary, junior and senior high school principals' groups. The total curriculum organization is built on the "grass roots" concept, with the majority groups in all councils being teachers who were elected by their fellow faculty members to represent them on the various councils.

ORGANIZATION FOR CURRICULUM IMPROVEMENT, DADE COUNTY PUBLIC SCHOOLS

It is the responsibility of the County Council to work on curriculum problems which have systemwide significance; to stimulate and encourage curriculum improvement within the individual schools; to recommend policies which require administrative action; and to appoint committees for special studies. Another important function is the promotion of systemwide communication concerning instructional matters by developing media for the exchange of ideas, new research, promising teaching procedures, and materials.

Area Curriculum Planning Councils are organized around the senior high schools and include the junior high and elementary schools which channel students to the particular area's senior high schools. Each school sends a representative to the Area Council, the principals being represented by a principal appointed by the chairman of the principals' group from each of the three school levels. The functions of the Area Curriculum Councils include coordination and communication between elementary, junior, and senior high schools. The Area Council also recommends projects which should be taken up by the County Council.

The School Curriculum Planning Council is selected by the faculty and the principal to represent the various instructional areas within the individual school building, such as elementary school grade groups or high school departments. The purposes of the School Council are twofold: to develop a coordinated curriculum and guidance program, and to recommend problems for consideration by the Area or County Curriculum Planning Councils.

Time for Curriculum Improvement

Special days are scheduled in the school calendar to provide time for curriculum planning within the individual schools. At least one monthly Tuesday afternoon after school is set aside by the schools for curriculum work. Area Councils and the County Council meet during the school day. If the work of these committees requires extensive amounts of time for research and writing, teachers with outstanding competencies in the specific areas under study are employed during the summer months to complete the work.

The "Little School" or school-within-school organization in the junior high school provides a common planning period for teachers who have the same five groups of pupils in their classes. Each pupil is scheduled with all the teachers in a "Little School." This arrangement enables the teachers to center their instructional planning around individual students. Planning becomes a cooperative process in which the time for working together is scheduled during the regular school day. Only the physical education teacher is unable to participate in this planning with the others at this particular time.

Curriculum coordination in the senior high school brings together department chairmen in a common planning period. This type of organization enables the principal to meet regularly with key personnel to plan improvements in the total program.

Curriculum Planning Councils in Action

The initiation of the systemwide study of listening skills illustrates the Curriculum Councils in operation. There was a need to share the successful techniques which teachers used to teach the listening skills. As materials in this area seemed to be limited, all teachers would be served by a collection of teaching procedures. A proposal for doing this resulted in a systemwide study coordinated by the Area Curriculum Planning Councils.

Each Area Council member conferred with his school principal and developed plans and a schedule for carrying out the study. Some principals used the School Curriculum Councils as the local coordinating group. In other schools, a curriculum assistant, a department head, or a teacher was appointed by the principal to serve as the local coordinator. In the smaller schools, the entire faculty was involved as a unit. It had been emphasized that extra meetings should not be scheduled but that this study should be a part of those regular faculty meetings routinely reserved for instructional purposes. In some of the buildings, grade level, departmental and total faculty meetings were used to accumulate techniques and practices. Reports from the schools were sorted into six listening categories: i.e., listening to directions, to conversation, for information acquisition, for evaluative purposes, for enjoyment, and miscellaneous. The Area Curriculum Councils screened and evaluated the procedures, eliminating duplication. In some cases, the Area Councils appointed a special subcommittee to carry out this task. Each of the Area Councils reported at the County Curriculum Council's final meeting of the year.

The West Laboratory School staff, working on a parallel study of effective procedures for teaching listening skills, volunteered to serve as a publication committee. This faculty carefully studied the Area Council reports, integrated the results with their own study, and prepared a report. The refinement and publication of the report for systemwide distribution followed. Since all Dade County teachers participated in this listening-skills study, the report should receive considerable attention for classroom use.

An Area Council at Work

The work of one Area Curriculum Planning Council which selected the improvement of spelling as its major project for the year will illustrate operations at this level. The results on standardized achievement tests in spelling from each member school were compiled, analyzed, and used to assess the status of instruction in the Council's area. Plans were then developed to improve the teaching of spelling in each school.

Each faculty, as a total staff or in grade-level groups, studied the county's curriculum bulletin on spelling instruction. Teacher-developed materials were shared among the schools. Research reports on teaching spelling were mimeographed and distributed. A list of the words most commonly misspelled and mispronounced was compiled and teachers stressed instruction on these. Senior high school teachers in the area developed spelling lists of words unique to particular subject areas. Here, too, understanding, pronunciation, and spelling were emphasized. Standardized achievement tests were again administered in the spring semester to ascertain the progress that had taken place as a result of the efforts—stimulated and coordinated by the Area Curriculum Planning Council—to improve spelling.

A Building Council at Work

An elementary school Curriculum Planning Council identified arithmetic as an area of instruction needing improvement. The

County Guidance Department's graphic item count of the diagnostic tests at each grade level indicated weaknesses in understanding the process of subtraction. The Council found that teachers wanted assistance with effective procedures for teaching the subtraction process.

A series of colored slides was brought in, showing the developmental steps in the teaching of subtraction from grades one through six. With the help of the curriculum assistant, the teachers allocated skills to be taught at each grade level. As the skills were taught, the curriculum assistant helped the teachers in arranging the materials and using the slides. The total staff worked on the preparation of a narrative which was tape recorded to accompany the colored slides. The sequence for teaching the subtraction skills, emphasizing their place in the total arithmetic program, was thus determined by the staff.

A Special Committee Assignment

Special committees are often appointed by the County Curriculum Planning Council to work on specific problems. Personnel for these committees are individuals who have particular competencies in the area of study. The activities of special curriculum committees include countywide surveys, comparative studies of the Dade County curriculum with those of other large school systems, curriculum bulletin preparation, and research projects.

One special curriculum committee was appointed to study the twelfth-grade social studies program. This committee found a number of problems: duplication in content; inadequate application of the understandings developed; a program too highly academic in nature and lecture dominated; course content lacking basic uniformity, varying from school to school. Students transferring had problems of adjustment and those doing make-up work in summer school differed in their needs, creating considerable difficulty in the organization of the course.

To solve these problems, the Social Studies Curriculum Committee developed a plan for the reorganization of the course. It decided to conduct a practicum during the school year which secondary school representatives would attend. A social studies specialist was employed as consultant. The central purpose of this practicum was to coordinate information and ideas from each school. Practices and proposals were screened and evaluated at the practicum meetings. Opinionnaires were prepared for students, parents, and social studies teachers in an effort to determine the interests of the students and the content which parents and teachers considered important for twelfth-grade students. Some 2,000 students, 600 parents, and all the county's social studies teachers responded. The results, tabulated by a graduate student at Florida State University, indicated that all three groups agreed on certain fundamental areas. These became the basis for replanning the course.

The committee considered it important to develop a balanced course in which all the important social sciences were covered. A tentative outline was submitted to faculty members of Florida State University, who were specialists in the behavioral sciences, including history, psychology, geography, and anthropology. These specialists evaluated the outline from the standpoint of their respective subject areas and offered many constructive suggestions for improving the course. During the summer, the teachers and a consultant participated in a workshop to develop problems around the eight major areas agreed upon. Several teachers worked together on the development of each unit. These teachers then tested the problem units in their own classes during the following school year. Recommendations submitted as a result of this tryout were given to a writing team composed of teachers and the social studies supervisor. The team spent a month developing a curriculum guide titled "American History and Government II (Twelfth-Grade Problems Course)." Follow-up studies and evaluations of the effectiveness of this revised program are in progress.

INSTRUCTIONAL LEADERSHIP

Systemwide leadership for instructional improvement begins with the Superintendent who participates in numerous instructional planning sessions. He spends many hours with groups, committees, and members of the Board of Public Instruction working on basic curriculum policies.

Every two weeks the Superintendent and his staff meet informally around the luncheon table with members of the Board of Public Instruction. At these luncheons, which precede the formal meetings of the Board, the group considers some phase of the instructional program with teachers, supervisors, or consultants. Time is always provided for a free discussion in which Board members study and analyze the program.

The Assistant Superintendent in charge of general education devotes the major portion of his time to the improvement of instruction. He welds the various branches of the school organization, including instruction, guidance services, and administration. It is his staff of directors who administratively implement the planning in guidance and instruction. His staff includes the Directors (Elementary Schools; Junior High Schools; Senior High Schools; Technical and Vocational Education; Special Education; Student Welfare and Attendance; Curriculum and Instructional Services; and Guidance Services). The three directors of the elementary, junior, and senior high schools coordinate the work of the principals in schools at these levels. The program of technical and vocational education is related to other phases of the curriculum through the director of this area. Arrangements for pupils who require special educational services are provided by a staff under the leadership of the Director of Special Education. The countywide guidance program is coordinated by the Director of Guidance Services. The Guidance Staff helps appraise the abilities and capacities of individual pupils through a systemwide testing program. This information is used in counseling pupils toward more self-understanding as well as for early identification of educational and vocational goals. Many schools use guidance information to initiate instructional improvement programs. The guidance services include those of school psychologists who, among other responsibilities, diagnose the pupils' emotional difficulties which severely affect their learning, making referrals to community agencies when necessary.

The Director of Student Welfare and Attendance supervises the work of a staff of visiting teachers whose job it is to bring about a cooperative relationship between the school and the home for those pupils who are not adjusting normally. In addition, this director maintains the system of pupil accounting, including an up-to-date school census. These data are used to establish and adjust school boundary lines as well as to assist in locating future schools. It can readily be seen that the work of these directors is so closely interrelated that a cooperative teamwork approach is basic to the success of this staff.

The Work of the Director of Curriculum and Instructional Services

The Director of Curriculum and Instructional Services coordinates the work of the supervisory staff and that of the various curriculum councils and committees. Supervision of curriculum research and the writing, editing, and publication of curriculum bulletins are also his responsibility.

The development of the bulletin on elementary school instructional objectives illustrates the job responsibilities of the Curriculum Director. Elementary school principals were requested by the Curriculum Director to meet with their faculties and identify and rank in order of relative importance the most pressing systemwide instructional problems. With few exceptions, the top priority problem listed by the schools was the need for instructional guidelines in the various subject areas at each grade level.

The supervisory staff, together with some of the administrative staff, held a two-day meeting in which the alternatives were carefully weighed, and it was pointed out that clearly understood, over-all objectives are essential to a coordinated instructional program. On the other hand, there was the danger of grade-level objectives being interpreted as rigidly applied policies which might result in a crystallized curriculum. A decision was made to develop grade-level instructional objectives but to place them in a context that recognized the individual interests and needs of pupils. It was stressed that there are always differences among individuals for whom the instructional emphasis must be adapted.

Tentative objectives were prepared by a writing team as a point of departure from which to initiate systemwide participation in the improvement of the instructional program. This team used consultants, research reports, textbooks, and curriculum materials from other school systems. The objectives were listed in a curriculum guide and presented to the elementary schools as tentative, with the request that they be explored and discussed by classroom teachers.

The Director of Curriculum and Instructional Services requested that each faculty carefully evaluate the proposed objectives and, at the end of the school year, send a summary report of their conclusions and recommendations to the Curriculum Office. These school evaluations were carefully analyzed and used as the basis for making changes. A revised guide was then issued. In this project, the work of the Director of Curriculum and Instructional Services ranged from initiating the survey to the publication of a bulletin and periodic evaluations of its effectiveness.

The Assistant Directors: Educational Radio and Television

Two Assistant Directors are assigned to the area of curriculum and instructional services. One is responsible for radio station WTHS-FM and the educational television station WTHS-TV. His responsibilities include the supervision and production of radio and television programs, the training of teachers for radio and television instruction, the coordination of programs with classroom schedules, and the preparation and publication of lesson guides and teaching manuals.

The second Assistant Director has full charge of the Educational Television Teaching Experiment. He coordinates the selection of on-camera teachers, the planning and production of the lessons and, with the building principals, supervises the television classes. One of the most important phases of his work is the constant task of improving the quality of the telelessons and their utilization in the classroom. From the camera side, it means regularly conferring with the studio teacher, and possibly the inclusion of subject area supervisors or commercial television personnel who may provide help. From the classroom side, the Assistant Director constantly strives to assist the teacher in working toward meaningful student participation for the total experience, including student activity preceding and following the telecast.

Supervisors as Instructional Leaders

The primary responsibility of the supervisory staff is to work directly with teachers, curriculum assistants, and principals on instructional improvement. Secondary responsibilities include such varied items as assisting with the publication of curriculum bulletins, advising on building plans, and making recommendations concerning classroom equipment. Every effort is made to relieve supervisory personnel of administrative details dealing with material things and to emphasize working with people.

Elementary schools are divided into geographical zones, each supervised by a zone supervisor, whose responsibilities are general and include all grade levels. The supervisors help both principals and teachers identify major instructional problems, select procedures for curriculum improvement, and evaluate the effectiveness of their efforts. In working with individual teachers, supervisors consider such facts as past experiences, interests, and abilities of teachers. Since the individual pupils, classrooms, and schools also differ from one community to another, one successful teaching method cannot always be transplanted into other situations. Some teachers are most effective when working independently and need little assistance; other teachers work most effectively with more direct help. Supervisory procedures must be flexible enough to meet the unique characteristics of each situation.

The work of an elementary school supervisor is illustrated by the development of an evaluation of a program for high-ability learners in one building. The school staff had identified a group of pupils who were acquiring their fundamental skills in about half the time required by the average child. For half the school day these high-ability pupils were in heterogeneously grouped classes with their regular teachers who worked with them in the basic skill areas. For the remainder of the day, a resource teacher endeavored to extend and enrich these skills through practical application and through creative activities. Considerable emphasis was placed on the pupils' responsibilities for service to their fellow pupils, parents, and teachers. The program was well accepted in the community and there seemed to be few problems connected with it in the school. However, the principal and the staff desired a thorough assessment of the program and called for the assistance of the elementary supervisor to help plan the evaluation. The supervisor planned cooperatively with the principal, consultants, teachers, and resource personnel from the central office.

After decisions had been made regarding evaluative procedures to be used, the supervisor served as the coordinator in following through on the plans. Sociometric measures, for example, indicated that the personal relationships and attitudes were normal between the pupils in the regular classrooms and those who left to attend the resource class. The arrangement seemed to have the values of special grouping for challenging the high-ability pupil plus the added advantage of retaining friendships and normal relationships with pupils in the regular classroom. Other data supported the resource class use. The supervisor also coordinated the follow-up studies on these high-ability pupils as they progressed into the junior high schools.

Subject Area Supervisors

The elementary schools have subject area supervisors in reading and arithmetic. These supervisors frequently work as a team, concentrating their efforts on a single grade level in one school. The team approach was used in one elementary school where the standardized test scores had indicated that most of the fifth-grade pupils were above-average in mental ability but their reading and arithmetic achievement levels were considerably below grade level. Plans were made with the principal and the teachers. After diagnostic tests had helped to identify the specific areas of difficulty, a series of weekly supervisory visits was planned. The supervisors worked as assistant teachers with those pupils who had been identified by the classroom teachers individually and in small groups, administering periodic tests to determine pupil progress.

The principal wrote to the parents explaining the work going on and asking for their cooperation in helping their children at home with specific supplementary learning activities. The instructional problems of the individual pupil were briefly analyzed and clear-cut directions given for the help by the parents. In conferences further explanations were given parents and understandings between home and school enhanced.

Each classroom session with the supervisors was followed by an evaluation meeting regarding the procedures used and plans were made cooperatively for the following week. Pupils kept individual charts of their progress, thus using arithmetical skills in which they needed practice. Their attitude toward testing changed from one of being threatened by measurement to one of eagerly wanting to be measured so that they could discover their progress.

As time passed, the supervisors gradually minimized their instructional role and the teachers increasingly assumed responsibility for the program. Teachers, reluctant at first about flexible grouping in arithmetic and reading, gained new confidence in these classroom procedures. When it became apparent that the teachers no longer needed the assistance of the supervisors, a faculty meeting was held where the results of the work were discussed. These fifth-grade teachers now help other teachers within the school as the program is extended to other grade levels. As the report spread throughout the school system, the two supervisors received many requests from other schools for assistance of this type.

Principals and teachers seem to appreciate supervision which neither tells teachers how to teach nor takes over the situation at the risk of impairing pupil-teacher relationships. The characteristics of this supervisory experience include cooperative planning, direct assistance with the more difficult phases of teaching, and continuous evaluation.

The supervisory staff also includes personnel in each of the important junior and senior high school subject areas. Although these people are specialists in a particular area, a continuous effort is made to coordinate their activities with work on the rest of the curriculum and to build on the foundation of the elementary school program.

All the secondary school supervisors, for example, were asked to assist one of the new comprehensive high schools with the organization of its instructional program. The principal and faculty of this school had spent most of the year studying and analyzing their curriculum. A series of departmental meetings was scheduled to develop further plans. The department chairmen served as the leaders for the meetings, with the principal and the supervisors serving as consultants. Standardized achievement test scores were analyzed and the areas in need of improvement were pinpointed. Plans were made to survey research related to each of the subject areas. Diagnostic test use was discussed as an aid to identification of individual pupil difficulties. The groups developed over-all departmental objectives for each grade level and arranged a flexible time schedule. The importance of coordinated planning between departments was carefully considered and a decision was reached to develop projects which would relate the students' learning activities in two or more departments. A specific example of this type of planning was the interdepartmental student projects between the language arts and other departments within the school. The language arts skills and the subject-matter content of the joint projects became the central concern of the appropriate department. Students who were enrolled in art classes received guidance in the preparation of illustrations and project covers. A student received a grade on a single research project in several different subject areas. The language arts teachers also identified as one of their major concerns the problem of teaching methods for fast and slow learners. The supervisors helped the departments to identify their major curriculum problems and to plan attacks on the various phases of these problems.

Special Responsibilities for Supervisors

The Supervisor of Special Reading Services has responsibility for helping develop a more effective reading program in the Dade County schools. This supervisor works with both serious reading problems and with programs designed to improve the visual and perceptive skills of high-ability readers. Seven assisting teachers supplement the work of the Supervisor of Special Reading Services by working directly with reading problems in the classroom and by planning with other teachers.

The Instructional Materials Department includes library services, audio-visual services, textbook services, and the instructional materials distribution center.

The total supervisory staff meets monthly at which time problems of systemwide concern are considered. The elementary school supervisors meet weekly. In addition, individual conferences are scheduled regularly with the Curriculum Director. All supervisors are in schools for four days each week. The fifth day is used for conferences, planning meetings, and office work.

Leadership at the Elementary School Level

The active leadership of the building principal, working cooperatively with his faculty, is an indispensable requirement for an effective program of curriculum improvement. It is the principal's responsibility to help initiate, develop, and follow through on instructional improvement activities. He must make certain that his teachers are working on real problems which are of genuine concern to them.

The principal in a school with a student population in excess of 1,000 is entitled to employ a currriculum assistant as a regular faculty member. The curriculum assistant works with the principal on program improvement. A large-sized school can diminish the conscientious principal's influence on instructional improvement but the provision of competent assistance helps to maintain this important function at an effective level.

The curriculum assistant spends most of his time in the classrooms working with teachers in the development of a more effective program. He meets with the teachers in grade-level or subject-matter sessions to help identify and work cooperatively on serious instructional problems. Teachers are encouraged to develop simple, uncluttered plans which include emphasis on major concepts, clear-cut assignments, reasonable amounts of homework, and definite instruction in study skills.

In one elementary school, the principal and the curriculum assistant were active in initiating a program to improve the teaching of arithmetic. Tests were administered by the classroom teachers to determine the areas needing immediate consideration. The curriculum assistant then prepared a schoolwide report which furnished an analysis of the strengths and weaknesses in the four basic computational areas and provided a springboard for the curriculum assistant to plan work with individual teachers on the improvement of arithmetic. The results were discussed with the teachers who requested help concerning plans, grouping, parent conferences, diagnostic testing, and teaching procedures. Individual progress records were kept on each pupil. In a short time there was clear evidence of more effective teaching resulting in increased pupil understandings as well as progress in achievement levels.

Consultants Used for Variety of Purposes

Consultants are used in many different ways in the Dade County schools—such as planning and evaluating specialized phases of experimental programs. One of the high schools, for instance, wished to develop a special course in science research and desired assistance in planning and evaluating the program. A science consultant had had outstanding success with a similar high school science program which seemed to fit the needs of the local situation. He shared his experiences with the planning committee and his suggestions were used as the basis for the development of a new course. Advanced science students were given opportunities for original experimentation, with time for reading in areas of the greatest interest to them. The Science Research Course was taken by these students, in addition to the regularly scheduled science course. After almost a year of operation, the same consultant was brought back to observe the program in action. At a follow-up meeting, the consultant listened to problems from the staff and recommended ways to improve the activity. The course was successful and demands by high-ability students to enter this class increased over 100 per cent. The Science Research Course is now being extended and adapted in other senior high schools.

Consultants often help to introduce new programs and to demonstrate effective teaching procedures in them. A newly developed secondary school mathematics program, initiated in Florida, has been adopted in the Dade County schools as part of the regular curriculum. Built on a logical development of mathematical concepts and cutting across traditional mathematics subject area lines, the program emphasizes inductive teaching methods. Students are not limited by artificial partitions of subject areas to study college-level mathematics. Traditionally separate branches of secondary school mathematics are integrated. While not designed exclusively for the gifted mathematics students, it does provide the opportunity for a student to study areas of advanced mathematics at a much earlier grade level than is possible in the regular program. Because it differed from the standard secondary mathematics program, one of the designers was brought in to serve as a consultant to the school system. Two all-day sessions were scheduled at the beginning and middle of the school year, at which time the consultant explained instructional materials related to this program and demonstrated procedures for helping students to explore and discover their own concepts. This mathematics consultant visited each of the schools, teaching classes while teachers observed his work. The class sessions were followed by meetings during which the teachers raised questions and discussed their observations.

Consultants are frequently residents of the community. A special program was developed because one of the local research scientists came to the schools with an idea for challenging and motivating gifted science students. After discussing it with school officials, a pilot program was initiated in which the main purpose was to provide gifted students with firsthand experience in working with research scientists in the community. The man who originated the idea for the program is serving as the community coordinator, securing commitments from other community laboratories to enable selected students to work side by side with research scientists. These students are thus able to become acquainted with outstanding research workers in the community, to develop extensive knowledge about an area of science, and to acquire research skills.

In-service Training on a Broad Basis

A variety of in-service education activities is offered to the school personnel for credit or noncredit. Frequent surveys are made to determine the needs and wishes of instructional personnel. The activities may take the form of practicums, seminars, workshops, institutes, or new courses offered by the universities at the request of the schools. Supervisory and administrative personnel participate in these activities but do not serve as instructors. The formal activities are coordinated under the general direction of the Assistant Superintendent for General Education.

The informal program is sponsored by various professional organizations, school faculties, and other groups.

The junior high school principals have been meeting biweekly, developing criteria for measuring an effective program. These criteria will be used in self-studies by individual schools interested in improving their curriculum. The principals first identified the various areas which they wished to evaluate with their faculties. These areas served as a working outline for the practicum in which subcommittees were organized to identify the characteristics of effective classroom instruction. Tentative reports were distributed to all the principals who took the rough drafts back to their schools and organized faculty study sessions. The proposed criteria were critically analyzed, suggestions were collected from the staffs, and the principals reported the recommendations of their faculties to the practicum. After further consideration and modification, the criteria were refined and pilot-tested in several junior high school self-studies.

Typical of the self-study practicum in action is the elementary school faculty which began studying the strengths and weaknesses of its curriculum. Standardized test results were analyzed and specific areas of instructional difficulty were identified. In the area of arithmetic it was discovered that pupils were having trouble understanding the concept of place value. Each grade level studied this problem and made plans for improving the teaching of this concept. A series of colored slides was developed which explained how each grade level taught this concept.

Another committee made plans to carry out improvements in the area of guidance. The efforts of this committee resulted in improved ways of using sociograms, anecdotal records, and parent-teacher conferences.

A third committee was concerned with inadequacies in the science program. It was not clear which concepts and skills should be taught and at what grade levels they were to receive major emphasis. The committee took one topic—the solar system—and made an intensive study of it. Determining the questions children at each grade level asked about the solar system, the teachers constructed a chart of concepts and skills. These concepts and skills were then tested in each classroom from grades one through six to find whether or not they were appropriate at the grade level. Adjustments in the chart were made by the teachers in the light of their classroom experiences. This staff also produced a list of helpful references, including films, filmstrips, texts, and supplementary materials that were related to the solar system.

During the practicum, short recreational periods were scheduled at which times one of the special area teachers assumed leadership. The teachers participated in activities designed to help them relax and to develop new understandings and skills in the areas of music, art, and physical education. These short periods had great "carry-over" value in the classrooms.

The school made use of resource people in the different subject areas, along with the school nurse, a university consultant, and people from the community.

SUMMARY AND CONCLUSION

Dade County's rapid growth exerts a powerful influence over curriculum improvement. It has made necessary some systematic plan for orienting a great number of new teachers who must be integrated into the school system. A continuous program of inservice training provides new principals with the opportunity to study policies and to do preliminary planning and organization. Periodic self-study practicums involving total faculty participation enable all the schools in the system to evaluate their instructional programs and to work on curriculum improvements at the school level under the leadership of the principals.

The Dade County system operates on the fundamental principle that the individual school is the basic unit of instructional improvement. Genuine curriculum development can come about only as it is cooperatively planned in schools and in the classroom. The systemwide framework for the improvement of instruction provides for over-all coordination and is designed to provide individual schools with wide latitude of choice in their instructional improvement activities.

Rapid growth creates many problems in developing and maintaining an organized and coordinated program of instruction, but it also provides the school system with one of its greatest strengths. New teachers with different backgrounds and experiences bring thousands of new ideas. These serve as stimuli to curriculum improvement activity. Traditions are being established for the first time in many new schools throughout the system. Each year new principals have the opportunity to initiate school programs which incorporate curriculum planning based on the systematic collection of evaluative evidence. The central objective of all of this organization and coordinated effort is to provide a continuously improving curriculum for the boys and girls in Dade County public schools.

7

LEWIS COUNTY, NEW YORK

IMPROVING THE EDUCATIONAL PROGRAM

TO MEET PUPIL NEEDS *

LATER in this chapter the reader will find a brief description of a
seminar for rural youth in a county where geography would seem
to be a formidable barrier to such an experience. This creative
program, as well as other developing programs, are logical outcomes of an established and accepted practice in Lewis County,
New York: namely, a systematic and continuing program of opportunity for in-service growth of administrators and teachers.

Although there is no special organization for curriculum development as such, improvements are taking place and others are
projected. Assuming that curriculum means any and all experiences which affect the development of the pupil as a self-directing,
thinking, responsible citizen, then there is continuing attention to
curriculum improvement. This is due to, and has given expression
in several ways to, a single emphasis without which a discrete
program of curriculum improvement cannot proceed very far.
This emphasis is the study of pupils and their needs. Perhaps the
motif which characterizes the Lewis County program best of all

---

* *This chapter was written by* GLYN MORRIS, *Assistant Superintendent, Pupil Personnel Services and Curriculum, Lewis County,
New York.*

is its guidance-oriented quality. The reader will see that this motif runs throughout the chapter. Discovering needs, studying individuals, improving group processes, role-playing, and developing adequate pupil developmental records are paramount procedures.

BACKGROUND

Lewis County,[1] covering an area of 1,270 square miles, is east of Lake Ontario and includes some of the foothills of the Adirondack Mountains. Much of the area is cutover timber land. The Black River, running north and south, divides the county roughly in the middle. About 24 per cent of the annual income of county residents comes from agriculture, supporting 31 per cent of the working population. Approximately 25 per cent of the population is employed in manufacturing, primarily of wood and paper products and related industries. The remainder of the population is engaged in trades and services, government and other occupations. The population in 1950 was 22,521, a figure which has remained almost constant for half a century. The next census may indicate a slight increase. Much of the land on the western plateau, with an altitude of 2,000 feet, was formerly used for agriculture but is now being reforested. The abandonment of this area accounts in part for the population trend. The county has the greatest annual snowfall of any region east of the Rockies, making it a popular winter sport area. There is abundant water power available. The county seat, Lowville, is the largest village, having a population of 3,800.

There are eight "centralized," one "union free school," and a few "common school" districts. With the exception of the Lowville school of 1,700 pupils (kindergarten through grade 12), the central schools range in size from 213 to 800 pupils. Two of the schools are sixty-six miles apart. All schools participate in the services made available through the Board of Cooperative Educational Services. A district may contract for service in such areas as art education, physical education, dental hygiene, driver education, music, health, elementary supervision, and guidance.

[1] George Armstrong, *The Forests and Economy of Lewis County, New York*. Bull. 33 (Syracuse: State University of New York, College of Forestry, 1954).

Formerly composed of four separate supervisory districts, the entire county became a single district in 1953 with one superintendent who also serves as the executive officer of the Cooperative Board.

While it would be gratifying to be able to state precisely what has resulted from the procedures to be described, this is not possible. That something has happened is reasonably clear as was demonstrated in several schools after the first two years.[2] Among other things, guidance services have been extended both in terms of personnel and quality of service; pupil developmental records have been improved; standardized testing has been made more uniform throughout the county and the test results put to better use; changes have taken place in details of program in individual schools; scheduling of classes has been improved; commencement programs have taken on new and deeper meaning; more appropriate experiences have been provided for more able students.

The strength and promise of the Lewis County effort, however, lie in the method by which the program is evolving: the leadership role and broad perception of the superintendent; the emphasis on pupil needs; the increasing involvement of administrators and teachers in planning and studying; the way in which elementary and high school teachers combine their efforts; and the excellent communication which prevails at all levels.

The program, procedures, and emphasis described in the following pages were formally begun in 1951 when the superintendent of the two southern districts sought a modest grant from the Kellogg Foundation through its Cooperative Project in Educational Administration. A grant for a two-year program made possible the employment of a coordinator who served part time as director of guidance for five schools. On the completion of the project, he became the full-time director of guidance. This accounts for the guidance emphasis throughout the program.

One more observation is necessary in order to describe the scope of the program. At many points, both elementary and sec-

---

[2] Don Donley, "A Study of the Influence of Administrative Leadership upon Educational Change in Supervisory District No. 2, Lewis County, N. Y., from September 1951 to June 1953." Doctor of Education Project, Syracuse University, Syracuse, N. Y., 1959. (Unpublished.)

ondary teachers meet together, especially in their discussion of matters appropriate to all pupils: for example, case conferences, pupil records, techniques of guidance, testing, and formulating school purposes. A consistent effort has been made to see the school program as a whole and to distinguish between elementary, junior high school, and senior high school only where functions are uniquely appropriate to these divisions.

THE ROLE OF THE ADMINISTRATORS

The strategic device for improvement of instruction is the regular biweekly meeting of the superintendent and his small staff (the director of guidance and the elementary supervisor) with the nine supervising principals. Rotating among the schools, where luncheon is usually served by a class in homemaking, this group meets for the entire afternoon to work on some problem of improving instruction. Fortunately, the temptation to discuss purely administrative matters was resisted early and overcome. Here problems in instruction, curriculum, and guidance are raised and a reasonable and sustained effort is made to find solutions for them.

Since 1954, the school term has been preceded by a three-day conference of the group during which the members explore a single problem that might possibly be the basis for study by the individual faculties throughout the year. Because of differing circumstances, the quality and extent of the follow-through have varied with respective schools. Considerable concerted effort is, however, put forth and some uniformity in program has been effected.

Getting Under Way

Reference has been made to the Cooperative Project in Educational Administration. The grant from the CPEA provided the impetus for the administrators to focus on a particular problem selected by them: "How to Improve Services Based on Pupil Needs." This proved important in the growth of the administrators and in subsequent developments in the county.

The group began by asking the question: "How can we find

out what our pupils need?" Initially, there was a strong inclination to view and list needs from the administrative rather than pupil point of view. In due time, however, the group realized the necessity of finding an objective way to discover pupil viewpoints and, after exploration and study, two procedures were adopted: (1) to give an inventory [3] to all high school pupils; (2) to find out what former pupils had to say through a follow-up study of graduates.

Analysis and appraisal of the results of these procedures proved worth while and took up a considerable portion of time during the first year. The results were thought-provoking. It was noted that the area of greatest concern to pupils was "Adjustment to School Work." Here the number of problems averaged 5 per pupil as compared with 1.2 in relation to "Home and Family." For example, to indicate just a few problems noted in this area, 44.7 per cent of the pupils were concerned about not spending enough time in study; 33.7 per cent indicated they were not interested in some subjects; and 27 per cent had trouble in making oral reports.

With consultants to help in interpretation, considerable time was given to trying to understand these data. The administrators were able to see the limitations as well as the implications of the findings. For example, the principals noted that even though a problem was checked by a pupil, there was no indication of its intensity or of its actual meaning for the student. Furthermore, the fact was recognized that problems checked may be currently pressing but of short duration while, at the same time, more obvious problems might obscure deeper and less clearly defined ones. Finally, the group recognized that pupils could have problems which would not be reflected in the check list. The meaning of the results of these studies for the faculties of some of the schools will be described later. The importance for administrators is reflected in their own statements, as, "This gives us something concrete to go on. We have a clearer understanding of what the problems are." [4]

During the following two years, progress in any given area was

[3] *The Mooney Problems Check List* (New York: Psychological Corporation).

[4] Glyn Morris, "How Five Schools Made Plans Based on Pupil Needs," *The Clearing House*, Vol. 29 (November 1954), pp. 131–34.

limited and efforts were diffused. Among other things, the junior high school program was examined in relation to the growth and development of that age group. This included a careful examination of a particular seventh-grade class in terms of data collected: personality tests; pupils' responses to two projective devices ("If I Had Three Wishes" and an incomplete sentence exercise); a sociogram showing the structure of class relationships; and the California Test of Mental Maturity.

The most fruitful experience of one year seemed to come from analysis of tape recordings of the group members' role-playing interviews with teachers who presented problems. Admittedly, principals have difficulty in a counseling relationship with a teacher. The process of discussing the personal attitudes, statements, and the approach to an interview proved both threatening and enlightening to all concerned. Later, when the principals were concerned with helping teachers make adjustments to slow learners in the areas of reading and social studies, analysis of tape-recorded interviews again proved helpful.

During this same period, the group shifted focus to the educational aspects of what seemed to them to be purely administrative problems: how to select cheer leaders or improve conduct on school buses on trips to athletic events. An effort was made to see that *all* pupil activities are grist for the educational mill and, somehow or other, can and should be viewed and worked out in relation to the purposes of the school. The touchstone for determining what to do in any situation involving pupils would seem to be: "How can this experience contribute to the well-being of the pupil?"

Four schools started or developed their existing student councils into more educationally meaningful experiences. There was considerable discussion among all concerned of the meaning of democracy within the framework of pupil maturity levels and the limits set by legal authority. Equal emphasis was placed on teaching pupils the skills and understandings necessary to function in a group, and on teaching a particular subject.

The Administrators at Work

In order to describe the Lewis County program adequately, the work of the administrators must be described in some detail.

Growth of the teacher is difficult, if not impossible, without the understanding, insight and leadership of the administrator. In 1954, principals started the custom of holding three-day planning sessions prior to the opening of the school term and these programs will now be described.

Helping to define goals.   In these planning sessions, problems posed by the administrators repeatedly led back to another problem: no school had a clearly defined statement of its purposes of education. To be sure, all had read and tacitly accepted the "Seven Cardinal Principles of Secondary Education." Each administrator thought he knew what his school should do for its pupils. But the overemphasis on some aspects of the program to the exclusion of others and the anachronistic nature of some assumed goals in the light of the nature of the pupil population caused strain, confusion, and frustration among all concerned. Furthermore, the application of accepted goals to specific situations had never been worked through.

Administrators admittedly had no experience in their leadership role in bringing the statement of school aims up to date or spelling these out in detail. The first of the three-day, preschool-term planning conferences was devoted to doing just this. Broad goals were stated, and then, because it was impossible to do more, one of the specific goals was applied to a particular segment of the pupil population and spelled out in terms of classroom and community experience. For example, one of the goals selected was: "The pupil should be able to assume an adequate citizenship role." This goal was examined in terms of a ninth-grade pupil and involved delineation of what could be reasonably expected of a fourteen-year-old boy: i.e., what kinds of behavior should the school expect of him? Details of classroom experience were described and their meanings explored as had never been done before by these principals. For the first time, attention was given to "developmental tasks" and their meaning for curriculum. Opportunities for more extended experiences were explored as the group sought for behavioral outcomes and more specific types of performance than those limited by textbook knowledge. The group kept asking, "Is this goal something which can be observed and evaluated?"

Planning the program.   During the year each faculty worked on this problem. Concurrently, the administrators continued their study at biweekly meetings, bringing in problems that had emerged in their local situations as they had worked with teachers. At the end of the year they selected the teaching of reading as the area of concern for the next preschool conference.

For this second conference, a reading specialist was brought in. Again, the group went through the step-by-step process of setting up a developmental reading program. It seems difficult to believe that in this most important aspect of contemporary education administrators felt such strong limitations with regard to what is involved in teaching reading. This group tackled the problem with both humility and eagerness. Diagnostic features of reading tests and their implications were studied; the distinction between a slow and a retarded reader was clarified and emphasized. Literature on reading programs as well as other resources were examined. The need to provide adequate reading materials on the pupils' psychological level was emphasized.

Taking action. As might be expected, sooner or later the administrators would be compelled to consider some aspect of evaluation. Up to this point, there had been no discussion of the desirability of considering either an examination of standardized tests or the values of a uniform testing program for the entire county. It was to these two concerns that attention was directed at the annual administrators' preschool conference, starting with the question: "What do we want the tests to do?" The discussion led to a consideration of other matters, such as the relation of national norms to an area, particularly a rural region, and the differences between tests purporting to measure similar objectives.

During the year all the biweekly meetings were given over to further understanding of testing. Various test-publisher representatives described their products and were questioned about them. As a result of this experience the principals learned that no standardized test was without its limitations; some tests were more useful in measuring certain areas or skills than others. Some members of the group developed a healthy skepticism about the usefulness of instruments which they had assumed were "scientific" and therefore infallible.

Meanwhile, some of the faculties were examining tests so that by the end of the year the principals were prepared to accept tentatively a countywide testing program. Among the tests included was an aptitude test battery for all ninth graders which was also to contribute to research about the predictive value of these particular tests for college success of rural youth.

Finally, the administrators turned their attention to the fact that in the entire county the experiences directly relating pupils to the world of work were limited to vocational agriculture and clerical work. Without studying the matter, it was obvious to all that vocational agriculture was anachronistic. In several schools, this was the only training available to boys for developing manual skills even though a large percentage would not be going into agriculture. Vocational agriculture was taken by many boys because nothing else was offered.

With this in mind, the 1957–1958 conference of administrators was devoted to a study of vocational needs and the possibilities for offering additional courses. A consultant was called on for definition of types of work-school experiences possible, to describe types and requirements of vocational courses, and to help lay the groundwork for the study of those experiences most appropriate for Lewis County youth.

A thorough follow-up study of former pupils was planned and a survey of the personnel needs of industry in and around Lewis County undertaken. The entire year was devoted to these studies. A committee of administrators designed instruments which were checked by experts. Of the three thousand questionnaires sent out, over one thousand were returned and analyzed. Meanwhile, the administrators continued to study the personnel needs of industry in the region, particularly in the county, to determine the extent to which personnel for certain types of skilled and managerial jobs must be secured outside the county and to ascertain training requirements which might be met by the public schools. Finally, during this same year, the administrators accepted and began to use the methods for computing the drop-out rate developed by the State Department of Education.[5]

Values of administrative participation. The foregoing paragraphs give the high points of the administrators' study. The custom of meeting together has been established. A congenial

[5] Division of Pupil Personnel Services, New York State Department of Education, Albany, N. Y.

and friendly atmosphere has developed, wherein ideas are freely exchanged and the leadership is quick to respond to needs as these are revealed. The climate of these sessions involving leadership personnel as set by the District Superintendent is contagious, so that this same tone is carried over into meetings of respective school faculties. The regular meetings of administrators are valuable in the following ways:

1. There is cross-fertilization of ideas. Participants learn from each other.
2. Without stifling individual differences in school needs and program, they tend to bring all schools along on certain fronts.
3. There is dissemination of resource material.
4. Time of consultants is effectively used at a strategic point.
5. There is possible improvement in morale and an antidote to the isolation of the rural administrator.
6. The superintendent is able to exert more effective leadership.

THE SCHOOL STAFFS AT WORK

The strategy that seemed appropriate in the early days of the program described above was that the principals would work with their own professional staffs on some aspect of the same problem under consideration. By taking turns at leadership within the principals' group, it was expected that they would then be better able to carry on with their respective faculties. In general, however, this did not work out exactly as planned. Occasionally, it did take place, as when the schools worked on improving reading and in developing a statement of school purposes. But individual differences exist both in the administrators and in the local situation, making it impossible to adhere exactly to a rigid plan. These differences and needs are carefully respected by the District Superintendent. For this reason, it is difficult to give detailed descriptions of the varied in-service programs carried on in each of the schools. However, this section will describe some of the most significant and interesting work of the respective faculties.

For the most part principals and faculties accept the value of holding regular meetings for discussion of educational problems.

These meetings are normally scheduled for every other week and in some cases oftener. In some schools classes are dismissed early for such meetings. In most, the faculty meeting is preceded by a refreshment period. The meetings are informal and, in all but one school, the faculty is small enough to make communication and group work relatively uncomplicated.[6] Generally speaking, it appears that the smaller the school, the easier it is to develop an effective program of in-service meetings.

Before proceeding with an account of staff participation in this program, an essential detail of administration through supervision and communication should be mentioned. Each principal, in planning regular faculty meetings, may obtain assistance from the superintendent's office, generally through the administrative assistant who also serves as director of guidance. More often than not, the principal of a school spends considerable time in conference with the director of guidance or, as the case may be, with his own counselor, making plans for the day's faculty meeting. In this way maximum effectiveness is achieved through adequate planning.

Using Check Lists

When returns on the *Mooney Problems Check List* had been summarized several faculties studied their implications. As might be expected at this early stage in the in-service program, the staffs took hold of those pupil problems which were related to teacher needs—for example, helping pupils study more effectively. As a result, one school made noticeable improvement in the area of supervised study. The practical way in which this was done not only set the pattern in this school for subsequent improvement in other areas but illustrates one good method for helping faculties grow in teaching skill.

The staff dramatized a study hall situation; they acted it out. Many teachers are at a loss to know how to meet the variety of pupil problems in study hall. These range from the pupil who is too sleepy to study to the one who finishes his assignments early and has time on his hands. With this in mind, teachers planned

[6] See Glyn Morris, "The Faculty Meeting as a Guidance Resource in Small Rural Schools," *Education*, Vol. 74 (April 1954), pp. 501–06.

and acted the parts of different pupils, while one teacher dramatized what might be done in response to these situations. This
included checking pupils' assignments, helping them find materials to augment their study, and counseling informally with
the pupil who needed help in motivation. By coming to grips
with the situation kinetically instead of verbally, teachers gained
confidence and found some practical answers to a problem. It is
interesting to note that later, whenever the in-service program
in this school seemed to bog down, teachers recalled the dramatization of the study hall as an example of the kind of experience
they would like to repeat.

Another faculty approached the matter by studying this same
study hall problem in some depth. They prepared a check list of
study habits and analyzed each pupil's responses, making a kind
of case study of the pupil's habits, resources, and liabilities in this
particular area of activity.

One problem revealed by the *Mooney Problems Check List*
and susceptible to immediate attention was the concern by a
large number of pupils with their possible duty in the armed
services. Responding to this, for several years a series of orientation classes were held for eleventh- and twelfth-grade pupils.

There were other important results of the *Mooney Problems
Check List* findings such as counseling pupils with problems of
some magnitude. Teachers began to recognize that pupils had
problems of which teachers were not aware. This viewpoint has
since been underlined in at least two well-known studies.[7]
Finally, through discussion, teachers were helped to recognize
that a check list of problems by no means gives a picture of the
depth or extent of a pupil's problems as he views them, either
consciously or unconsciously.

Developing a Statement of Goals

It is difficult to describe or appraise this experience adequately, but it can be safely stated that for the majority of

[7] W. H. Ivans, W. H. Fox, and D. A. Segel, "A Study of the Secondary
School Program in Light of the Characteristics and Needs of Youth," *Bulletin
of the School of Education* (Bloomington, Indiana), Vol. 25 (November 1949),
p. 6; and H. H. Remmers and D. H. Radler, *The American Teenager* (Indi-
anapolis: Bobbs-Merrill, 1957).

teachers this was both a new and complicated experience. Only a beginning has been made here. Again, the quality of the result varied with individual schools, depending on their understanding of what was involved and the effort put forth. One faculty, unable to make adequate distinctions between purpose and method, hardly began; another faculty, by effective committee work, prepared a mature statement of purpose and some plans for implementation.

In all cases, faculties were forced to examine some of their assumptions and to appraise these in the light of the characteristics of their pupils. One good feature which characterized several of the statements of purpose was that they were written in terms of what the school should do to "help the pupil learn *to do*." This emphasized the functional nature of the curriculum, particularly in areas where emphasis had primarily been on education which was presumed, rightly or wrongly, to lead to favorable action at some future date. In other words, wherever possible the focus was on behavior which could be observed and accurately appraised. To some extent, teachers were helped to dispel the degree of vagueness which persists with respect to detailing aims and objectives in terms where appraisal is possible. Granted that appraisal in many areas of presumed growth and development is elusive, much more accurate evaluation than is currently practiced is possible.

Improving Reading

Until the reading program began, administrators only vaguely realized the need to give systematic and continuous attention to the teaching of reading beyond the sixth grade. At the same time it was recognized that many pupils were unable to meet school requirements because of deficiency in the language arts. As a result, the faculties concentrated for one entire school year on trying to understand how reading could be improved.

Three significant steps were taken. (1) The distinction, which had been hazy, between retarded and slow readers was made clear. A majority of high school teachers had not realized that a pupil of high intellectual potential could be reading at grade level or above and still be retarded. (2) The diagnostic features of reading tests were used to locate areas where special attention was needed. (3) The teachers used the case-conference method to place the pupil's reading problem in its proper setting.

Each school attacked the problem in its own way and consequently there were differences in details of the program. In two schools, counselors working with pupils on an individual basis for the first time saw considerable progress made by the students, and found the experience personally worth while. From that time on the counselors gave better leadership to programs for improving reading. Another school did a thorough job of identifying retarded readers and held extensive case conferences which led to better understanding of these pupils as a whole and resulted in more and improved counseling. In still another school teachers demonstrated how to check informally on specific weaknesses in the reading pattern of individual pupils. A number of these demonstrations were tape recorded and discussed by the faculty. In another case, after the principal had tabulated the diagnostic test results for a single grade, the staff examined carefully the social studies textbooks in terms of the abilities of slow learners to read and master their contents. The faculty then spent considerable time in suggesting how contents of a particular chapter might be presented effectively and in agreeing on minimum and essential facts which a slow reader might be able to handle. Much of these discussions revolved around the problems of sorting out nonessential information—coming to grips with the plethora of material contained in social studies texts— and of helping teachers feel comfortable in a situation where it is physically impossible to expect many pupils to benefit from instruction which requires learning all these details. Many good ideas were set forth for using methods and experiences not requiring reading. For example, teachers listed many local resources which might be used for field trips prior to reading a particular chapter and showed how these might motivate pupils to better understanding of the related reading. Among other benefits, teachers saw that it was not essential to begin with the material on the first page of the chapter. In several secondary schools, elementary school teachers were brought into the discussions to demonstrate how reading is taught at the primary level. One staff dramatized the right and wrong way to assist a slow reader who is called upon to read aloud.

One school in particular has continued its attack on this problem in a special and effective way with all teachers participating to the extent of using three periods weekly for developmental reading. Periods are rotated and all pupils participate. The evidence of the program's effectiveness is found both in the results of standardized test scores and in pupil and parent enthusiasm. In turn, the interest of other administrators has been aroused and they are watching the program closely.

In trying to improve reading, the teachers were led to consider standardized tests and their use. One of the most useful outcomes in this respect was the practice of looking carefully at the distribution of pupil abilities as these were reflected in the typical classroom. In each case a wide range of ability was apparent. This led to more thorough classification of pupils and eventually to identification of pupils at both ends of the curve of ability. Now all schools are not only identifying talented pupils, but are trying to plan more specific programs in the light of these findings. One administrator found that his teachers became more willing to spend time on in-service training and they now have something tangible to go by. This has helped bring their work into focus, and instead of trying to raise the level of all pupils indiscriminately, their efforts are more concentrated. They have discarded the "buckshot" for the more accurate "rifle" approach.

Using Role-Playing and Dramatization

Reference has been made to role-playing in connection with some meetings of the administrators, and to dramatization. This device was also used in several of the schools, particularly where the teachers seemed comfortable in experimenting. The situations which lend themselves naturally to role-playing are those involving a face-to-face relationship between two persons: teacher and pupil or parent; principal and teacher, pupil, or parent. For instance, teachers in one school wanted to know how they might learn about a pupil's interests directly from him. As they tried this through role-playing, they gained insight into the implications of their questions and responses to the pupil's statements. Immediately the teachers recognized how frequently their own comments and questions left very little room for pupil expression as the nature of the questions asked and the unwitting judgmental character of teacher responses restricted him. Words took on new meaning for these teachers, as they, playing the part of pupils, reacted to teacher questions.

Dramatization played an important part, too, in helping teachers act out situations. In one school, teachers wanted help in a classroom exercise of developing the implications of a selection from literature. Actually, the experience turned out to be a lesson in the art of group discussion. In doing this, a group of teachers assumed the roles of respective pupils, trying as best they could to respond to the discussion in much the same manner as they believed the students might, i.e., they tried to view the scene from the standpoint of some of the major environmental and psychological factors affecting a particular pupil's life. A typical selection of literature was chosen which contained a conflict of values, and one teacher led the group discussion. Several times it became clear to the "teacher" and the "class" that the teacher tended to ask questions and to respond to pupil statements in such a way as to channel answers directly and speedily into a "right" or "wrong" category. This was evident, for instance, in a story where action resulted in apparent unethical behavior by the hero but where his motivation was obscure. It became clear that teachers need help in structuring responses to pupil statements in such a way as to permit the pupil to develop ideas and implications adequately in much the same way as a counselor encourages a client to solve or understand his own problem.

Since dramatization and role-playing are used increasingly in this program, a further word may underline their value. Frequently teachers burlesque a situation so effectively that its incongruous aspects take on real meaning. For instance, in acting out the way a poor reader reads aloud, and the way in which a poor teacher tries to help, teachers inject humor into the situation. Since humor and tragedy are related in an intimate but strange manner, the plight of the suffering pupil takes on added dimension.

Using the Case Conference

Because guidance is so central to the Lewis County program, the case conference has, from the beginning, played a strategic part in its development. Probably no other single procedure does quite as much to modify teacher attitudes and therefore pave the way for curriculum change as does proper use of case conferences. Consequently, many conferences are held in Lewis County schools.

When the case conference is systematically done it has several advantages:

1. It focuses on the needs of an individual in his unique environment.
2. It requires adequate data about a pupil, hence helps teachers see the importance of good pupil developmental records and the collection and use of data.
3. It sharpens awareness of the pupil's needs in relation to the curriculum and by implication points to change in both method of teaching and content of program.

The logical starting point is a teacher's concern about an individual pupil. That is, the teacher wants to do something to correct a situation such as the student's failure to respond to a segment of the curriculum. For instance, one teacher, disturbed by her inability to cope with the misbehavior of a precocious eighth-grade student, appealed to the guidance counselor for aid. The counselor in turn suggested that it might be beneficial if a group of teachers who knew the pupil, together with the school principal and nurse, met to discuss the pupil. Because this was the first such conference, records proved to be inadequate, although some standardized test scores and other fragmentary information were available. The conference revealed that the pupil was reading at least four years above his grade level and that part of his difficulty was due to an unchallenging program. Several changes were suggested and carried out. Most important was the change in the teachers' attitudes toward this pupil as they began to realize that he was not willfully mischievous but was reacting to conditions over which he had no control and of which he was unaware. After several similar experiences this faculty became enthusiastic about such conferences. The principal, in turn, told other principals about their value, so that it was not difficult to initiate conferences in other schools. Now it has become axiomatic that whenever a pupil needs special attention no plans are made without first holding a case conference on him.

One small central school holds a conference on all pupils in grades 9 through 12 each year. At another school the personnel of the New York State Traveling Guidance Clinic assisted the school faculty at several conferences, and significantly evoked enthusiasm from several teachers who had previously found faculty meetings unchallenging. In fact, the wise and understanding way by which the psychiatrist helped the teachers understand something of the causes of a particular pupil's behavior suggested this procedure had undeveloped potentialities. This faculty continued to hold case conferences on its problem pupils for nearly an entire year.

Partly as a result of the emphasis placed on such conferences and on other guidance procedures, Lewis County was selected by the State Heart Assembly to do a pilot program on guidance for children with cardiac trouble. The program culminates in a case conference on each child. This involves the cooperation of the family physician who provides a detailed prescription regarding all the school activities of the pupil. The forms and procedures developed have already been adopted by a large city in the state. The value of this procedure which coordinates all the school resources for the best development of a handicapped pupil cannot be overestimated, affecting as this does not only the pupil in relation to his current program, but looking ahead to vocational planning and his future activities.[8]

Another procedure related to the case conference, which has some of the features developed by the Institute for Child Study, University of Maryland,[9] has been followed by Lewis County teachers. Here the teachers learn how to observe one pupil accurately and to keep a diary of his behavior. Teachers take turns reading their diaries aloud; these are then discussed by members of the group in relation to their scope and accuracy. In one school where teachers in the primary grades had been doing this, the high school teachers followed suit assisted by the experienced elementary teachers. After accumulating considerable material about a pupil the teachers then suggest a number of

[8] For information on the case conference see Glyn Morris, *The High School Principal and Staff Study Youth* (New York: Bureau of Publications, Teachers College, Columbia University, 1958).

[9] Daniel A. Prescott, *The Child in the Educative Process* (New York: McGraw-Hill Book Company, Inc., 1957).

hypotheses to account for some characteristic behavior. The data in the diary are then classified, item by item, as either supporting, contradicting, or not being applicable to any one or more of the hypotheses. Inevitably teachers discover that their explanation of pupil behavior is inadequate and are led to realize that full understanding of a pupil requires much more care and objectivity than is usually displayed by them. Teachers unfailingly develop a healthy respect for the technic of accurate observation and reporting of pupil behavior.

Working with Talented Pupils

One of the most interesting developments in Lewis County is the work done to meet the needs of talented pupils in a rural area. The first formal attempt to do this was in the elementary department of one school. Here a committee met to explore the problem and work out a plan of attack. Some explanation of this approach must be given because it represents a strategic device applicable to similar situations in other areas of improving instruction. The principal selected a committee to work through many of the "angles" and details of the problem before repeating the same procedure with the entire faculty. In other words, he had a trial run with a small group who were then capable of serving as resource persons on the committee of the whole.[10]

The elementary school teachers mentioned above discussed the needs of talented pupils in a general way, pointing out what could be done within the current structure of the classroom. At the same time, the school is moving ahead to provide enrichment for groups of pupils; this may require administrative changes in schedule and better use of teachers as resources.

Meanwhile, this and other developments stimulated among the administrators a concern for talented pupils in the secondary school. In 1955 they launched a project called the Lewis County Youth Seminar.[11] In this, 25 to 30 high school pupils, grades 9 to 12, from six schools (two of which are forty miles apart) are

[10] Glyn Morris, "Helping the Mentally Superior Child in Rural Areas," *Journal of Exceptional Children*, Vol. 22 (January 1956), pp. 161–62.

[11] Glyn Morris, "A Stimulating Seminar for Rural Youth," *Journal of the National Association of Women Deans and Counselors*, Vol. 21 (October 1957), pp. 31–34.

brought together at a central point for an afternoon seminar once a week. A theme is selected and a problem formulated. Individuals and groups are permitted to work intensively on one segment of this problem, but much of the focus is on discussion resulting from special reading, field trips, observation of selected commercial TV programs, and listening to good music. For two years the seminar has focused on "Communication" in its broadest sense. One year the goal was to correlate communication with the development of civilization. In this experience, pupils are encouraged to develop vocabulary, see relationships, make generalizations, deal with concepts, and learn how to participate in group discussion.

The project was first discussed at a meeting of the administrators; a committee of teachers was then selected to explore possibilities. This resulted in a series of eleven meetings devoted to planning. The Talented Youth Project of the Horace Mann–Lincoln Institute of School Experimentation at Teachers College, Columbia University, has provided consultant and research help to the group since the beginning of the project. As the seminar got under way, the small group of teachers involved became increasingly interested in what they were doing with the result that their efforts went far beyond the call of duty. They volunteered for a planning session each Friday afternoon as they found themselves reading and planning in order to provide experience for the group, and they have continued in this to the present time.

Patterned somewhat after the Youth Seminar one school has made it possible for eleventh- and twelfth-grade pupils to meet with three teachers for an experimental course that would:

1. Provide an opportunity to learn the practical side of dealing with crucial social, economic, and political problems they were certain to face, such as voting in a village election, buying or building a home.
2. Give them a chance to meet with people engaged in such fields as law, insurance, personnel, manufacturing, and ask questions in an informal atmosphere.
3. Help them to develop ease and poise in social situations.
4. Develop the ability to plan methods for a group attack on mutual problems.

The course may be taken with or without credit, depending on the amount of work done, and involves taking field trips of limited distance which make possible using out-of-school personnel. The teachers are from the fields of homemaking, commerce, and social studies. Before getting the course under way there was considerable planning by the teachers and they continued to meet regularly once or twice a week through the year for charting new directions and for evaluation. When evaluated, the course proved to be highly worth while to the pupils.[12]

Changing Patterns of Commencement Programs

Two Lewis County schools have responded to suggestions that commencement ceremonies might be more meaningful to all concerned and have been experimenting with more functional programs. After four programs, the board, faculty, and pupils of one school have accepted a more creative approach; they will probably never return to the traditional-type commencement program.

Generally speaking, they proceed as follows: sometime during the school year the senior class is asked these questions: "How can we convey to our parents and others what our school experience means to us? Is there a theme around which we can develop a program?" After some searching, a theme or idea usually emerges. Then comes the experience of developing its implications and exploring all possible ways of effective presentation. For instance, the theme "Our Heritage: Freedom Under Law" was developed, using a combination of narration, choral speaking, historic scenes presented as live pictures, interpretive dancing and, finally, the passing on from the senior class to the junior class of a mantle (an academic gown) as symbolic of the heritage.

No small part of the value of this experience is in the discussion and research and writing done by the group as they develop the theme. In some respects, and unfortunately so, this is the only opportunity they have for utilizing art, music, drama, history, and literature in a unified way. Other themes have been: "Not by Bread Alone"; "Always Climbing Higher"; "Let There Be Light."

[12] William Kellerhals and others, "Report on a Special Course Initiated at the Constableville Central School in 1957–1958." On file at the office of the District Superintendent, Lewis County Schools, Lyons Falls, N. Y.

OTHER DEVELOPMENTS

The reader must judge to what extent the Lewis County program contains worth-while features similar to those in comparable situations elsewhere. The leadership of the superintendent, however, by supervision and adequate communication through the pattern of group meetings, should result in a maximum of growth in many areas. In other words, there is a belief that an alert leadership will stimulate creative effort and will continually utilize and develop a wide range of human and other resources. Such leadership is involved in developing community programs related to the well-being of youth and adults. Below are brief descriptions of some salient developments and procedures.

Making Use of Films

Throughout the years of the program described, films were used extensively to acquaint teachers with aspects of the emotional life of pupils and teachers. The films included "Preface to a Life"; "Angry Boy"; "Learning to Understand Children"; "Shyness"; "Feelings of Hostility"; "Feelings of Rejection"; "Overdependency"; "Feelings of Depression"; "Individual Differences"; "Meaning of Adolescence"; "Near Home"; "Unconscious Motivation." [13]

Films such as these have the advantage of leading teachers into consideration of important aspects of human development and then relating these to individual students. Teachers have frequently volunteered the information that they found the film helpful for these purposes. Films make excellent sources for stimulating discussion during interims when the in-service program slows down, as well as between more clearly focused aspects of the program.

Orientation of the Faculty

Early in the fall the faculty of one school takes an afternoon ride over the major school bus routes which cover the district. Teachers are provided with maps showing the location of pupils' homes. The trip, covering seventy miles, enables them to have

[13] A nearby film library can supply details about these films and the means for securing them locally.

firsthand knowledge of pupil environment, and is particularly useful in sensitizing new teachers to the extreme rurality and environmental limitations of some of their pupils.

Working with Parent Groups

In two communities long-range programs of parent education have proved beneficial. In one, showing a series of ten films on behavior and child growth followed by discussion did much to increase parent understanding of the complexity of a modern school program which has been developed with the idea of taking account of all kinds of pupils. In another very small rural community a series of ten meetings for discussion of the school program in relation to the needs of boys and girls resulted in a notable change of parent attitude toward the school. Initially critical, parents of this school visited other schools under guidance, organized a community library, provided some new forms of recreation and, most significant of all, took a critical look at themselves as a community group. Several important services, including a fire department and more adequate garbage disposal, were initiated. The parents were amazed to discover human resources in their own community eager to be tapped when direction and purpose became crystallized under school leadership.

Pupil Inventory of Community Resources

In connection with the Citizenship Education Project of Teachers College, Columbia University, Lewis County pupils made an inventory of resources in the area with a view to promoting industrial development in the county. A complete report was published and presented to industrial leaders. Not only was this practical from the standpoint of itemizing human and other resources, but it sensitized businessmen to some of the functional aspects of educating pupils for participation in citizenship.

Making Use of Television

Beginning with a conference of all teachers in the fall of 1957, the use of television for reinforcing and supplementing the classroom program has slowly developed in Lewis County. During the last part of the year, several programs on the teaching of science were presented over the local television station. A committee of teachers continues to work on plans for further use of the local commercial station in ways that will be of maximum help to the classroom teacher, keeping always in mind the limitations and strengths of such a resource. A person has been employed full time to direct this television program.

CONCLUSION

Curriculum development proceeds in Lewis County on many different levels without too highly structured an administrative organization. Guidance and curriculum are inextricably bound together. A sound curriculum is not something in isolation. Even after the most careful planning, its effectiveness depends on some "fitting and alteration." The kind of alteration necessary is determined by guidance—a continuous process. By the same token, a systematic and detailed guidance program can be effective only as curriculum resources and flexibility are possible in view of individual needs. In Lewis County there is increasing recognition of the value of a guidance program; the implications for the curriculum are emerging, but not with the clarity and force with which, it is hoped, they will eventually appear.

8

DENVER, COLORADO

CURRICULUM DEVELOPMENT IN

THE PUBLIC SCHOOLS *

THE present pattern of curriculum development in the Denver, Colorado, public schools is generally dated from the school year 1922–1923, when Superintendent Jesse H. Newlon appointed committees in subject fields at the elementary, junior high, and senior high school levels. During the next ten years these committees produced a series of "Course of Study Monographs" which attracted considerable attention from educators throughout the United States.

Gradually the work of committees came to include consideration of materials, methods, evaluation, policy recommendations, sequence of learning, and guidance as aspects of the curriculum. Committees other than curriculum committees were organized. Membership, at first made up of teachers only, now includes supervisory personnel, school principals, such specialists as psychologists, experts from outside the school system, and lay persons.

In short, curriculum development in the Denver school system has taken form through an evolutionary process which has been

* This chapter was written by LLOID B. JONES, Director of Department of General Curriculum Services, Denver Public Schools.

traced in an earlier book.[1] A number of important changes have occurred since 1950, when that book appeared, and it seems certain that changes will continue.

The essence of Denver's curriculum development procedure is free-thinking, outspoken participation by large numbers of people, particularly classroom teachers, in shaping the school program. Neither an account of evolution nor a chart of committee structure and relationships brings out clearly this essential ingredient. This attitude or habit, this quality—somewhat intangible but nevertheless real—is the actual moving force which gives the Denver way of working at curriculum development its distinguishing characteristics.

THE SCHOOL SETTING

Perhaps a brief look at Denver itself may help to give this broad notion more substance. Denver is a city of about half a million people, situated on the high plains just east of the Rocky Mountains. A hundred years ago there was no habitation, no settlement, on this site. Fifty years ago Denver was a sprawling big town, a frontier metropolis. In the past twenty years Denver has become a large city. In other words, the city and the school system have grown and continue to grow at a tremendous rate; change has piled upon change; much of the city is new and many of the people are newcomers.

It is by far the largest city within a radius of 600 miles. About a third of the people of Colorado live within sight of the state capitol dome, a fact which affects the thinking of Denverites, and the attitudes of other people in the state and the region toward them. It is a spread-out city, covering a very large territory for its population. The typical residence is a one-family house, reflecting perhaps a certain "don't-fence-me-in" attitude that to some extent carries over into the schools. The population is largely Anglo-American, although there are sizable segments of Spanish-background, Jewish, Negro, and other ethnic groups; mostly middle-income, with some poverty, and considerable wealth.

As compared to many cities, Denver is not yet heavily industrialized, though industry is now expanding rapidly. Transporta-

[1] Hollis L. Caswell and Associates, *Curriculum Improvement in Public School Systems* (New York: Bureau of Publications, Teachers College, Columbia University, 1950), pp. 151–69.

tion, distribution, trade, and government agencies figure heavily in its economy. Trade includes service to tourists, since the climate and scenery attract people on vacation.

Politically, the city and county of Denver are identical, and the city government is largely independent of the state. The Board of Education is also almost entirely autonomous. The seven members of the Board are elected from the city at large, in elections separate from state and national elections, and reference to political affiliation is specifically barred. Alternate elections of school board members are combined with city government elections.

The School System

The school system comprises 87 elementary schools, 15 junior high schools, 5 senior high schools, the Boettcher School for Crippled Children, and the Emily Griffith Opportunity School for adult and vocational education. Several new schools are under construction and more are in the planning stage. About 85,000 pupils are enrolled in kindergarten through grade twelve. The school population has increased by several thousand pupils each year during the past decade.

Two important facts should be noted here. Because of the nature of the city conditions of employment are probably more favorable in this school system than in any other for hundreds of miles around. As a result, Denver teachers tend to have a high level of professional competence. Furthermore, after three years of satisfactory service a teacher is placed on permanent tenure, subject to dismissal only in the event of proved charges of immorality or incompetence. Their sense of security encourages teachers to speak their minds freely on matters of school policy and practice. These facts explain at least in part why Denver teachers do in reality exercise a large measure of influence over curriculum practices and curriculum development in the Denver public schools.

In a larger city or a smaller one, or in an older city, or one that lacked the frontier tradition of informality—in a different city the program of curriculum development would probably be different. The Denver plan is presented not as a model, but rather as the plan that suits Denver.

ADMINISTRATIVE ORGANIZATION

The Board of Education of the Denver public schools has, with a few minor constitutional limitations, complete authority and responsibility for operation of the schools. This means the Board prescribes the subjects to be taught; the course of study in each; the textbooks; and the organizational plan of the schools. It provides equipment and materials for instruction; regulates practices in teaching, guidance, and discipline; and selects the teachers. All this the law prescribes.

In its actual operation, the Board of Education acts chiefly on matters of broad policy. Carrying out these policies is left to the Superintendent appointed by the Board. For more than a decade, the Superintendent has been Dr. Kenneth E. Oberholtzer. This has meant that a continuity in ways of working at the process of curriculum development has been maintained.

The Board of Education does take an active interest in instruction. At each of its regular monthly meetings some phase of the instruction program is reviewed by teachers, supervisors, students, or parents—someone who knows the particular program well. The Board members discuss the program and, if appopriate, give official approval by formal action.

Central Office Personnel

The central offices of the school system were reorganized in 1951 into three divisions: instructional services; business services; and personnel services. Heading each division is an assistant superintendent. The Assistant Superintendent for Instructional Services is also the Deputy Superintendent. These divisions operate in their respective spheres at all levels from preschool through adult education. That is, the Division of Instructional Services is responsible for the teaching and learning of pupils at whatever age. This differs from the organization of many large school systems, where there are assistant superintendents for elementary schools, for junior high schools, and so on.

Continuing the line of delegation of authority, the Assistant Superintendent for Instructional Services has three Administrative Directors of Instruction working with him, one each for elementary schools; for secondary (junior and senior high) schools; and for adult, vocational, and special education.

Under this triumvirate of administrative directors are fourteen departments, each with a director and such other supervisory personnel as may be necessary to meet its responsibilities, namely, art education; general curriculum services; health and physical education; health (medical, etc.) services; home economics; industrial arts; library services; military science and tactics; music education; radio and television activities; social work and psychological services; special education and pupil personnel; special services (audio-visual education); and vocational and adult education. Personnel in these departments work from the central offices.

School Building Personnel

Other administrative and supervisory personnel function in the school buildings. These include building principals and coordinators of instruction.

Building principals. Each school principal is responsible for the total operation of his school with regard to instruction, business, and personnel. Officially, and in fact, the principal of a school is recognized as the instructional leader of that school. This statement has considerable significance.

It means that principals are the persons chiefly responsible for seeing that all Denver public schools provide pupils the basic, or foundation, program of instruction. This basic program is built around six fields of study which are taught in all grades: English or language arts; mathematics; the social studies; the sciences; health; and guidance and counseling. The scope and sequence of these areas are indicated in kindergarten through twelfth-grade program guides. The intent is that all pupils, in whatever part of town they live and whatever school they attend, shall have full opportunity for a complete and adequate school program. Central office personnel and school principals, working together, devote a great deal of their time to assuring this equal opportunity.

The curriculum, or program of instruction, in the Denver public schools is flexible from school to school and even from classroom to classroom. That is, beyond the basic program, instruction is adapted according to such factors as the pupils, the parents and community, the facilities of the building, and the size of the school. Obviously such factors are not uniform in a school system as large and as rapidly changing as Denver's.

The principal's considerable authority and responsibility mean that curriculum changes are made a part of classroom practice at different times, in different degree, and in different manner from school to school and sometimes from classroom to classroom.

It should be made clear that the absence of rigid uniformity is not due to reluctance of the central administration to exercise authority. Rather, the acceptance of variability among the programs of individual schools is a matter of basic philosophy. Members of the central office staff believe strongly that an instructional program or practice or change is in fact put into operation only to the extent that the principal and the teachers in the school see a need for it, understand it, recognize its value, and undertake energetically and intelligently to use it. The inference is that this is true anywhere, however much a school system may appear to be subject to strong central direction or however dutifully orders may be carried out.

The foregoing is an attempt to state a principle of curriculum development, one that is considered to be fundamental to the curriculum development program in the Denver public schools. The principle in operation gives each building unit a central place in program development.

Coordinators of instruction. The coordinator of instruction is, in effect, a local school supervisor. Each junior high and each senior high school has one coordinator assigned to work with the faculty in that building. Among the more than eighty elementary schools there are some thirty coordinators who go from school to school, regularly helping teachers in their first and second year to improve their work and serving occasionally as resource consultants to experienced teachers. A coordinator is an acknowledged leader, an expert in instruction placed at the scene of operations.

CURRICULUM MAKING

For purposes of this account, it may be useful to think of the curriculum improvement process as having two phases: curriculum making; and improvement of instruction. Each phase can be looked at, first, in terms of the machinery and second, its operation.

The Machinery

Instruction committees. A cluster of organizations known as the Instruction Committees is maintained to study continuously the program of instruction in all its aspects; to define problems and propose ways and means of studying and solving them; and to serve as a channel of communication among school faculties.

There are eight Elementary Instruction Committees, each comprising a group of schools in a neighborhood or area of the city. Each school is represented by the principal and one teacher elected by the faculty. Each committee includes, also, an elected representative of the elementary school coordinator group. The North Area Elementary Instruction Committee, for example, is composed of one teacher and the principal from each of the fourteen elementary schools in north Denver plus one representative of the elementary school coordinators. Each of the eight elementary school Instruction Committees elects a chairman, a secretary, and a member at large. These twenty-four persons make up the Central Elementary Instruction Committee, which meets to draw together the. actions of the several area committees.

Similarly, there is a Junior High School Instruction Committee made up of the principal, the coordinator, and one teacher elected by the faculty of each of the fourteen junior high schools. The Senior High School Instruction Committee is set up on the same pattern, except that three classroom teachers are elected from each senior high school faculty. Each Instruction Committee meets four times a year, usually in October, December, February, and April. Each meeting lasts for half a school day, the classroom teacher members of the committees being relieved of their regular duties by substitute teachers. Central office personnel meet with all instruction committees, some regularly and others as occasion arises.

Following each series of meetings the Executive Board of the Instruction Committees meets. The Board consists of elected representatives from the Central Elementary, the Junior High, and the Senior High Committees. All committees working on instructional matters are responsible finally to this Executive

Board which authorizes the committees' appointments, defines their responsibilities, and recommends dismissals when committees have completed their tasks. Obviously, the Executive Board carries great weight in the whole organization for curriculum improvement.

Curriculum committees. The kind of committee with the longest history and, in some respects, representing the purest "democracy" is the curriculum committee. The members of curriculum committees are classroom teachers, elected by their department in the junior or senior high school faculty. (There are no comparable groups for the elementary schools.) Usually the chairman of a department is elected as curriculum committee member. Each curriculum committee also has one staff member, who is a supervisor from the appropriate department at the central offices. Curriculum committees report to the Instruction Committees and their Executive Board. Curriculum committees have responsibilities primarily related to the improvement of programs of instruction in the classrooms. These responsibilities are described on page 203.

Program committees. Certain committees are set up primarily for the task of curriculum building. In fields of study that are part of the curriculum in all grades, there are K–12 (kindergarten through grade 12) committees. Among others, there are a K–12 English Program Committee; a K–12 Mathematics Program Committee; a K–12 Evaluation Committee; a K–12 Guidance Committee; and a K–12 Study Committee for the Gifted. In a subject such as home economics, taught only in junior and senior high, the committee is not K–12 in structure.

The program committee is different from the curriculum committee in that each of its members is appointed by the staff of the appropriate department at the central offices on the basis of the individual's interest in the field, his experience, competence, and previous activity (such as special study or experimental work related to the field). Membership is also arranged to provide broad representation of all points of view. The typical K–12 committee will be made up of a primary-level classroom teacher from each of the five main geographic areas of the city; five intermediate-grade teachers similarly distributed; five junior high school teachers; five senior high school teachers; an elementary principal and a principal or other administrator from the junior and the senior high schools; a coordinator from each of the three levels; and members from the staff of the central offices whose specialties are in this subject. As new high schools are opened, the geographic areas will be reorganized along the same principles.

Since 1952, each K–12 committee has had one or more members who are lay citizens appointed by the Denver County Council of Parent-Teacher Associations. The program committee is thus designed in order to include the widest possible representation of the many points of view that should be taken into account during curriculum making.

An interesting type of organization set up for the same purposes is found in the Lay Advisory Committees used by the Emily Griffith Opportunity School—Denver's school for adult and vocational education. The Lay Advisory Committee is composed of citizens directly concerned. For example, if a course in television repair is to be offered, a committee is organized consisting of an equal number of television repairmen and owners of television service shops plus a coordinator from the school. This committee outlines the content of the course, the skills to be taught, the projects to be undertaken by the students, the materials and equipment to be used, and the related information from such fields as electricity and electronics to be presented. The committee recommends the amount of time to be devoted to the course and to each topic or section within the course; devises, in its essential elements, the examination to be given; and states the standards of competence the students should attain. The committee also assists in finding and recommending qualified instructors.

Special committees.   The Executive Board of the Instruction Committees from time to time has occasion to recommend appointment of a committee to work on some aspect of curriculum that is not within the province of either a curriculum committee or a program committee. The names of a few special committees will indicate the varied nature of the work they undertake. In the past few years there have been, among others, a Committee on Time Allotment in the Elementary School; a Committee on Nomenclature of Courses in the Senior High School; and a K–12 Pupil Personnel Records Committee.

The Denver Summer Workshop.   Another means of curriculum building is a workshop operated jointly by the Denver public schools and the University of Denver. Here, for a period of five weeks during the summer, members of the Denver teaching staff (including principals, coordinators, and others, as well as classroom teachers) may go to study curriculum problems which they have not had opportunity to work out fully during the school year. A staff of consultants is provided to advise with members of the workshop. Those who seek credit to assist them toward a salary increment pay tuition; those who do not receive college credit are assisted by the Board of Education to meet the cost of attendance.

National projects. The Denver public schools have for a long time participated in national studies on curriculum projects. Among such projects may be listed the Eight-Year Study of School and College Relationships; the Stanford Social Studies Investigation; the Study on Teacher Education of the American Council on Education; the Chicago Inter-Group Study; several projects of the Horace Mann–Lincoln Institute of School Experimentation at Teachers College, Columbia University; and, most recently, the Advanced Placement Program of the College Entrance Examination Board.

Because of Denver's geographic location at a great distance from other cities of comparable size, the opportunity for exchange of ideas with other people working on similar tasks is particularly valued.

Curriculum writers. Still another useful procedure in curriculum building is the hiring of persons from the regular instructional staff, teachers or others, to prepare curriculum guides and reports. Working during the summers, they receive extra pay on an hourly basis for the time they work, within certain established limitations.

Curriculum writers have proved particularly useful in carrying forward work started by committees during the regular school year. They assemble, organize, and prepare for committee use data that have been gathered through testing, surveys, and other such means. Most frequently, perhaps, writers are used to prepare guides for which the basic outline has been established by a program committee. Writers have also been assigned to study and to abstract for reporting the professional literature on various subjects and the published programs of other school systems. Finally, writers often prepare instructional materials for the use of pupils —such as workbooks, tests, and reference materials when these are not available from commercial publishers.

Besides active personnel hired for curriculum writing during the summer, retired personnel may be similarly engaged either in the summer or during the school year. The work of the curriculum writers is of course subject to review by the committee concerned.

Such is the basic structure of the professional staff that is provided for curriculum building. It is now in order to give some picture of how this machinery operates.

The Operation

There are at least three sources from which a proposal to undertake a curriculum-building project in the Denver public schools might come: the grass roots or general interest among the professional staff or the community at large; instructional leaders in status positions, such as members of the central office staff; and the continuous program of curriculum development whenever there comes a time when it is desirable to bring up to date the instructional program in a given area. An example of each point of origin will illustrate and clarify how such proposals originate.

Grass-roots example. Around 1949 there developed in Denver among both lay citizens and members of the professional staff an opinion that pupils in the schools were not learning mathematics as well as they should. The results on standardized tests showed there was some basis for the feeling. The problem was discussed in meetings of mathematics departments in the schools and in general faculty meetings; it was called to the attention of Instruction Committees. Soon the Executive Board of the Instruction Committees authorized the appointment of a K–12 Mathematics Program Committee. The committee was set up according to the general structure described previously and in 1951 produced a new (i.e., modernized) mathematics program.[2] This was pre-

[2] *The Mathematics Program of the Denver Public Schools.* 1951 ed. out of print. New edition available January 1960. (Denver, Colorado: The Mail Room, Denver Public Schools.) Inquiries about any publication of the Denver Public Schools hereinafter mentioned should be referred to The Mail Room, Denver Public Schools, 414 14th Street, Denver 2, Colorado.

sented to the Board of Education, given careful consideration, and adopted.

Administrative-level example. Some years ago the Assistant Superintendent for Instructional Services became concerned about the adequacy of instructional provisions for gifted pupils. Early in 1954 certain members of the Board of Education also expressed an interest in the problem. The Assistant Superintendent asked a supervisor to make a preliminary study of this subject. The supervisor prepared a report that was presented to the Board of Education. The Board concurred in the opinion that here was a curriculum project which merited full consideration by a K–12 committee. This opinion was communicated to the Executive Board of the Instruction Committees, which authorized appointment of a K–12 Study Committee for the Gifted. The question was then discussed widely in Instruction Committees and in the faculties of schools.

On-schedule example. The K–12 English Program,[3] published in 1953, was evaluated in 1957–1958 simply because it was five years old. However, the evaluation showed that the program was not out of date and the Guide need not be revised. Some of the related published materials were reorganized, and some new ways of operating the program were devised, but the basic publication will remain in use for another five to six years.

In short, it is intended that the process of curriculum development shall so operate in Denver that anyone with a sound idea for curriculum improvement will be heard and his proposal acted upon if it proves valid.

When a project is undertaken, the persons selected to work on it meet together, for the most part, during school hours. The classroom teachers in the group are relieved of their regular duties by substitute teachers provided through the Department of General Curriculum Services. Scheduling meetings and providing substitute teachers constitute two of the services of this department.

Occasionally a committee will hold a one-hour meeting after school to transact business that can be handled quickly; some-

---

[3] *Program in English, Kindergarten through Grade 12* (Denver, Colorado: Denver Public Schools, 1953).

times meetings are held in the evening or during a week end. In the main, however, the business of curriculum making is considered to be important school work that should be done during school hours.

IMPROVING INSTRUCTION

What has been said so far in reality describes the preparation of guides, handbooks, resource units, and the like. Curriculum workers will recognize an occupational hazard: having a seemingly excellent program on paper, with any resemblance to what goes on in classrooms being apparently, if not wholly, coincidental. The larger the Denver public schools become, the more difficult it seems to bring together policy and practice. Again, descriptions will be given in terms of machinery and of its operation.

The Machinery

Curriculum committees. Curriculum committees make their chief contribution in improvement of instruction rather than curriculum building.

Instruction committees. Instruction committees function in improvement of instruction to some extent, although policy formulation and recommendation are the purposes they are designed primarily to serve.

Area organizations of school principals. Because the Denver public schools are rapidly increasing in size with the result that communication and putting policy into operation are increasingly difficult, the school system is organized for certain purposes into five areas or geographical districts. Each area is composed of a senior high school and its associated junior high schools and elementary schools. All, or nearly all, the boys and girls in the elementary schools of the North Area, for example, will go to one of the junior high schools in that area and then on to North High School. (Three more senior high schools will be opened in the near future and the areas will then be revised.)

The principal of the senior high school is the area chairman, responsible for leadership when all the schools in that area work together on certain common undertakings. Thus far, four kinds of common enterprise have been identified; namely, putting instructional programs into operation; working with lay citizens in the community to promote better understanding of school programs and to improve school programs; gathering current information on population and school building needs; and studying annually, again with citizens of the community, the school's budget and the budget decisions that have to be made.

To accomplish these purposes, the area chairman calls together his fellow principals about once a month, excepting June and July, for discussion of common concerns. This group sponsors area meetings of other personnel. For example, the principals might request the evaluation chairmen from the several schools to meet, or such a meeting might be requested by the evaluation chairmen and approved by the area principals. Evaluation chairmen, incidentally, are special personnel responsible for testing and measurement in the school.

Working with each Area chairman as a liaison person or executive officer is an Area representative. The five area representatives are members of the staff of the central offices, their services being made available to the area half time (the other half is devoted to supervision in a subject area).

When the area organizations were established in 1951, the functioning body was an area articulation committee whose members were teachers, principals, and coordinators, after the fashion of Instruction Committees. Experience proved, however, that the school principals make a more practicable standing committee for the area.

Central office personnel. People in the central offices take an active and considerable part in the work of improving instruction as well as in curriculum design, development, and preparation.

The Operation

Curriculum committees. Since classroom textbooks to some extent determine, as well as limit, the teaching and learning in the class, they are selected with great care in the Denver public schools. Examining and recommending textbooks are the responsibilities of curriculum committees for junior and senior high schools. At the elementary school level these responsibilities have been delegated to certain other committees. Seldom is there a meeting of a curriculum committee (or other committee with similar responsibility) when some consideration is not given to a newly available textbook. In other words, the scrutiny of textbooks is a continuous process. Sample copies of the textbooks are taken to the schools and discussed with other members of the faculty who might use them.

Certain criteria have been developed and every book considered is examined in light of these criteria. At an appointed time, then, the committee prepares a recommendation for each textbook it believes should be made available for use. This recommendation, together with a copy of the book, is then forwarded to the appropriate Instruction Committee. All textbook recommendations originate with committees of teachers in the schools.

In some cities textbook selection is considered a part of curriculum making. In the Denver public schools, however, there is a strong tradition of first determining what the curriculum shall be and then seeking the instructional materials which are best adapted to the curriculum. When no commercially published materials are available, "home-grown" publications have been prepared. Conspicuous examples are arithmetic workbooks for the elementary grades [4] and English workbooks for grades seven through nine.[5] In recent years there has been some sentiment that an unnecessary amount of publication work has been done.

Besides recommendations on materials there is a second way in which curriculum committees help to improve classroom practice. As representative teachers meet together, they exchange information on promising methods that have been developed in their respective schools. Often these exchanges take the form of reports such as "Managing Group Work in Eighth-Grade Social Studies" and "The Values of a Science Club." There are also many informal discussions as, for example, "one of our teachers has found that a trip to the museum is a good way to start this unit"; "instead of sending in those old books to be discarded, we have

[4] *Arithmetic Exercises and Problems,* 8 books (Denver, Colorado: Denver Public Schools, 1955).

[5] *Language Skills for Americans,* 3 books (Denver, Colorado: Denver Public Schools, 1951).

taken them apart and used some of the pages for individual homework assignments." Members of the committee carry these ideas back to their own schools, tell other teachers about them, discuss their values and possible use, and often devise even better means of reaching a similar end. The result, again, is better teaching and learning.

In brief, curriculum committees operate as a force in unifying instructional practice among the schools of Denver and in promoting that unity at the level of the best discovered about teaching and learning.

Instruction committees. Instruction Committees review all proposals for adoption and deletion of textbooks, considering the recommendations of individual committees in the total perspective of such suggestions. This serves to keep the textbook lists balanced as to quantity and to prevent hasty adoptions. The decisions of the Instruction Committees are sent on to the Assistant Superintendent for Instructional Services who reports them to the Superintendent. The Superintendent, in turn, presents the books to the Board of Education. After a month of study and review, the Board proceeds to formal adoption, as required by law.

Another way in which Instruction Committees promote improvement of instruction is through communication. A policy or decision designed to improve instruction cannot be carried out until teachers know and understand that policy or decision. Since every school is represented in Instruction Committees by its principal, one or more teachers, and in the case of the secondary schools by the coordinator of instruction, the faculty is informed by these representatives of actions taken by the Instruction Committees and the thinking behind such actions is explained. A considerable part of the meetings of whole faculties or faculty groups is devoted to consideration of such matters.

As a further aid to communication, the Division of Instructional Services at the central offices publishes *The Instructional Meetings Reporter*. This mimeographed publication is produced after each series of meetings of Instruction Committees and carries the official record of proceedings. It is distributed to all members of the professional staff in every school and in the central offices, usually at the same time members of the Instruction Committees make their reports.

Besides the *Reporter,* a newspaper called *Instruction News* is brought out four times a year. *Instruction News* reports promising practices that have been developed in the Denver public schools. These issues have likewise proved very useful aids to teachers in finding better ways to do their work.

The area organizations. The original purposes of the area organizations were twofold: to promote continuity of teaching and learning through use of the K–12 programs; and to develop *esprit de corps* and a spirit of cooperation within a workable-size segment of the professional staff.

When the K–12 Mathematics Program was produced, for example, each area representative from the central offices was briefed on its purpose, content, and application. The area representative, in turn, presented it to the principals of schools in his area. Then the principals, the area representative, or mathematics specialists from either the K–12 Mathematics Committee or the central office presented the guide to teachers of the area schools. Follow-up discussions for further clarification, suggested solutions to problems, and reports of results were made.

This way of working provides a flexible but well-coordinated method of achieving improvement in instruction. Thoroughly experienced teachers can make use of a new program much more quickly and easily than new teachers. Where particular difficulties are met, as in a school with considerable numbers of less able pupils, consultant service is brought in by the area representative. Junior high schools learn what is going on in elementary schools and in senior high schools, and so on. Adjustments in program are proposed, considered, and decided on by common agreement.

The area organization is especially important to a large school system because each group of schools is of a size such that it is possible to work effectively at the operational level. A total of nearly 3,500 teachers cannot work together as one group on an instructional problem in a way that brings much actual benefit to their pupils. The area groups are small enough so that members of the faculties in each group of schools can be fairly well acquainted, can become accustomed to working with each other, and can reach agreements and carry out decisions with dispatch. Each area has certain common concerns that are individual to it and certain problems characteristic of the community it serves.

This organization by area also serves as a channel for directing classroom supervision to the points where it is most needed. Classroom supervision is most useful when directed toward an instructional problem the teacher already recognizes; when the supervisor is familiar with conditions under which the teacher and class work; and when there is opportunity for thorough study and consideration. Therefore, the staff specialist in science does not make a visit to every science classroom in the city, a visit that would necessarily be brief and of small value. Rather, the area representative calls on the science specialist to visit those schools and classrooms in his area where help in science is particularly needed or wanted.

In making his request, the area representative will also present the nature of the problem, the strengths and limitations of the school or the teachers, and the kinds of help he believes they most need. These are known to the area representative because of his frequent visits and consultations with the principal and faculty of each school.

All efforts to improve curriculum practices in each one of the schools are drawn together in a report on instruction prepared by the principal and faculty therein. These reports, made annually to the Superintendent of Schools, describe the chief activities of the faculty in improving instruction during the year, summarize the results that have been achieved, and indicate what the faculty believes are the important next steps to be taken during the coming year.

Central office personnel.   The central office staff helps with the improvement of instruction in many ways that are probably common to most school systems. One rather unusual procedure is the annual instruction conference in each school. A team consisting of the Assistant Superintendent for Instructional Services (Deputy Superintendent), the Administrative Director of Instruction for either elementary schools or for secondary schools, and the area representative visits each building once a year for a conference on its instruction program. The principal and instructional leaders from the faculty (the coordinator of instruction, chairmen of faculty groups, etc.) take part. In some schools, community leaders and parent representatives are also invited.

Each of these conferences lasts at least two hours and may extend over a day and a half in the larger senior high schools. The school's entire instructional program is reviewed: current activities, special projects, results of evaluations, plans for improvement, and problems, difficulties, or impediments to progress. The Deputy Superintendent and the Administrative Director offer comments, suggestions, and recommendations. The area representative notes particularly any needs for help, and later, with the principal, works out the specific arrangements for securing such help.

These conferences are considered a major factor in improvement of teaching and learning in the schools. Here the school staff has an opportunity to talk over its own progress and problems with top-echelon personnel, to receive recognition, and to seek advice and assistance. At the same time, the central office people have an opportunity to explain and stress the importance of citywide programs, problems, and concerns.

THE RATIONALE FOR CURRICULUM DEVELOPMENT

In 1955 the Superintendent of Schools appointed a group to describe what happens as people in Denver work on curriculum development. The report [6] of this group sets forth six steps that are taken by the instructional staff in the process of curriculum development. These steps are as follows:

1. *Purposing:* defining the objectives of the program or the outcomes expected or the benefits that the pupils should receive.
2. *Surveying:* gathering evidence as to how well the objectives are being attained currently and then analyzing the results for indications of strong points and weaknesses in instruction.
3. *Planning:* devising measures that, if taken, should help to maintain strengths and overcome weaknesses.
4. *Organizing:* gathering the resources of people, time, facilities, materials, and the like needed to put the plans into operation.
5. *Operating:* using the plans in day-to-day work.
6. *Evaluating:* measuring the results of instruction to find how well strengths have been maintained and weaknesses overcome.

[6] *The Denver Program of Instruction: Its Development, Application, and Improvement* (Denver, Colorado: Denver Public Schools, 1957).

These six steps tend to occur when curriculum development takes place. Sometimes curriculum workers are conscious of the steps, and at other times the steps are taken without such realization. The point of view is held in Denver that if these necessary steps are undertaken consciously, each phase of the operation is likely to be carried out more carefully, thoroughly, and effectively.

The Denver public schools make intensive efforts to reach common understanding of purposes not only among the professional staff but also with the citizens of the community. When in 1953 the present social studies curriculum [7] was being developed, a statement of the fundamental point of view was taken to every school in the city and discussed with groups of parents and other lay citizens invited for the occasion. An estimated total of 20,000 citizens took part in these discussions. In 1957–1958, as the program of guidance and counseling in the schools was receiving major attention, again a statement of basic premises and desired goals [8] was submitted to citizens throughout the city for their comments, questions, and suggestions. This is a means to effective public relations, to be sure, but—more important—the result is a better program and one more readily put into classroom operation.

Both of these statements, as finally worked out, were presented to the Board of Education, where they were given thorough consideration. They were then approved as official documents of the school system.

There are two points at which Denver school people believe lay citizens can and should take active part in curriculum development. The first point might be described as lay citizens joining with school people to state their aspirations for children and youth—what they hope will be accomplished through education. The second point at which lay citizens should help is in evaluation—giving their judgment as to how fully their aspirations are being realized. Denver's procedure in this matter is described below (see p. 215).

---

[7] *The Social Studies Program of the Denver Public Schools,* 4 vols. (Denver, Colorado: Denver Public Schools, 1954).

[8] *Guidance Viewpoint of the Denver Public Schools* (Denver, Colorado: Denver Public Schools, 1958).

WAYS AND MEANS

Two continuing problems confront a large school system in its curriculum improvement efforts: where to utilize its considerable resources to greatest advantage and how to unify the activities of its numerous workers so that real progress is achieved throughout the whole school system. In the Denver public schools, choice of projects to improve instruction is based on evidence of strengths and weaknesses in the program. Reliable evidence is not always easily come by.

Tests

One way to gather evidence is through testing, and the Denver public schools make extensive use of tests. Two schedules are in operation, one called the Minimum Testing Program and the other the Survey Testing Program.

The *Minimum Testing Program* is made up of standardized tests in the various subjects given each year to all pupils in specific grades. For example, all fifth graders will be tested in the sciences and social studies; all sixth graders will take a battery test on reading, arithmetic, and mechanics of English. The tests are so distributed among the various grades that each pupil is examined periodically in the major subjects as he progresses from kindergarten to high school graduation.

The results of the tests are analyzed to determine what aspects of the subject the pupils in a group—or class or school—are learning well and which aspects they are not achieving as well. To do this, item and error analyses are carried out.

In the item analyses, tabulation is simply made of those questions most (i.e., about two thirds) pupils answered correctly and those that most pupils answered incorrectly. The questions are then grouped according to the area of learning they represent and a decision is made as to whether most pupils *should* have been able to respond correctly.

In error analysis, the pupils' responses to the questions in a specific area of learning are examined to see what kinds of errors they made. Carefully done, this process shows what the difficulty is and suggests what should be done to correct it.

To illustrate, several years ago item analyses revealed that many sixth-grade pupils were not able to multiply correctly when the multiplier contained two or three figures. There was little doubt that sixth-grade pupils should be able to do this. Many schools reported the same types of difficulty, so an error analysis was made. The common cause of error was mismanagement of partial products. Curriculum change was indicated. The particular change devised was a ten-day plan of reteaching multiplication, primarily as an aspect of place value, with relatively little attention to the "times tables" since most pupils showed little evidence of difficulty with the multiplication facts. The procedures for the reteaching were worked out, tested in some sample classes, and then described in a bulletin.[9] All teachers of sixth-grade arithmetic undertook the quality control project. The following year sixth-grade pupils substantially exceeded the national norms of the test so far as multiplication was concerned.

Quality control projects in appropriate phases of arithmetic have been developed for each half grade from the fourth through the eighth. They serve three purposes: to get the semester's work under way well and quickly; to give the pupils a sense of substantial accomplishment; and to give the teacher evidence of how well the pupils understand the mathematical concepts basic to the coming semester's work.

Quite as important to curriculum development as the Minimum Testing Program is the *Survey Testing Program*. Since 1950, during April of every third year, all pupils in grades 3, 6, 9, and 12 have been tested thoroughly in all academic subjects. These particular grades were chosen because in each instance students are completing a phase of their school work. Pupils in third and sixth grades take an entire achievement test battery. Pupils in ninth and twelfth grades take an entire battery of tests of general educational development. In addition, pupils in grades 6, 9, and 12 do an inventory for mental health analysis. In order to assure completely objective findings, the pupils' papers are sent out of the city to test-scoring agencies to be marked. Cost prohibits so elaborate a program being used more frequently or in more grades.

[9] "Quality Control Projects," No. 92000–92005 (Denver, Colorado: Denver Public Schools).

The results of survey testing are used in providing specific, accurate, objective information to the public which supports the schools and to the professional staff which operates them. Measures are taken to prevent comparison of schools or of teachers and any consequent erroneous rating or fixing of blame.

Pertinent, however, to the problem of curriculum development is the use made of these test results in the same way as described above for the Minimum Testing Program. Item and error analyses can be made on a citywide scale, and considerable extra weight is given to survey-testing results because of the special care taken in administering and scoring the tests.

Surveys

Curriculum building requires the use of many kinds of evidence besides test results. For example, in the recent survey of the English program, the judgment of teachers, coordinators, and principals was sought through questionnaires, interviews, and conferences. A study of the programs of other cities throughout the nation, as represented by their curriculum guides, was made and recent professional literature on the teaching of English surveyed. Expert consultants, recognized authorities in the field of English instruction, have been asked to analyze and evaluate the program. All these data are types of evidence upon which to base judgments.

In certain fields additional tangible evidence can be gathered. In art, music, physical education, industrial arts, and home economics, the performance of pupils can be added to test evidence. Drawing a picture, playing an instrument, and baking a cake are concrete evidences of learning.

As many kinds and sources of evidence as possible are continuously being sought, as well as ways of using the evidence more knowledgeably in reaching decisions on where the curriculum needs improvement; what the nature of such improvements should be; and how these improvements can be accomplished.

Tables of Expected Achievement

Another means of improvement used in Denver are Tables of Expected Achievement. These tables propose a goal of learning for a pupil according to his age and his IQ. The goals are determined by formulas adapted from well-known research studies on the relation between IQ and achievement in the subject fields. Two sets of Expectancy Tables, as they are commonly called, are in use: one sets the goal as a grade placement on a standardized test; the other sets the goal as a grade-point average of report-card marks. For example, a pupil of 100 IQ, age 9.3, should achieve a grade placement of 4.0 on a standardized test, whereas a pupil of the same age with 120 IQ should reach 5.2. This is from the Grade Placement Tables. From the Grade-Point Average Tables, a tenth-grade pupil with 102 IQ should achieve a 2.0 (C) grade average while a pupil with 120 IQ should reach a 3.8 grade average (nearly all A's).

The value of these devices is that they furnish a pupil, a teacher, and a parent with a tangible goal. That it is also a reasonable goal is demonstrated by the fact that about as many pupils exceed their expectancy as fall below it. The youngster with 80 IQ who is working up to expectancy is to be commended, even though his classmate with 120 IQ may be reading or doing arithmetic at a level three or four grades in advance. Further, expectancy is a source of security to teachers: a teacher whose fourth-grade pupils have a median IQ of 90 may find that she is doing a good job even though her class is not doing "fourth-grade work"; another teacher may find that her pupils, with IQs ranging from 115 to 150, seem to be loafing, even though they are breezing through the fourth-grade curriculum.

Many people recognize hazards in the use of the expectancy concept. IQ and age or grade are not the only factors that control a pupil's ability to learn: such matters as emotional development, physical condition, and home background come immediately to mind. Another common question is, "What about the teacher whose pupils do not reach expectancy?" Again, it is recognized that a pupil has varying interest and aptitude in different subjects. It is quite common, for example, for an individual pupil to exceed expectancy in arithmetic and fall below it in geography.

None of these reservations is any more applicable to expectancy than to any other standard of achievement. The arbitrary use of national norms or the curriculum guide or—perhaps most common—the teacher's or principal's subjective opinion of what constitutes good work may be challenged on the same bases. Whatever standard a school system chooses (unless it chooses to abandon standards) must be used with good sense and good will. The fact is that since the Denver public schools began using the expectancy tables there has been a marked improvement in the general level of achievement.

Bulletins

Mention has been made of the problem of organizing and coordinating the program of curriculum development for the schools as a whole. In this undertaking the Denver public schools use a bulletin which has come to be known as *Points of Emphasis.*

Points of Emphasis is prepared after careful consideration of suggestions from the Instruction Committees, from curriculum, evaluation, and program committees, from individual teachers and study groups, and particularly from school faculties in their annual reports on instruction. Every teacher, coordinator, supervisor, director, and school principal shares in the work of these groups either directly or by representation. Thus in a very real sense, *Points of Emphasis* in any year represents the consensus of the thinking of all professional personnel, the common tasks which are generally regarded as of major importance.

Points of Emphasis, Number 4, asks schools to aim at "Challenging every pupil to achieve to the best of his ability by providing a strong regular program with suitable modifications for the less able, suitable enrichment and extensions for the more able and ambitious." This objective was then elaborated briefly with a description of the chief aspects of current concern in the regular program, ways of teaching the less able, and new methods and materials recommended for the able and ambitious (i.e., the gifted).

Points of Emphasis is stressed by the Superintendent of Schools in an address before the total school staff the first day of school each September. Then throughout the year it continues to serve as a basic guide in curriculum development work and a frame of reference by which the community and the Board of Education can appraise instructional progress.

The foregoing sections have contained some explanation of the process of curriculum development in the Denver public schools with respect not only to curriculum making but also to the actual improvement of teaching practice and pupil achievement. Following such an analysis there arises naturally the question, "How well does the process work?" Some light on that question is shed by the public opinion survey which has become an important part of the evaluation of curriculum and instruction in the Denver public schools.

THE SURVEY OF PUBLIC OPINION

Reference has been made to the triennial survey of pupil achievement—the Survey Testing Program. Every three years, at the same time as the testing program, a survey of public opinion about Denver's public schools is also made. This survey is an attempt to get an impartial scientific analysis of what the citizens of a very large community think about their schools. The method used is that of the public opinion poll which has come to be rather widely accepted in recent years as a reasonably accurate way of measuring people's attitudes.

The Board of Education contracts for the services of an independent company. This company's staff, working with the schools' central office staff, prepares a list of questions which are judged likely to be significant. The company selects a sampling of the residents of Denver, using its regular methods to assure balance and proper proportion of the people interviewed as to income, education, location of residence, and the like. The company's interviewers are then sent to talk with those selected for the sampling. The information obtained by the interviewers is transferred to punch cards, and statistical analyses of the findings are made by the company. These data are reported in detail to the Board of Education.

From the rather formidable mass of data thus obtained, a digest of the basic information is prepared and published under the title *Denver Looks at Its Schools*.[10] Thus the whole professional staff of the Denver public schools and any interested citizen in the community may be informed as to what the public

[10] *Denver Looks at Its Schools* (Denver, Colorado: Denver Public Schools, 1959).

thinks of the quality of its schools and what it wants from the schools. That information has proved to be not only interesting but valuable.

In the three surveys so far made, public opinion of the public schools in Denver has been found generally favorable. On the whole, the residents of Denver feel that they have good schools, with good teaching and learning going on in them. There are some matters which the public questions or criticizes, indicating a thoughtful appraisal rather than indifference or unthinking acceptance.

Even more important than the general approbation are the rather clear aspirations the people of Denver have for their public schools as those aspirations emerge from the total volume of data. As indicated in the report of 1956, the people expressed their convictions as follows:

1. The fundamental subjects are the essential foundation of an educational program.

2. Good character and well-rounded personality should be developed by education.

3. Broad backgrounds of learning should be encouraged through a wide range of subject offerings.

4. Continuous guidance and counseling of boys and girls are important.

5. Good behavior and habits of work should be stressed.

6. Personal attention and thoughtfulness should be given each pupil.

7. Less crowded schools are desirable.

The first six items define rather well the scope of a substantial curriculum program for this—perhaps for any—school system. It is to achieve these broad objectives that the total process of curriculum development in the Denver public schools is aimed.

9

NEWTON, MASSACHUSETTS

IMPROVING THE CURRICULUM *

THE SETTING

Any educational program, to be understood, must be viewed in relation to its setting. One reason for this is that the quality of education is determined to a considerable extent by the level of community expectation and support. In order to understand the Newton schools one must first know something of Newton as a community.

Newton as a City

If there is such a thing as unity of diversity, Newton may well serve as an instance of it. About 85,000 middle-class citizens live in eleven villages. Each has its own post office and shopping center and each has slight but real differences in social and ethnic patterns. As a city it is held together by a city government and its services, and by various civic and social organizations such as Kiwanis, Rotary, Chamber of Commerce, and Community Chest which cut across village lines.

---

* This chapter was written by J. Bernard Everett, Coordinator of Instruction, and by Wilson C. Colvin, Coordinator, Junior High School Education, Newton Public Schools.

In many respects Newton is a typical middle-class and upper-middle-class residential suburban community. Its population is divided about equally among adherents of the Protestant, Catholic, and Jewish faiths. Most of its adult working population are commuters, many of whom hold professional and managerial positions. In home ownership and in proportionate numbers of school children it leads the cities in Massachusetts. At least three-fourths of its children, year in and year out, have college ambitions which they successfully pursue.

A significant characteristic of the city over a period of many years has been its tradition of good government. All city elections are nonpartisan, and although some political maneuvering does go on behind the scenes, the caliber of political office seekers seems to be the primary consideration of the voters. This has been particularly true in the election of School Committee (i.e., school board) members.

It is also significant that in Newton the School Committee is financially independent of the Mayor and Board of Aldermen (city council). The Committee is empowered to develop the school budget and once the budget is established it cannot be cut by the mayor or any other branch of city government. Neither is it necessary to submit any increases in the budget to voters for their approval. Thus, the School Committee has a greater degree of independence than is true in many parts of the country.

Tradition of Good Schools

Just as Newton has always had good government, so also does it enjoy a long tradition of good schools. This reputation goes back at least to the superintendency of Francis Spaulding in the early 1900s. His annual reports are still considered "classics" in school administration.

Probably the most important causal factors have been the high caliber of the elected school committees and the resultant freedom from political pressure of any kind. The school committees have consistently drawn the line between lay and professional responsibilities. Selection of teachers, approval of textbooks, de-always resulted from the recommendation of the superintendent. velopment of courses of study, promotion within the ranks have there was unanimous agreement on the best course to follow. To what extent the foregoing conditions have been the result of good professional leadership or of capable nonpolitical lay leadership one cannot determine precisely. In most instances, it probably has been a combination of both.

Newton's public schools follow a K, 6–3–3 plan. The twenty-five elementary schools enrolled nearly 10,000 pupils in 1959–1960; the five junior high schools, about 4,000; and the senior high, including the technical high school, about 3,500. Enrollment has increased about 15 per cent in the past five years. A new senior high is now under construction. In 1958–1959, the total educational staff was approximately 860, an increase of 25 per cent during the past five years. Including replacements as well as expansion, the over-all change is such that nearly one-half of the total staff had fewer than four years of local experience when school opened in September 1959. With these rates of change, it can never be assumed that any task is done. Continuing and perhaps increasing attention must be given to the orientation and indoctrination of new teachers.

Salary Schedule

The School Committee has consistently provided a salary schedule which is adequate to attract good teachers and to maintain a good competitive position in the New England area. It is a "training and experience" schedule and requires recurrent study in each five-year period of service. It is not difficult for teachers to meet the training requirements because of the ease of access to collegiate and graduate schools in the area. Many of the teachers, in fact, come to Newton because of the opportunities nearby for graduate study. Moreover, area professional schools place 300 to 350 practice teachers in Newton schools annually. As a *quid pro quo*, the master teachers with whom the students work are given opportunity to obtain "Practice Teaching Vouchers" which entitle them to tuition-free courses at the institution from which the students come.

Newton Teachers Federation

The Newton Teachers Federation is an all-inclusive professional association affiliated with the National Education Association. It has a long record of interest in, and promotion of, professional improvement. From time to time its Professional Development Committee, as a result of teacher surveys, has suggested new directions and courses for the in-service education program. All courses not initiated by the Divisions of Instruction or Counseling are cleared with this committee as to specifications and standards. They are then accepted by the Division of Instruction which administers all courses wherever initiated.

Lay Organizations

Citizens' awareness of their stake in good public education is shown by the number of lay organizations concerned with the schools. Every school has its own Parent Teacher Association, each of which is represented on the board of the citywide Council of PTAs. In addition, a group known as "Operation Education" was formed a few years ago to serve as an unofficial liaison between the general public and the schools. "Operation Education" includes representatives of the local League of Women Voters, Federation of Women's Clubs, Community Council, School Committee, Teachers Federation, and PTA Council. The group is the nucleus of a larger Committee on Community Characteristics which supplies background data for other civic enterprises. From the schools' point of view, just as important as the number of lay groups and persons involved is the way they operate. Rather than maintain permanent inspectorial committees which might conflict with professional activities, these citizens' groups work through *ad hoc* committees selected to collaborate with professionals on specific projects. Decisions and recommendations are arrived at cooperatively.

Recently the PTA Council, with the cooperation of members of the professional staff, conducted an extensive survey of parent opinion regarding elementary education. A similar study is now going on at the junior high school level. In both instances the studies were instituted at the suggestion of professional staff members who assisted in the development of the questionnaires. A great deal of the actual work, however, was done by lay persons. Much worth-while information derived from the elementary survey has provided substance for PTA meetings in the schools. It also has pointed the way to a reconsideration of certain school policies.

Dramatic evidence of the interest of Newton's citizens in their schools came in March 1956, when 500 of them struggled through the midst of the worst storm in a decade to attend a "Little White House Conference" which had been four months in the planning. The Conference opened on this note: "Education being the blessing of all is likewise the responsibility of all and we know that in a democracy there is a correlation between good schools and a good community." The conference group endorsed and recommended exploration of potential usefulness of teacher aides; classroom television; the loan of industrial experts and scientists as school consultants; increased emphasis on science instruction (but not at the expense of the humanities); extension of the Advanced Placement Program to earlier grades; continuation of the administrative policy of individual school autonomy; and special provision for gifted children. These recommendations illustrate the breadth of citizens' interests in education.

INTERNAL ORGANIZATION

Professional Staff Organization

The present structure of staff organization has been in effect since 1946. At that time the school system was reorganized into four major divisions: Business Services; Personnel; Instruction; and Counseling Services. The Personnel Division is headed by the Assistant to the Superintendent, the other three divisions by Directors.

Because of a shortage of office space, the Division of Instruction and the Division of Counseling Services have been housed in one building; the offices of the Superintendent, Assistant to the Superintendent, and Director of Business Services in another. This has proved to be both an asset and a liability. It is an asset in that it has tended to dissociate in the minds of principals and teachers Instructional and Counseling Services from line organization and thereby to strengthen their roles as service agencies. It is a liability in so far as it hampers close central staff communication (a mile can be a long way sometimes) and tends to establish too arbitrary a line between administration and supervision.

Newton schools are organized administratively on a line and staff basis. The line of authority runs from School Committee to superintendent to principal to teacher. Each school is an autonomous unit, except in matters of finance and personnel. Division of Instruction personnel are staff. Their relationships to individual schools, principals, and teachers are consultative and service in nature.

Roles of Principals and the Director of Instruction

The role of the Director of Instruction and the relation of Division services to schools are described as follows in the *Principals' Handbook:*

> The Director of Instruction coordinates the services of the Division of Instruction, directs the study and selection of textbooks and materials of instruction, and guides citywide efforts to improve instruction. These include the development of teaching guides and courses of study and the establishment of programs of in-service education . . .
>
> However, responsibility for coordination of these services within each school rests with the principal. It is the principal's responsibility to initiate conferences and faculty meetings designed to promote a better understanding and teamwork among the various specialists who serve his building and between these specialists and the classroom teachers.
>
> If systematic and continuous improvement of Newton's instructional program is to be effected, it will be the result of the cooperative efforts of teachers, principals, and members of the central staff. It is true that, within his own building, the major responsibility for developing an effective instructional program rests with the principal. However, to implement this responsibility and to make the best possible use of the central staff services and resources, the principal should:
>
> 1. Recognize and make use of the superior technical background and experience of the various specialists on the central staff.
>
> 2. Be familiar with all materials which are available at the

Division of Instruction and encourage teachers to use them intelligently.

3. Support actively all citywide meetings, in-service courses, workshops, and committee work designed to coordinate and improve the systemwide instructional program.

General Supervision

The Director of Instruction is responsible for general supervision. To assist him, he has a Coordinator of Elementary Education and a staff of four full-time consulting teachers, a Coordinator of Junior High School Education, a staff of six part-time teacher consultants, and one full-time consultant in General Education. The major part of their services goes to newer teachers; responsibility for classroom supervision of more experienced teachers rests primarily with the respective school principals. Supervision in the high school is provided by the several department heads and housemasters.

Special supervision. Supervisors of Art, Music, and Physical Education; Coordinators of Audio-Visual Education and Library Services; and Consultants in reading, and in science and conservation provide supervision in special areas of instruction. In general they and their respective staffs of consultants and special teachers work on the basis of scheduled visits to the several elementary schools, but their services—as well as those of general supervisors—also include conferring with teachers and principals; assisting in faculty meetings and workshops; arranging for classroom intervisitation, demonstration teaching, and in-service courses; working with PTA study groups and speaking at PTA meetings; and providing materials and resources in their respective fields.

Instructional materials. Each of the special department supervisors and coordinators maintains an extensive loan collection of teaching materials. This includes a library of several hundred films and nearly 2,000 filmstrips, an extensive collection of art objects, a circulating library of over 1,000 professional books and 25 current educational magazines, and several hundred recordings. The audio-visual collection is being greatly expanded under grants from the National Defense Education Act. The loan collection in science and conservation will be described in more detail later in this discussion (see p. 234).

ORGANIZING FOR CURRICULUM IMPROVEMENT

Newton has no central curriculum council which is a clearinghouse and coordinating body for all curriculum problems. Hence, recommendations for curriculum changes originate from many sources—grade-level meetings, faculty meetings, principals' meetings, and central staff meetings. A number of generalized attitudes, however, run through the whole operation of coordination, supervision, and in-service education. These points of view reveal as much about the nature of the operation as do details of function and activities.

The curriculum worker, to be effective, must always keep in focus the different dimensions involved in his work: society, the teacher, the child.

Society. The curriculum worker must continuously re-examine the why and what of education as an institution in its social context. In our present context vast bodies of knowledge have been added to what is needful to know. New skills to practice and new problems to be attacked parallel the tide of things to know. This is a time for pruning and compressing traditional content, for introducing much that we have not taught before.

The teacher. The curriculum worker must realize that improving the curriculum means improving the quality, meaningfulness, and continuing effect of the learning experiences of children and youth. Since the classroom teacher is the chief change agent so far as pupils' learning experiences are concerned, curriculum change means change in the teacher's perceptions, purposes, and classroom tactics. These perceptions, purposes, and tactics are functions of the teacher's background of personality, knowledge, and skills. Curriculum change is, therefore, a problem of teacher growth and is subject to all that is known about individual differences, motivation, and learning through doing.

The child. The curriculum worker must never forget that the beginning and the end of the product, purpose, and process of education is the child. The child's needs and interests—how, when, and why he learns—are the indispensable determining conditions of all aspects of curriculum improvement.

Involvement and Participation

Participation of teachers in any new development, from its inception to its culmination and evaluation, is a goal of Newton's Division of Instruction. This does not relieve others of the responsibility for initiating projects whose need is more visible to them because they see a broader picture. It does mean that scanning the grass roots is a continuous process. Whether or not initiative stems from the grass roots, great care is taken to arouse interest and disseminate information through bulletins and communications. Even so, efforts sometimes founder on the rocks of poor communications.

Creating Leadership

Leadership is where you find it, not where you bestow it. A wise status leader is one who is quick to recognize a functional leader and is able and willing to work with him. Opportunities to display leadership capacity are many—in the activities of the Teachers Federation, the PTAs, the committee structures of schools. All textbook committee chairmen and subgroup chairmen of the materials selection committees are classroom teachers.

Time for Curriculum Work

If teachers are to carry heavy responsibilities in addition to their classes, time must be provided. Five expedients are used: (1) lightening the teaching load in terms of the pupil-teacher ratio for a year; (2) transferring the teacher temporarily to the Division of Instruction; (3) employing a full-time substitute temporarily; (4) paying the teachers to use vacation periods for school work; and (5) occasionally closing school early to permit teachers to take part in schoolwide workshops.

To encourage teachers to take active part in national and regional specialized professional associations, classroom teachers who hold office, committee membership, or have special responsibilities in connection with meetings are usually given released time to attend meetings and reimbursed for their expenses by the School Department.

Of major importance as a factor in curriculum improvement at the elementary school level has been the use of Tuesday and Thursday afternoons. A policy calling for the earlier opening of school and the dismissal of classes at noon on Tuesdays and Thursdays was instituted approximately fifty years ago at parents' request. Their purpose was to provide time for private lessons in art, music, and dancing as well as for medical and dental appointments. Now, although many of these functions have been absorbed by the school, the policy has been continued and is woven firmly into the fabric of community, family, and school life. The practice provides unusual opportunities for carrying on remedial, enrichment, and recreational programs for children. It has proved to be even more valuable as a time for instituting curriculum work and in-service education at the elementary school level without the time pressures usually accompanying such activities.

Research and Experimentation

Freedom to try out new ideas is the prerogative of individual teachers and schools. As a rule, when ventures new to Newton are undertaken they begin in a small way. Before personal-use typing in grades seven and eight was adopted as general practice, it was preceded by a survey of research, tried out in two schools on different plans, tested and evaluated by pupils and teachers. Foreign languages for elementary pupils is now the subject of similar, varied try-out studies in several schools, as are a variety of new approaches to mathematics and to the education of gifted children. During the summer of 1959 a team of teachers was employed to develop both teacher and pupil materials in mathematics to be tried out in selected schools during 1959–60.

In this connection, the parent-opinion studies of Operation Education and the PTA Council mentioned earlier have indicated directions in which the Newton community was ready to move and changes for which additional preparation or information was needed. Recently completed is a parent-teacher report on homework policy for elementary schools. An extensive study of how pupils use out-of-school time showed that time is available. The results of an interview-questionnaire prepared by parents for parents showed that more of them favor homework than oppose it but that there is great difference of opinion as to what constitutes useful homework. An agreement on policy has been reached on the basis of this information.

"Broken-Front" Approach

For many years Newton has been committed to a "broken-front" approach to curriculum improvement. Activities are generally moving forward at different rates on several different fronts. Such a program can never be as neatly organized and administered as one which puts a premium on uniformity. However, it appears to be the method most likely to use the creative potential of teachers and principals and to recognize individual differences among staff members and variation among the respective school communities.

The Teaching Personality

To some unmeasured degree the quality of teaching depends on the quality of the teaching personality—breadth of intellectual vision and interests; love of humanity; vigor of satisfying personal life; and insight into the interplay of emotional drives, age interests, and personal fulfillment needs of children. To suppose that in-service education or supervision can supply these traits would surely be overly optimistic but to suppose that it cannot help would be equally pessimistic. The Division of Instruction does sponsor a number of courses intended to meet personality and interest needs of teachers.

The Teachers Federation, jointly with other community agencies, has tried to give new teachers a feeling that they belong, by providing various services such as finding places to live; sponsoring a picnic for new teachers; publishing lists of recreational facilities and hobby groups; and taking new teachers on a trip through the city.

A few studies that have been made support the tentative conclusion that the most important influence on job happiness or unhappiness in Newton is the quality of human relations. Perhaps most effective in meeting problems of this order have been a series of building study groups on "Emotional Problems." They are generally led by a psychiatrist with experience in group work.

The key to what usually becomes the real agenda is found in the questions of one psychiatrist: "Shall we examine this further? What is there in *your* experience which makes it necessary for you to react so violently to this child?" Taking such a course is a strenuous experience, but follow-up evaluations have revealed that most teachers feel it is an enriching one.

COORDINATION OF INSTRUCTION

The problem of coordination is to strike a proper balance between autonomy and uniformity. The major responsibility for this rests with the Director of Instruction. The roving roles of his staff (described on p. 222) establish an orderly system of ground rules. One way in which the organization is made operationally effective is by a definite schedule of regular and frequent meetings of the Director and Coordinators of Elementary and Junior High School Education with elementary principals and secondary principals; of the Elementary and Junior High School Coordinators with head teachers of elementary schools and consultants for junior high departments respectively; and of the Director with all coordinators and supervisors.

Responsibility for making arrangements for citywide committees concerned with instruction and in-service education is delegated by the Director to various members of his staff. To avoid conflicts, an informal agreement has been reached that normally Monday afternoons will be reserved for Teachers Federation meetings; Tuesday for building-faculty meetings; Wednesday for in-service courses and workshops; and Thursday for citywide and service committees and for departments and grade-level meetings. Tuesday and Thursday meetings are facilitated by the fact that there are no afternoon sessions on these days in elementary schools. Junior high schools reserve the first period daily for faculty planning and coordination meetings.

Obviously, this structure places a heavy premium on "keeping in touch" and on operating in an atmosphere of consultation and cooperation. This appears to be the only way to avoid excessive unilateral action by principals and to make sure that the several parts of the broken-front attack on curriculum problems do not become entirely disengaged.

IN-SERVICE EDUCATION

Use of Consultants

Whenever persons with the necessary talent and experience are available from Newton's own professional staff, they are used as consultants. Otherwise the services of the faculty members of nearby colleges or schools of education are secured. Usually a planning committee of teachers or a representative of the Division talks with several such potential "outside" consultants, and final choice is a mutual decision based on a clear understanding of needs and the kind of service the consultant is prepared to offer.

Newton is fortunate in having an arrangement with Boston University for the use of "Practice Teaching Vouchers" in financing courses through the Harvard-Boston University Extension Division. Being transferable, their vouchers make it possible to meet the cost of consultants obtained through the Extension Division with a minimum burden on the school budget or the pocketbooks of teachers.

Recent In-service Courses

In a later section (see p. 230) there are more detailed accounts of a few major projects, but the next few paragraphs provide a sketch of the scope of the in-service offerings in the past few years.

On the college and graduate level, courses have been offered in recent years on the teaching of arithmetic and reading as well as subject-matter refresher courses in geography, in science, and in American literature. There have been workshops on group processes, classroom guidance activities, creative writing, current social problems, and elementary science. An interesting departure from standard practice has been an intercommunity summer workshop in which teachers from neighboring cities were invited to participate. Other activities include a workshop in administrative leadership problems. For leadership and consultant services, staff members from the Boston Museum of Science and Industry as well as the nearby colleges of liberal arts and graduate schools have been used.

Courses are frequently offered for "local credit." Division of Instruction Service Workshops in elementary school art, music, physical education, arithmetic, and science are technique-and-materials courses designed especially for the orientation of new teachers, under the leadership of local supervisors and consultants. During the past three years, mathematics teachers have worked through the materials prepared by the University of Illinois Mathematics Projects in local Newton courses and at UICSM centers for instruction. Quasi-professional courses for parents also fall in this category and have included two seminars for prospective substitutes and a course for prospective teacher aides in "Contract Correcting of English Papers."

MATERIALS OF INSTRUCTION

Curriculum Guides

The variety of materials produced ranges from pamphlets and bibliographies for pupil use to publications explaining aspects of the instructional program to parents. Most materials, however, are resources and instructional guides for teachers.

In arithmetic and written expression, the guides supply the basic scope and sequence necessary from grade to grade if pupils are to develop skills and mastery with continuity and without confusing gaps or changes in direction. To this extent, the guides are prescriptive and teachers are expected to base their teaching on recommendations contained therein. In elementary science, spelling, reading, social studies, handwriting, and home-and-family living, the guides delineate objectives, suggest a variety of successful teaching plans, and present sample unit organizations. Teachers are encouraged to vary and supplement these ideas to the limit of their talents and resources. The practice of writing detailed teaching units for general use has been discontinued because too often they were used only by the people who produced them.

Curriculum materials originate in many ways: from individual teachers; from in-service workshops; from appointed curriculum committees. When the need for a particular guide is identified by principals, teachers, or members of the central staff a general steering committee takes over the tasks of organizing its content and of distributing the various jobs to be done among subcommittees. The several parts and the whole are reviewed and revised by many teacher groups until pressure of time or satisfaction with the product makes it desirable to issue a tentative edition. This edition is tried out, parts are deleted or added, and it is revised in light of experience with its use. A permanent guide is then issued; "permanent" usually means five to eight years of useful life before the whole process begins again.

Textbooks

Each school principal is supplied by the Division of Instruction with a list of textbooks recommended by textbook committees and approved for purchase by the School Committee. Standing, citywide textbook committees with representatives from all grade levels are maintained in all subject fields. Committee membership is on a rotating basis with classroom teachers as chairmen. Systematic, annual examination of new textbooks is carried on, usually in March and October; previously approved books are reviewed periodically as necessary. Standardized work sheets based on criteria and policies agreed upon by the committee chairmen are used by all work groups to the extent that they are pertinent to the particular subject. Publishers' representatives are consulted when it seems wise to do so.

Multiple, rather than single, adoptions is the accepted practice in all subject fields at the elementary level and in most subjects at the secondary level. Approved books are classified as basic or supplementary, the distinction being that the latter will usually be ordered in smaller numbers. Textbooks not yet on the approved list may be ordered in trial sets with the understanding that the teacher will send an evaluation to the Division of Instruction.

FERMENT OR CHAOS IN EXPERIMENTATION?

On how many different fronts is it possible to move with purpose and coordination? In a school system where the possibility of initiating curriculum improvement is so widespread and the process of pursuing it is bounded principally by limits of ingenuity and energy, it is permissible to wonder at times whether the results are ferment or chaos. The following reports of a few of the programs in progress were chosen because they are indicative of major recent emphases in curriculum improvement.

Experimenting with Television

As an example of regional cooperation, a member of the School Committee and the Director of Instruction of the Newton Schools have played key roles in securing the cooperation of school systems in the Greater Boston area to finance in-school television. The educational television channel had been in operation for approximately three years but it had been restricted, because of its basis of financial support, to adult programing in the evenings only. As a result of organizational efforts by the persons mentioned above, the Eastern Massachusetts Council for School Television was established. Now entering its second full year of in-school telecasting it is supported by a budget of $100,000 contributed by the 120-member school systems, and supplemented by approximately $250,000 from foundations and federal research grants.

In promoting the use of school television in the Boston area, Newton's purpose has been twofold: (1) to use television for enrichment rather than direct teaching; (2) to place major emphasis on quality rather than quantity of programing.

To minimize difficulties of scheduling and because of the conviction that there were greater needs at the elementary level, all the programing during the first year was directed to the elementary schools. A pilot course in sixth-grade science was offered during the spring of 1958. During the school year 1958–59 enrichment courses were offered in physical science, natural science, children's literature, music, art, and local history. Some of the courses were video taped and will be repeated a second year. Carefully prepared teaching guides were developed for each series. During 1959–60 the first cycle of a three-year sequence of aural-oral French for grades four, five, and six was offered. Two fifteen-minute lessons per week will be supplemented by a half-hour weekly telecast for the teachers involved in the program. Also offered in 1959–60 was a course in natural science, developed under the sponsorship of the Massachusetts Audubon Society, and biweekly programs on critical world problems for Problems in Democracy classes, with the cooperation of the World Affairs Council.

The most interesting feature of the entire project is the cooperation of over one hundred metropolitan school systems in program planning. This involves the agreement of representative committees on subject matter to be covered, grade levels to be emphasized, and teachers to teach the proposed courses. Representation includes public, independent, and parochial schools and the State Department of Education. If the quality of teaching remains high, the project could well raise the educational sights of many communities.

School Camping Program

An extensive program of school camping has been carried on since 1950 with the major emphasis on field science and conservation education. The setting is Camp Union, owned by the Young Men's Christian Union of Boston, and located in the beautiful mountain region of southern New Hampshire. Two science specialists attached to the Division of Instruction devote full time to the program. Their services are supplemented by a resident staff at the camp. All Newton's sixth grades spend a week at camp during the school year and the program is in operation from September through May. Approximately a fourth of the cost is subsidized; pupils pay the rest.

Ever since the inception of the program, classroom teachers have played a key role. The week at camp has provided a major focus for the entire year's work in many classrooms. Teacher education was a major factor in getting the program started. During the first three summers, teacher workshops in science and conservation were held at the camp, and were attended by approximately a hundred classroom teachers. Division of Instruction staff members in art, music, physical education, and audio-visual education participated. From the start, opportunities for an integrated program were recognized.

No blueprints for the program were drawn in advance. During

the first two or three years the experience consisted mainly of overnight or one-day science field trips to nearby conservation areas although a few brave souls pioneered in a full week's experience at camp. The activities gradually expanded but never became formalized so far as their curriculum content was concerned. Capable leadership has been provided but teachers accompany their classes to camp and play a major role in planning the experience. Summer workshops have been discontinued; weekend workshops are still held. All new sixth-grade teachers spend a full day and night at camp observing the program in operation with other classes before they start planning with their own.

Although initially teachers favored the spring season, now many ask for the fall or winter since it provides both a unique opportunity to get to know their children better and an effective point of departure for many follow-up learning experiences.

In analyzing the factors which have contributed to the success of the program, it appears that two were particularly important.

1. *The major role of the classroom teacher.* The week's experience is planned by the teacher with the children in the classroom. Initial and continuing emphasis has thus been placed on teacher education and involvement.

2. *Capable, creative leadership.* The consultants in the science and conservation program have had broad experience in camping, science, and classroom teaching. They are not content with a static program and constantly are trying new ideas.

As a result of these factors, there has evolved a rich, flexible, stimulating program for children worth much more than the actual amount of money invested in it.

Science Materials Center

During the past several years and under the leadership of the consultants in the science and conservation program, a Science Materials Center has been developed at the Division of Instruction. In September 1957 an additional staff member was added to serve as general consultant in elementary science and to expand the materials center.

A major feature of the center is a "lending library" of live animals and other natural science materials for classroom use. The collection includes hamsters, guinea pigs, rabbits, chinchillas, parakeets, rats, turtles, lizards, goldfish, and flying squirrels. Adequate housing, food, and instructions for proper care are also provided. Easily assembled terraria are available as are an increasing number of physical science kits and materials. Binoculars, microprojectors, and microscopes are available for loan. A careful record is kept of the use teachers make of these materials, their evaluations, and their suggestions for further additions to the center.

All three members of the Science and Conservation Department operate as a closely knit team. Although the newest member of the team frequently fills in at camp as an additional counselor, he devotes most of his time to the development of the center, classroom demonstrations, and teaching in-service courses for teachers. The Science Materials Center is also an evolving program based on the assumption that the development of effective teaching of science in the elementary school depends more on leadership and resources than on the development of a printed course of study.

The Newton Plan

The Newton Plan was conceived by the Senior High School English Department as a study of staff utilization. The initiators probed themselves and their co-workers with these questions: "What have we been doing? Why have we done it? Have our goals changed? Does our traditional approach help us to reach these goals? If not, what new approach is necessary?" They proposed to follow the answers they found to whatever conclusion they might lead. The Fund for the Advancement of Education found their proposal unique and helped with fundamental questioning and financial aid.

The staff rationale rested on five assumptions which seemed self-evident: (1) Students must accept a share of the responsibility for their own education. (2) Until a pupil has mastered the fundamentals of a subject, his work with more subtle aspects is often unreliable and unrewarding. (3) Uniformity of class size is unrealistic. (4) Since teachers vary in their effectiveness at teaching different topics, each pupil should enjoy the best work of several teachers. (5) Equipment too costly for small groups is economically justified for large-group classes.

To help teachers accept the new role which these beliefs imply, three steps were necessary. First, the teachers had to have released time to re-examine their goals, subject matter, and methods and to integrate these three. Second, equipment such as cameras, projectors, facsimile duplicators, and Vu-Graph projectors had to be made available as tools. Third, where materials of instruction did not exist, teachers had to have time and help to create them. These steps were taken.

The Newton Plan got under way in 1956–1957 with thirteen large-group lectures in the field of English. Classes ranged from 65 to 400 in size. Instruction was given on a now-or-never basis. In 1957–1958 the four weekly meetings of sophomore English classes comprised (1) a regular class, meeting for study of advanced topics; (2) a large-group lecture in fundamentals and special topics; (3) a reading and writing period used for working assignments; and (4) a speech period. While greater responsibility for carrying through on his assignments was placed on the pupil, he was given additional help in the way of advance assignments, outlines of material to be mastered, and class time to work on them. Moreover, he had the benefits of the best teaching of many teachers. The Newton Plan is still in its infancy but continuing evaluation of it is encouraging. It is being tentatively extended to other departments. Among varied developments are these:

1. *Foreign language.* With financial help from the Harvard School and University Program for Research and Development (SUPRAD), a set of long-playing records in French prepared by a Newton Plan teacher is loaned to pupils for home use.

2. *Mathematics.* A series of large-group lectures on such topics as problem solving, nature of proof, number systems has been opened to selected sophomores.

3. *Music.* Three lectures with visual and auditory demonstrations for each grade offer interpretation and techniques of classical, popular, and jazz music.

4. *Social studies.* A series of large-group lectures in each major social studies course was introduced in 1958–59, plus small seminars for more able students, in place of regular courses.

Junior High School Organization Study

This study grew out of the conflict of dissatisfactions and convictions: (1) dissatisfaction with the impasse between heterogeneous and homogeneous grouping and the conviction that the values of either should not be discarded entirely; (2) dissatisfaction with the rigidities of the 40-minute period, 6-period day, and 30-pupil class and the conviction that a more flexible schedule can preserve the advantages of both ways of grouping pupils; (3) dissatisfaction with an approach to content that exposes all pupils to the same subject matter without regard to ability and the conviction that differentiation of subject matter can be devised without sacrificing the basic aims of the common learning program; (4) dissatisfaction with the irrational distinction between curricular and co-curricular activities and the conviction that the purposes of so-called co-curricular school activities can be integrated with curricular activities.

Two school faculties agreed to make a joint effort to devise and operate a plan of organization which would be more in keeping with their convictions. They agreed that two conditions would permit the experiment to be significant to persons other than those taking part in it: once under way, it must be possible to operate under existing pupil-teacher ratios; a plan for evaluation must be created to weigh the achievements of the experimental organization against those of the present organization.

In search of expert advice as well as financial help, staff members proposed the plan to the Harvard School and University Program for Research and Development as one which it might support. The Directors of SUPRAD agreed to devote both money and personnel to it and the Coordinator of Junior High School Education was appointed as coordinator of the project. The following grouping and program changes constitute the working objectives of the plan:

1. To regroup regular English classes, which are normally heterogeneously grouped in a combined English-social studies program for several periods each week, bringing together—for advanced literature, for corrective help in composition, for developmental reading, and for remedial reading—those pupils who can best benefit from concentrated instruction in those areas in new groups that are relatively homogeneous in need and interest.

2. To teach mathematics, science, and foreign language on two or three levels in groups that are relatively homogeneous on the basis of ability in these subjects, with extra periods for pupils identified as having exceptional talent and interest in science or mathematics.

3. To teach certain specialized aspects of art, music, industrial arts, and home economics in elective, homogeneous groups to pupils who have a high degree of what may be called producer interest.

4. To teach social studies, physical education, and common learnings in English, art, music, industrial arts, and home economics in constant, heterogeneous groups.

5. To provide time within the school day for meetings of clubs, service groups, student government committees, and for intramural sports.

6. To devise a program schedule which will establish periods of varying lengths set up in multiples of 30 minutes, the result being a school day 45 minutes longer than previously.

7. To develop and apply criteria for grouping pupils.

Development of grouping and evaluative techniques and of teaching plans and material has been time consuming. During the summers of 1958 and 1959 a team of ten teachers received a modest stipend for taking part in a six-week workshop to propose plans and materials. SUPRAD has also supplied consultant service beyond the community's local resources. Evaluation has been a knotty problem. At present it seems likely to take the form of a comparison of achievement test scores in the respective schools in 1958–1960 and in 1956–1958; of teacher-opinion studies; of student-attitude studies; and of follow-up studies of student success in senior high school.

Special Reading Program

In 1955–1956 the Laboratory for Research in Instruction of the Harvard Graduate School of Education was engaged to make a study of factors relating to underachievement and overachievement in reading in the Newton public schools. The reading achievement of all children in grades one, three, six, and nine was analyzed in relation to their age and mental ability. A detailed analysis was made of samples of underachievers and overachievers in the third grade. An extensive series of special tests was given to over 150 children; data were also obtained from teachers and parents by questionnaire and by interview.

Although overachievers in reading outnumbered underachievers about two to one, the number of underachievers identified was found to be substantial. The Laboratory's analysis of causal factors, including school and home experiences, clarified difficulties of the underachieving third-grade child. Problems cluster generally in such areas of skill and ability in which the school can and should furnish instruction: word analysis, articulation and speech rhythms, association of sounds with symbols. No statistically significant relationships were found between underachievement and many factors which are often suspect—rate of early motor development, personality adjustment, warmth of family relationships, methods of discipline, age at school entrance, time spent with TV and movies, indoor or outdoor play.

The data were studied carefully by elementary school principals. Several plans for providing help were considered. The one recommended to, and accepted by, the School Committee called for the appointment of four reading teachers for elementary schools and two for the junior high schools; increasing the facilities of the reading clinic; and offering additional training in the teaching of reading to classroom teachers who need it.

In general, the reading teachers are assigned to a particular school for a semester and work with a limited number of children who are average or above average in intelligence but a year or more retarded in reading. During their stay in a building, they also work closely with all teachers on the improvement of the total reading program.

Boston University cooperated with the Newton schools in setting up a remedial reading school in the summer of 1958 for 100 selected children in one of the elementary school buildings. A number of elementary school teachers served an internship in remedial reading methods under the leadership of Boston University instructors in this program. A similar program was offered during the summer of 1959 in cooperation with the School of Education at Tufts University.

SIGNIFICANT TRENDS IN CURRICULUM DEVELOPMENT

Among the trends in curriculum improvement in Newton which seem most significant are the following:

Experimentation at the secondary school level. New arrangements are being sought for more economical utilization of time, space, and personnel; for new ways of grouping pupils and for methods to combine traditional subject areas for greater effec- tiveness in instruction. This experimentation represents introduc- tion of some subject matter in grades earlier than normal: French and personal-use typing in grades 7 and 8; the Illinois Mathe- matics Project in grade 8; college preparatory biology in grade 9; and more physical science in grades 7, 8, and 9.

Evaluation of the program at all levels. This appears not only in more frequent use of standardized tests but in the more sys- tematic analysis of test results and growing concern about equat- ing ability with achievement. It is related to the studies of parents' opinions and attitudes, to the Harvard Study of Reading in Newton, and to the necessity of passing judgment on experi- mental programs. There is also a growing tendency toward self- examination on the part of individual school units and toward more emphasis on evaluation of processes of teacher-change in curriculum improvement.

Increased emphasis on subject-matter achievement. The sen- ior high school is firmly committed to the Advanced Placement Program (Kenyon Plan) and the junior high schools to multiple tracks in foreign language, mathematics, and science. Among ele- mentary schools this trend is clear from the growing interest in both horizontal enrichment and vertical acceleration for small groups of more able students.

Provision for systemwide coordination. Perhaps the influx of new teachers accounts in part for the recent growth of systematic study and evaluation of textbooks, and the production and revi- sion of curriculum guides. More central staff services have been made available for general supervision; a junior high school coordinator, a consultant in general education, and four elemen- tary consulting teachers have been added.

Concern for maintaining a well-informed public. This trend is evident in administrative and teacher cooperation in such formal activities as the Little White House Conference, Parent Opinion Surveys, and PTA and League of Women Voters committees. The novelty and complexity of current experimentation and change have led to more frequent and fuller use of newspaper publicity about what is going on in the schools. A special effort has been made to publish an annual report which is readable, interesting, and informative.

Close working relationships with universities and foundations. Much of the experimentation which goes on would be impossible without the consultant and financial help made available by universities and foundations. There has been a tendency to plan in terms of acceptability of projects to such sources of aid and to accept leadership from them when it is offered. In the fall of 1959 administrative and supervisory personnel participated in a three-day workshop to evaluate the effect of such projects on the total educational program and on policies and procedures of curriculum development in nonsubsidized areas.

De facto lengthening of the school year. The Harvard–Newton Summer School and Intern Program has expanded both upward and downward from the junior high school level. At the same time the regular summer school, originally a "second-chance" enterprise, has evolved into an enrichment and acceleration program. With the addition of the Summer Reading School, there may well be a trend toward an eleven-month school year on a voluntary basis.

WEAKNESSES AND STRENGTHS

It is always difficult for persons participating in a program to analyze it objectively. Because of the lack of a clear-cut pattern for initiating curriculum improvement this is particularly true in the Newton public schools. Therefore, this lack of complete objectivity must be acknowledged. What is regarded here as a weakness may be regarded elsewhere as a strength, and vice versa. Subject to these conditions, the following section outlines what seems to be certain weaknesses and limitations of Newton's program as they appear from the "inside."

Weaknesses

The Director of Instruction should be a "line" rather than a "staff" officer. Since he is not, principals frequently go directly to the superintendent to discuss curriculum problems. It would seem that a more clear-cut definition of the authority and responsibility of the Director of Instruction would provide for more effective coordination without seriously limiting the autonomy of the principal.

Inadequate attention has been given to communication and planning at the top staff level. This refers particularly to the superintendent and the heads of the four major divisions. All have great freedom of operation but in the past all have planned more or less in isolation. Much serious consideration is currently being devoted to this problem. Communication and planning would certainly be improved if all the central staff were housed in one building.

Frequent use of unilateral methods of operation hampers effective coordination. In the desire to free teachers and principals from the bonds of "line" operation in curriculum improvement, it has been made possible to by-pass staff personnel in initiating new projects. This could be regarded as a strength of the program, but it sometimes leads to a situation where no one has a complete picture of projects under way. Perhaps all that is here reflected are some of the usual frustrations of staff personnel attempting to coordinate an educational program which is constantly in a state of flux.

Too much attention is devoted to the spectacular, the newsworthy, the public relations angle. Too little recognition is given to gradual, systematic efforts to improve the learning program. In the efforts to secure foundation support for projects or to develop cooperative relationships with universities, there is a tendency to overlook the fact that this may limit to some extent the nature of projects attempted and may channel the energies of staff members away from other projects which may be equally important but less novel or spectacular.

Too little attention is devoted to careful scientific evaluation of projects undertaken. Seldom are plans for evaluation built in.

They are more likely to be undertaken as an afterthought without adequate "bench marks" on which to base judgments.

In final analysis and retrospect, it is fair to note that at least some of these weaknesses are present in most school systems. Perfect paper-organization schemes seldom guarantee equally perfect operation. As long as organizational patterns are operated by human beings, some of these weaknesses will persist.

Strengths

Candor about weaknesses perhaps justifies equal frankness about strengths. These five appear to be the most impressive strengths and probably outweigh the weaknesses.

Many and varied services are available to assist in the improvement of instruction. Services are available in general supervision, art, music, physical education, library, audio-visual education, science, and reading. In the Division of Counseling Services, there are psychological counselors, hearing and speech counselors, special-education counselors, a part-time psychiatrist, and clinical reading services.

Structurally the organization is so designed as to coordinate effectively the functions and services affecting instruction. All supervisory and consultant services are coordinated by the Director of Instruction. He also is responsible for citywide leadership in the development of curriculum materials, the direction of study and approval of textbooks and materials, and the administration of in-service education.

There is unusual freedom to initiate, invent, and experiment. Principals and teachers enjoy a great deal of autonomy. Invention and diversity are encouraged and recognized. Mere conformity is seldom rewarded. A principal need only clear a new idea with the superintendent, a teacher with her principal. In many instances even these clearances are not necessary. Curriculum policies are discussed in meetings and written policy statements are kept to a minimum.

Principals occupy key positions and enjoy unusual status. Principals are not only the chief supervisory officers of their respective schools; collectively, they play a major role in curriculum planning, policy development, and personnel selection. Thus, they have every opportunity for continued professional growth and leadership.

There is strong public support of education in the community and a genuine pride in the quality of its schools. This is perhaps Newton's greatest asset, for upon it all the other strengths in some measure depend. So long as local schools continue to deserve and enjoy such support from the lay public, continued growth and improvement remain possible.

In conclusion, it may at times be frustrating to serve in a staff relationship in a school system which puts a premium on diversity and experimentation. Yet it is also stimulating and few staff members would want it to be otherwise.

10

GALENA PARK, TEXAS

DOME OF MANY–COLORED GLASS *

THE DISTRICT

TUCKED in a bend of the Houston Ship Channel, the Galena Park
Independent School District consists of a cluster of communities
in the east central part of Harris County, largest and richest in
Texas. In addition to two incorporated towns of 10,000 population each—Galena Park and Jacinto City—the district includes
smaller communities as well as frontier strips of Houston which,
like tentacles, encircle the thirty-nine-mile area. The area is in
the shadow of the San Jacinto Ordnance Depot; it is the heart
of large steel and other industrial and manufacturing plants.
Through the Washburn Tunnel, one passes to oil refineries,
chemical plants, paper mills, and industrial plants located along-
side forty miles of the channel to Galveston and the Gulf of
Mexico.

Although but twenty minutes from the heart of downtown
Houston, Galena Park retains a breath of country air. The atmos-
phere is reflected in the motto of the Chamber of Commerce:
"Big City Efficiency; Country Hospitality." Incorporated only

---

* This chapter was written by RAYMOND J. FREE, Director of
Curriculum, Galena Park Public Schools.

thirty years ago, Galena Park and Jacinto City, with the other communities, represent the suburban swell of metropolitan Houston. Like an oasis, Galena Park feels no traffic congestion either from the north where cars roar over the Old Spanish Trail and the new highway to Port Arthur, or from freeways leading into Houston and on south to Galveston.

As Houston and the port—third largest in the nation—continue to grow, Galena Park is destined to become a heavily populated suburban community. Residents work in the district, in Houston, in Baytown, and in Pasadena. Galena Park maintains independence through its mayor, councilmen, police, newspaper, post office, fire and water departments; Houston furnishes electricity, gas, and telephone service. Residents have access to the cultural advantages of Rice Institute, the University of St. Thomas, the University of Houston, art galleries, museums, concerts, theaters, and operas in Houston.

The Schools

Serving this district are nine elementary, three junior high, and two senior high schools. Of these fourteen, four have been built under a $4,000,000 bond issue of 1953, which also financed additions to four of the existing schools. A 1958 bond issue of $3,790,000 guaranteed two additional elementary schools, another high school, and additions to seven of the existing schools.

Growing from an enrollment of 401 pupils in 1930 to 9,200 in 1959, and with a projected enrollment of 12,000 by 1962, the schools have experienced many problems in curriculum and instruction. The changing nature of the staff—which increased from 192 in 1950 to 400 in 1959, and will require 500 by 1960—has complicated the development of any coordinated program of instruction. Between 1940 and 1950 the district employed 160 additional teachers. Expansion brought problems in transportation, in maintaining enough buildings, and in providing for the needs of widely differing scholastic groups. Before 1954 the administrative organization of the schools did not include a separate curriculum division. There was no emphasis on the development of a system-wide program. Under leadership of the building principal, individual teachers developed their own plans; schools developed their own programs, selected their own teaching materials, and evaluated methods of instruction.

The Gilmer-Aikin laws, passed in 1949 by the Texas legislature, guaranteed to the district minimum salaries for teachers and other professional personnel; provided for the cost of transporting children residing more than two miles from school; and partially paid for other costs of maintenance and operation. In 1958–1959, the per capita apportionment amounted to $82 per pupil. The Minimum Foundation Act provides $350 per teacher for instructional materials. In addition to the state's $350 per teacher, Galena Park spends on maintenance and operation an additional $800 per teacher. This includes utilities and insurance; teaching, shop, band, choir, homemaking, library, and physical education supplies; and janitorial and maintenance services. State funds met a little more than half the total cost of operating the schools, excluding debt service and revenue from sales of bonds. Galena Park now employs more professional persons than it is eligible for under the minimum program; it pays in excess of the minimum salary schedule; it spends more for maintenance and operation than the present state allotment. In 1959 Galena Park was eligible for 302 classroom-teacher units, but actually employed 326 units; eligible for 46 special-service units, it employed 47; and, eligible for 24 administrative units, it had 32 units. The district paid for the extra units from its own funds. The number of classroom teachers whose salaries the state guarantees is determined by the average number of pupils in daily attendance. The ratio for the number of teachers is one for every 26 pupils. Employment of special-service teachers is on the basis of one to every 20 classroom-teacher units; supervisors and counselors, one to 50. Galena Park's schedule for beginning salaries and increments is far beyond the state minimum scales.

In addition to providing a large share of the funds for operation, the state certifies teachers; furnishes textbooks; and maintains a staff to serve individual schools as special consultants. The local district retains authority to select teachers; to provide its own buildings and equipment; to insure attendance; to decide on teaching methods; to organize individual schools; and to develop instructional programs which meet the requirements of its own locality and of the state. Twelve lunchrooms, financed approximately 90 per cent by local funds and the remainder by federal funds, serve the fourteen schools. In two cases, lunchrooms are used jointly by an elementary and a junior high school since they are on the same campus. The state provides liaison with the United States Department of Agriculture and furnishes consultant services. Menus are planned in the central lunchroom office and are standard throughout the system.

EMERGENCE OF CURRICULUM COORDINATION

Pressed by a general shifting of population within the district and by the schools' rapid growth, the School Board saw a need for evaluating the program of the Galena Park schools. Teachers were asking for uniformity in textbooks and some coordination of the courses of study in the various schools. In answer to these requests, a curriculum division and a special education department for exceptional children were added to the administrative organization in 1954. The division responds to expressed needs of teachers and principals. Rather than incorporating the program of some other system, the philosophy has been to develop, through teacher meetings or groups, a program tailored to Galena Park—designed by the teachers themselves. The curriculum division was created to serve teachers—without conflicting with any individual school program or instructional or supervisory procedure used by the principal. All work is initiated by teacher groups; it follows, therefore, that such a program develops slowly.

THE CURRICULUM PROGRAM

Curriculum coordination represents a service involving the application of scientific methods of problem solving, participation in the solution of problems by all who are concerned, and testing of the solutions against the realities of the classroom or school program. Such a service, designed to help teachers improve their classroom practices, focuses on day-by-day problems and seeks to open new opportunities for teacher participation in the solution of problems.

The Central Council

In 1954 a coordinating council was first organized. This Central Curriculum Council is composed of a representative group of faculty members selected from all divisions of instruction of the Galena Park schools. The Council is composed of 26 members representing the administrative staff, the elementary school and the secondary school principals, the teachers, and the faculties of the individual schools. Meetings are held the first Monday of each month.

The purposes of the Council are to study the total educational program; to promote cooperative effort in recommending school policies; to develop discussion and study groups; and to study, recommend, and prepare materials for teachers to relate to systemwide problems.

Four members of the central office are ex officio members—the superintendent, the director of curriculum, the director of special services, and the director of elementary education. The elementary schools have nine members; junior highs, three; and senior highs, two. Terms of office are for three years. The terms are staggered so that one third are new each year. The duties of these school representatives are to report to the Council curriculum activities going on in the schools, to report to the faculty they represent the activities of the Council, and to serve on one or more of the Council committees.

There is one teacher representative from each school in the system. The method of selection of these representatives is left to the discretion of the building principal. The Council in no way attempts to influence the manner in which school representatives are selected.

With representatives of the principals, however, selection is a matter of rotation. A senior high principal serves once every two years; a junior high principal and an elementary principal, once every three years. Principals originally drew lots to determine the pattern, which now is more or less automatic.

Officers—chairman, vice chairman, secretary—serve for only one year. They are selected by a nominating committee, usually headed by the immediate past president. No chairman has ever served for two years. Since 1954 chairmen have included an administrator, an elementary school principal, an assistant principal from an elementary school, an assistant principal from a senior high school, an elementary teacher, and an assistant principal from a junior high school. With one exception the vice chairman has become the chairman the following year.

Committees of the Council, which cut vertically through all six grades in all schools, were organized with a classroom teacher as chairman of each group. Representatives polled teachers in their respective buildings for suggestions; principals served as resource persons in their chosen areas. The result of this work was a tentative sequence of offerings in each subject in the elementary schools. This study furnished the nucleus for curriculum development which, from this beginning, was expanded the following year to include the secondary schools.

The philosophy and objectives of the schools were revised and stated as follows:

> The general aim of the Galena Park Schools is to prepare the pupil physically, mentally, socially, and morally to take his place in an ever-changing, complex society. The school should be a pupil-centered school; that is, the individual is the chief interest. It should be realized that differences form the pupil's personality and that his needs and abilities should be the principal concern of the school.
>
> Since the pupil faces many complex situations, the school should assist him in making the necessary growth and adjustments to these situations. This may be accomplished by proper guidance and counseling. In this training the facilities of the school should be used by all the pupils and teachers for a fuller realization of the aims.
>
> The schools are a vital factor in the growth and development of the well-rounded citizen, who will take his place in the democratic way of life.[1]

As its horizons broadened to include representatives from both elementary and secondary schools, the Central Council began studying problems common to all schools. Most often requested by teachers was an outline of the policies applicable to all schools. By suggesting topics for inclusion and assisting the building representatives in the writing, editing, and revision of this outline

[1] "Philosophy and Objectives of the Galena Park Independent School District." Adopted March 28, 1948; reissued October 1, 1955.

teachers advanced the project. In the fall of 1957, after a two-year study, a 48-page copyrighted *Teacher's Handbook* was distributed. This handbook dealt with organization and administration, policies and practices relating to both personnel and the school, to the activity program, and to professional services. It also included organizational charts and a description of the course offerings in every grade and in every subject. The handbook is a ready reference for all teachers, especially those new to the system.

The Galena Park schools have a film library of over 500 films which are centrally housed and processed. In answer to a second expressed need, the Central Council in 1956 annotated, catalogued, and classified by grade level the films in the school depository. A catalogue showing subject area, grade level suitability, and order number for each film was issued to all teachers the following fall.

In the fourth year of operation the Council, polling teachers for problems for study, located three prime areas: programs for the gifted; a developmental reading program for grades 1–12; and a study of promotion policies. Committees with representatives from all schools began a survey in 1958 of the reading problems and of the superior pupils in all schools. The results of these surveys and tests will provide the basis for implementing a program to meet the needs shown in the study.

Some work has been done with individual pupils of superior ability. Studies in secondary school mathematics and science showed the need for an eighth-grade course in mathematics, which was initiated; teachers have participated in conferences on education for the gifted; secondary school English teachers are working with colleges on the content of a senior English course. There is, however, no systemwide program for identifying and providing for talented pupils. The Central Council, with a second survey, will formulate the principles for organizing programs for these pupils. The results will be presented to principals, teacher groups, and administrators for study. Courses for slow learners have been organized in the primary grades; courses in practical English have been introduced in junior and senior high schools.

The Council has become a clearinghouse for problems that relate to all schools. Identification and resolution of specific problems involving instruction and courses of study are assigned to teacher groups who work to produce guides and other teaching aids. The Council, to assist with the many meetings that this assignment necessitates, publishes a monthly calendar of all professional meetings and school activities. Table 1 (p. 254) shows the actual calendar for a typical month.

Organization for Teacher Participation

Believing that the best in-service program encourages teachers to participate in meetings, in discussion groups, in sharing ideas, the School Board approved an organization that would include all teachers and give them released time from classroom duties to work on curriculum improvement. In 1954 all elementary school teachers began meeting monthly in general meetings scheduled at a different school each month. At these meetings new publications, educational news, and speakers were presented to the group by the curriculum director.

Following the general meeting, there were grade level or special subject meetings, with a teacher acting as chairman and a principal as resource person for each group. In these group meetings, textbooks were studied for adoption; policies were discussed; films were previewed; and recommendations for curriculum revision were made. More important, they were the beginning of meetings which included all schools and brought together as a working unit all teachers of the same grade. Since time was required for teachers to get to the given school, classes were dismissed early one day a month to allow teachers to meet during school hours. Two problems were encountered: some teachers did not feel that time taken from actual classroom instruction was justified in these meetings; and teachers who served as chairmen of the groups felt that they were not adequately performing as leaders of the group.

In the spring of 1955 the Texas Education Agency asked each school system to conduct a self-appraisal of the program of instruction, using an outline prepared by the Agency. The results of a study in Galena Park showed the need for continuous planning and coordination in all schools and the development of courses of study. This evaluation helped chart the course for the second year when the meetings were extended to the secondary schools. At that level, teachers were grouped by subject areas: language arts, mathematics, science, social studies, homemaking, art, music, physical education, business education, vocational and industrial education, special education. A teacher was selected to serve as coordinator of each group for the meetings. Special-education staff held separate meetings for all their personnel once a week. (See chart, p. 257.) The school secretaries also organized an Educational Secretaries Association and met once a month to study ways to serve the schools better.

From 1954 to 1956 one person coordinated the entire curriculum program. It was difficult for this individual to do more than organize the program, schedule meetings, get background information, and plan with teachers who were acting leaders of the group meetings. Elementary school and secondary school staff meetings were held one week prior to the general meetings to plan the agenda. Chairmen of each grade and elementary school principals formed the elementary school staff; area coordinators and secondary school principals formed the secondary school staff. The curriculum coordinator met with both staffs on different days to plan the meetings. This meant that the coordinator's contact with the sectional groups was very limited.

In 1956 a consultant in elementary education was added to the curriculum division. Grade-level meetings were scheduled on different days of the week to allow the consultant to work with each group. Elementary school groups now find it necessary to assign the work of writing resource units to small committees of one representative from each school. These groups, on released time, work one half day a month. The initial project has been to develop units for the social studies: home and school life; neighborhood activities; the expanding community; Texas; the United States; peoples of the world; citizenship; world neighbors.

All secondary school groups still meet on the same day. As a result of study by secondary teachers, graduation requirements were changed to include driving theory for all ninth-grade pupils; civics for all seniors; office practice; two years of science; and applied science. Special studies were conducted in the teaching of mathematics and science, with plans made for tal-

TABLE 1

CALENDAR OF MONTHLY ACTIVITIES

February 4. Central Council will meet at 3 P.M. in the Administration Building.

Woodland Acres Junior High School PTA will meet at 3:15 P.M. in the Choir Room.

Council for Exceptional Children will meet in the Speech Room of the Galena Park High School at 7:30 P.M. The program will consist of a quartet, film and a discussion.

February 5. The Area PTA Council will meet in the Board Room at 9:30 A.M.

There will be a curriculum meeting of all first-grade teachers at 2:30 P.M. in the Jacinto City Elementary School.

The CTA Executive meeting will be held in the Board Room at 3:15 P.M.

February 6. The Special Services will have a staff meeting (all phases) at 2:30 P.M. in the Board Room.

February 7. The School nurses will meet from 8:30 to 9:30 A.M. in the Board Room.

The Pyburn Elementary School PTA meeting will be held in the cafeteria at 3 P.M.

February 11. There will be a curriculum meeting of all second-grade teachers at Jacinto City Elementary School, 2:30 P.M.

The teachers of special rooms will meet in Mr. Orr's room at Galena Park Junior High School at 2:30 P.M.

The Galena Park Senior High School PTA will meet in the library at 3 P.M.

There will be a meeting of the School Board at 7:30 P.M. in the Board Room.

February 12. There will be a curriculum meeting of all third-grade teachers at 2:30 P.M. in the Jacinto City Elementary School.

The Educational Secretaries will meet at Fidelity Manor at 3 P.M.

The CTA regular meeting will be held at 7:30 P.M. in the High School Speech Room. The program will be a panel composed of a doctor, lawyer, teacher and industrial personnel discussing the question, "How Can Teachers Grow More Professionally on the Job?"

February 13. The Special Services Staff, other than teachers of special rooms, will meet in the Board Room at 2:30 P.M.

There will be a curriculum meeting for all secondary principals and coordinators at 3 P.M. in the High School library.

The Galena Park Junior High School PTA meeting will be

held in the cafeteria at 3:05 P.M. The program will be, "We the People Achieve Effective Home, School, and Community Relations."

February 14.   There will be a curriculum meeting of all fourth-grade teachers in Jacinto City Elementary School at 2:30 P.M.
The Cimarron Elementary PTA will meet at 3:15 P.M. in the cafeteria.
The MacArthur Elementary PTA will meet at 3 P.M. in the cafeteria.

February 18.   There will be a General Curriculum meeting of all elementary teachers at 3 P.M. in Jacinto City Elementary cafeteria. Guest speaker will be Margaret E. Brown of Allyn and Bacon, Inc.
Teachers of special rooms and speech will meet from 4 to 5 P.M. at Baylor Clinic.

February 19.   There will be a curriculum meeting of all fifth-grade teachers at 2:30 P.M. in Jacinto City Elementary School.
The Galena Park Elementary PTA meeting will be held at 3:15 P.M. in the Music Room. The subject will be, "We the People Learn Civil Defense."
The Woodland Acres Elementary PTA will meet at 7 P.M. in the cafeteria. The topic will be, "We the People Achieve Effective Home, School, and Community Relations."

February 20.   School will be dismissed for the Fat Stock Show parade.

February 21.   The Cloverleaf Elementary PTA will meet at 2:30 P.M. in the auditorium. The program will be a Founder's Day skit.
There will be a curriculum meeting of all sixth-grade teachers at 2:30 P.M. in Jacinto City Elementary School.
The Jacinto City Elementary PTA will meet in the auditorium at 3:10 P.M. The topic will be, "We the People Achieve Effective Home, School, and Community Relations."

February 26.   The ACE will meet at 4:30 P.M. in the Museum of Fine Arts.
The North Shore Junior High School PTA will meet in the library at 3:15 P.M.
There will be a meeting of all elementary music teachers in Jacinto City Elementary School at 2:30 P.M.
The Family Life Institute, sponsored by the Area PTA, will meet in the Galena Park High School auditorium from 7:30 to 9 P.M.

February 27.   The Family Life Institute will resume at 9 A.M.

February 28.   There will be a curriculum meeting of all elementary PE teachers at 2:30 P.M. in Jacinto City Elementary School.

ented pupils. Art exhibits, science fairs, Texas history fairs, and career days were planned for in these meetings.

Guides for Teachers

The elementary school teachers, working in grade-level meetings, have produced experimental teaching guides for each grade which are now being revised. Resource units in the social studies have been mimeographed and distributed to teachers. Secondary school teachers have worked out the objectives for their courses and have agreed on units to be taught. All teachers are now engaged in developing resource units for all grades and subjects.

The appointment of eleven study commissions by the Texas State Board of Education for the purpose of examining all areas of the curriculum throughout the state proved helpful to local committees. Each of the state commissions was composed of six teachers, three college instructors, three principals, two curriculum directors, three superintendents, and two school board members. While the commissions did not work out details of resource units, they made recommendations concerning balance, content, scope and sequence, textbooks, and materials. The Science Commission, for example, initiated a study of the science education needs of noncollege students, of college-bound students who do not plan scientific careers, and of college-bound students preparing for professional fields definitely concerned with science. The Mathematics Commission directed study toward mathematics programs for the superior pupil.

Beginning with a sequence chart, proceeding to grade outlines of what is taught in all subjects and, finally, culminating in resource units for each area of instruction, the publications now completed represent several years of work. To the enthusiastic teacher progress seems slow. The time element still presents a problem even though teachers are relieved from duty for the monthly, half-day meeting. All work must be done during the school year since no summer workshops are maintained.

A state study of public schools—authorized by the Legislature and headed by the Hale-Aikin Committee of Twenty-Four—has also submitted recommendations. In connection with this study, a local committee, composed almost entirely of laymen, recom-

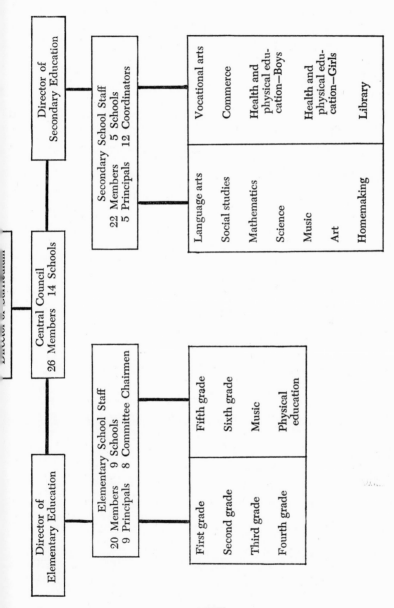

ORGANIZATIONAL PLAN FOR MEETINGS, GALENA PARK SCHOOLS

mended that all teachers be employed for ten months instead of nine. This group felt that the quality of the instructional program would be improved if teachers could have a two-week workshop before the opening of school and a two-week workshop at the end of the school year. At the opening workshop, teachers would prepare materials for classroom use. At the close of the year, they would evaluate the year's work, prepare curriculum guides, develop teaching aids, study new textbooks, preview films for purchase, plan more variety in methods of teaching, and study the latest developments, trends, and research in each area.

Publications

The Curriculum Division provides all teachers with mimeographed monthly announcements of recent trends in education, educational news, summaries of books and special magazine articles, notes on educational television programs, reports on current projects by classroom teachers, and news of state and national activities that affect teaching. Illustrative of the topics included are improvement of reading; textbooks; criticisms of public education; studies of superior pupils; special days and weeks; summer programs for science and mathematics pupils; precautions in building and launching rockets; space language; International Geophysical Year; structural analysis for language arts; and homework.

Meetings with the secondary school staff usually consist of discussion of preplanned topics. Since much of the contact the curriculum coordinator has with the staff is through directive or written communication, a tentative agenda for each meeting is forwarded, prior to the meeting, to staff members who have studied the needs of the secondary schools. Reports from area meetings and from personnel attending professional meetings are discussed and the local program is studied in relation to state requirements. Various patterns for developing teaching guides are examined and the one which seems best suited to a specific area is chosen. For example, the science teachers have adopted the following "Organizational Pattern for Science Resource Units":

1. Desired outcomes
   a. Knowledge and understandings
   b. Habits and skills
   c. Attitudes and appreciations
2. Overview
3. Outline of content
4. Suggested activities
   a. Laboratory work
   b. Demonstrations
   c. Projects
   d. Discussion
   e. Committee work
   f. Reports
   g. Evaluation
5. Materials
   a. Apparatus
   b. Supplies
6. Provision for individual differences
   a. Special assignments
   b. Special materials
   c. Special reading
   d. Special examinations
7. Films, filmstrips, and audio-visual aids
8. Bibliography for teachers
9. Bibliography for pupils

A house organ, *Curriculum Chat*, is published semi-annually. In December, it features innovations, plans, and orientation for new teachers. In May, the highlights are summer activities, evaluation, and a résumé of the year. By reporting activities of the entire school system, describing individual teacher projects, and giving news of personal interest about staff members, *Curriculum Chat* is one of the means for coordinating the school units. The first issues were 75 per cent concerned with state and national news articles; the present issues have reversed the percentage and now three-fourths of the articles report local activities.

Handbook for Parents

The first-grade teachers have published an illustrated booklet, *Happy Days Ahead*, which is sent to all parents with children entering the first grade. The handbook explains school policies regarding immunization, age, and attendance, and includes suggestions for parents to help first graders adjust to school.

THE ROLE OF CURRICULUM COORDINATORS

Under direction of the superintendent and in cooperation with the principals, curriculum coordinators serve as leaders of the professional staff in the development of the program. Their duties include the following:

1. Maintaining programs of in-service education in improving education

2. Evaluating the effectiveness and outcomes of the instructional program

3. Assisting in the selection of textbooks

4. Conducting research projects for selecting teaching methods and procedure

5. Serving as consultants in all phases of the instructional program

6. Reporting to the superintendent on the condition and progress of the instructional program and recommending changes and improvements

7. Assisting, on call, individual classroom teachers with instructional problems

8. Serving as administrative assistants to the superintendent on special assignments [2]

All five secondary schools dismiss school early on the same day for study committees and meetings in which coordinators have the major responsibility for leadership. Elementary school committees have meetings on different days; they may ask for additional assistance from the central office. The chairmen of the Central Council committees likewise can expect help from the curriculum division.

Since the individual school is the basic unit for improving instruction and since the principal is the instructional leader working directly with his teachers to develop the best instructional program possible for the pupils in that school, those engaged in

[2] *Teachers' Handbook,* Bulletin 2 (Galena Park, Texas: Galena Park Public Schools, 1957), pp. 3–4.

coordination enter school buildings only with the principal's knowledge and consent. Unless previous arrangements are made, a coordinator will not visit a school when the principal is away. Even on special assignments from the superintendent, central office personnel contact the principal so that on every occasion he knows the specific purpose of the visit. In confidential cases in which a teacher requests a conference or classroom visit, the principal is informed of the reason for the visit. Good relations with the instructional leader of the school are important for improvement of instruction.

TESTING PROGRAM

A 1955 status study of the testing program indicated that a great deal of testing was going on in the individual schools but that there was no pattern for the type of tests, the grade level, or time of year administered. Elementary schools reported the use of a very wide variety of readiness, achievement, and intelligence tests, plus reading tests which accompanied the books in current use. Junior and senior high schools reported an even greater variety of intelligence, special aptitude, and achievement tests as well as interest and personality inventories.

A study indicated that while it would be best for each school to continue its own testing program, a minimum testing program should be introduced gradually and at the rate at which schools saw the need and requested the service. With the acquisition of a scoring machine and with assistance from the Director of Guidance Services, the following prospectus was accepted as basic for all schools:

Grade   *Type of Test*
1 Social maturity; lateral dominance; hearing and vision; reading readiness
2 Vision; general achievement; mental maturity
3 Hearing and vision; general achievement; mental maturity
4 Vision; general achievement
5 Vision; general achievement; mental maturity
6 Vision; general achievement
7 Hearing and vision; general achievement; mental maturity; problem check list

8   Vision; general achievement; interest inventory
9   Vision; general achievement; mental maturity
10   Hearing and vision; reading; problem check list
11   Hearing and vision; mental maturity; reading; interest inventory
12   Vision; general achievement

This minimum testing program, using tests of the California Test Bureau, measures general intelligence in the second, third, fifth, seventh, ninth, and eleventh grades—six measurements for each pupil during his school career. Nine measures of general achievement are made. These fall in the second, third, fourth, fifth, sixth, seventh, eighth, ninth, and twelfth grades. Since one part of the general achievement tests deals with reading, scores are available in these grades for vocabulary, comprehension, and total reading. Special reading tests are given in the tenth and eleventh grades and a readiness test in the first so that a reading score is available for every year of a child's school attendance. This plan offers a uniform, coordinated testing program which makes interpretation and evaluation easier as the pupils move from one school to another and advance from elementary to secondary schools. Administration of the tests is supervised by the Guidance Director. Scores, computed by machine, are made available to teachers and recorded on pupil's cumulative records.

How the minimum program was unexpectedly changed is illustrated by a request made to the superintendent by the Central Council Committee for the Improvement of Reading when the members in a survey found that teachers preferred to have twelve measures of reading—one a year—instead of the nine proposed by the testing committee. To make reading scores available every year, the reading tests in the tenth and eleventh grades and the readiness test in the first were added in order to comply with the request. Comparisons are now available from year to year for the same classes and for individuals. It is expected that the testing program will expand naturally as it meets the requests of and answers other needs for teachers and counselors.

THE ROLE OF THE PRINCIPAL

The individual school is the ideal unit for improving instruction. The principal is the instructional leader and works with his teachers to develop the best program possible for the pupils in that school. Whereas it is the responsibility of the curriculum director to develop the over-all program, the specific assignment of supervising, evaluating, and improving the program remains with the principal. Under the general direction of the superintendent, the specific duties of the building principals are the following:

1. Recommending, to the superintendent, personnel for employment
2. Supervising the care of the buildings, grounds, and other school property to which they are assigned
3. Administering within each school the approved administrative policies for that school
4. Maintaining pupil welfare and desirable school-pupil and school-community relationships
5. Utilizing effectively the services of the supervisory personnel
6. Supervising and directing the service of the teachers assigned to their respective buildings; the general instructional program and classroom management; assisting in textbook selection
7. Preparing class schedules; assigning teachers; keeping records showing scholastic, social, and health history of all pupils
8. Keeping accurate attendance records; making annual textbook reports
9. Conducting fire drills that meet the requirements of the Texas Insurance Commission
10. Assisting in the development and execution of policies governing the classification, promotion, failure, and progress of pupils
11. Maintaining affiliation with educational accrediting agencies
12. Supervising the extracurricular school program and coordinating the building activities with those of other schools in the system
13. Assigning administrative and teaching duties to assistant principals.[3]

All principals have clerical assistants; none has teaching assignments. Through faculty meetings in their buildings, they review

[3] *Ibid*, p. 6.

school problems following the general guides as outlined in systemwide teacher meetings. Projects in individual schools have included the preparation and maintenance of vertical file material for social studies and a museum of natural history; activities to increase listening skills; art workshops; study of reading problems as related particularly to the school; study of retentions, distribution of grades, causes of failure; programs for American Education Week and Texas Public Schools Week.

For any or all of these activities, personnel from the curriculum or special education divisions may be called in as consultant or resource persons. Bibliographies of material available from the curriculum library are furnished. Every effort is made to encourage activities designed to improve the curriculum and to assist individual teachers in their own efforts to experiment with different teaching methods or materials.

Each year, principals attend either the conference of the Texas Elementary Principals and Supervisors Association or the Texas Secondary Principals Association. Every elementary school principal attends the National Elementary Principals Conference at least once every three years. Every secondary school principal attends the National Association of Secondary School Principals Conference at least once every two years. Other meetings include the Texas Association for Supervision and Curriculum Development, the Texas State Teachers Association, and district and state PTA meetings.

IN-SERVICE EDUCATION ACTIVITIES

Superintendent's Breakfast

On one day each week, all members of the administrative staff meet together for breakfast and discussion of problems. Reports of current activities in the various schools and departments are heard; announcements are made; policies and problems are discussed. Guests are invited to speak to the group. In discussion, school policies are formulated for presentation to the school board. All directors of special divisions (curriculum, special education, pupil accounting, lunchrooms, music, athletics, transportation), divisions of physical properties (maintenance and custodial, business management) and of instructional services functioning through the principals of all schools attend these meetings.

The threefold value of these meetings is primarily in the human relations effects of informal meetings; in the reduction of the number of written directives, reports, and announcements to these members; and in effective communication to the staff of the activities going on in the system.

Consultants

Consultants are invited to work with teachers in small meetings at individual schools; to speak to all teachers in general sessions; and to conduct workshops for teachers. Areas served by consultants during a five-year period have included reading, art, and arithmetic in the elementary schools; mathematics, social studies, library services, and science in the secondary schools. The Texas Education Agency, the Hogg Foundation, local colleges and universities, the state university, and publishers have furnished the schools with consultant assistance.

Assisted by the Citizenship Education Project (Teachers College, Columbia University), representatives from junior and senior high schools made their teaching on freedom more effective. They became acquainted with *The Premises of American Liberty*, a booklet listing fundamental principles and basic beliefs as set forth in the Declaration of Independence, the Constitution, and major court decisions; a Materials Card File containing over 1,200 cards bearing annotations of books, films, records, and pamphlets dealing with specific premises of American liberty and related current unsolved issues; a Laboratory Practices Card File containing 315 practice suggestions that have been used effectively by teachers; filmstrips dealing with the "concept of citizenship" and the "teaching of active citizenship." The teachers developed material on such topics as respect for property; attitude toward authority; taking responsibility; choosing leaders; exercising group membership; and attitudes and skills of democratic behavior.

The workshop on conservation of natural resources—open to all elementary, junior and senior high school teachers—enabled them to study the problems involved; to learn about available materials; and to evaluate suggested activities and procedures. Discussions centered on animals, flowers, birds, water, forests, soil. Teachers were furnished with packets and bibliographies showing sources of free and inexpensive materials on conservation of natural resources and soil conservation.

One of the services of the Texas Education Agency is to provide consultants in all areas of the curriculum. Their visits include conferences with all teachers of an area, with small groups, with individual teachers. Sometimes they visit classes. An illustrative schedule of a three-day program of one consultant is shown below in Table 2.

TABLE 2

ILLUSTRATIVE THREE-DAY SCHEDULE OF ONE CONSULTANT

Monday, February 18

9 A.M. to 2 P.M.	Galena Park Junior High School Individual conferences with mathematics teachers Visits to algebra classes
3 P.M. to 4 P.M.	Meeting of all mathematics teachers and principals Topic: "Difficulties Encountered in Teaching Mathematics"—Galena Park Senior High School, Room 220

Tuesday, February 19

9 A.M. to 2 P.M.	North Shore Junior High School Individual conferences with mathematics teachers Visits to classes
3 P.M. to 4 P.M.	Meeting of all mathematics teachers and principals Topic: "New Trends in the Teaching of Algebra"— North Shore Junior High Library

Thursday, February 21

9 A.M. to 11 A.M.	Woodland Acres Junior High School Individual conferences with mathematics teachers Visits to classes
1 P.M. to 3 P.M.	Fidelity Manor High School Conferences with individual mathematics teachers Visits to classes
3 P.M. to 4 P.M.	General meeting with all mathematics teachers Topic: "Evaluating and Improving Instruction in Mathematics"—Fidelity Manor Library
4 P.M.	Conference with W. C. Cunningham, Superintendent

The recommendations for the mathematics program evolving from these activities were as follows:

1. Utilize bulletin boards in the classroom
2. Improve orientation and presentation of new material
3. Develop a professional library
4. Encourage science-fair activities for junior high schools. Hold separate science fairs for the junior high schools prior to the high school fair. Include exhibits in mathematics as well as science
5. Plan in-service workshops at regular intervals
6. Attend the Conference for Advanced Science and Mathematics Teachers at the University of Texas
7. Study Cooperative Sequential Tests of Educational Progress in Mathematics and Science
8. Participate in Interscholastic League activities: (a) number sense; (b) slide rule; (c) Activities Conference, the University of Houston
9. Inaugurate a field day in mathematics
10. Visit other schools for definite purposes
11. Stimulate mathematics club activities
12. Provide storage space for project work
13. Use films for teaching

Consultants have assisted in setting up improvements for the driver education program; the adult education program; the summer recreational program (including summer camp); the "learn-to-swim" program; and the 1959 summer program for the handicapped, in which 112 children participated, including 84 mentally retarded. There is no charge for the swimming program. Pupils must, however, be 42 inches tall.

The Galena Park School conducts one-week summer camps at Garner State Park, 75 miles from San Antonio, for four sessions during June. One counselor is assigned to each eight campers. The school sets up the little tent colony, furnishes the tents and cots, and transports the children. Pupils in the fifth grade or above are eligible. Letters are sent to parents extending invitations to have their children participate in this healthful program of swimming, hiking, horseback riding, cooking out, excursions, and sightseeing. The only expense is the $12 for the balanced meals that are served. About 400 boys and girls attend each summer.

Reading Workshops

Fifty-eight representative teachers participated at school expense in the annual reading conferences held at the University of Houston and at Texas Southern University during the summer of 1959. These three-day conferences are part of the program of the Texas Association for the Improvement of Reading. Outstanding authorities from all over the nation participate. The teachers attend general and discussion group meetings; visit publishers' exhibits; and report back to the teacher groups they represent. Following one summer workshop, the participants discussed the conference highlights at the first program of the general teachers' meeting in the fall. In 1958 the members of the newly formed reading committee of the Central Council attended the reading conference.

Orientation Program

Two days prior to the opening of school, teachers hold general meetings with the administrative staff and, in individual buildings, with their principals to prepare for the opening of school.

Teachers new to the system report one day earlier than others for special orientation to school policies. They meet the members of the administrative staff, principals, coordinators, and chairmen of committees. The *Handbook* is explained at this time. The teachers are welcomed by the mayor of Galena Park, the presidents of the professional organizations, the treasurer of the Galena Park Federal Credit Union, and the president of the Area Council of the PTA. These new teachers then report to their respective buildings where the principals acquaint them with the local building policies. This extra day gives the new teachers an opportunity to become acquainted with the schools and leaves time for the two-day meetings for all teachers.

The percentage of new teachers is always high because of the number leaving for personal and family reasons; for employment in other school systems; and because of the tidal expansion which is still highest at the seventh-grade level. New teachers usually constitute 25 per cent of the total personnel. Only eight teachers have 25 years of service; nine have 20 years; and 77 have 10 years. Less than one third have been in the system 10 years.

The two-day orientation session has been very helpful to teachers and to principals in preparing for the opening of school. At present, there is not adequate time for curriculum personnel to help teachers get started. There is a definite need for more time before the beginning of school to allow teachers to study curriculum guides and new textbooks; to prepare bibliographies of resource materials; and to plan units of instruction for the year.

REFLECTIONS AND CONCLUSIONS

Day by day the population in the district increases; new residential sections are built; there is a constant influx and shifting of pupils; teacher turnover is high; resistance to change must be overcome; there are problems of coordinating the existing school programs, developing an all-school program, and at the same time leaving to each school its individuality as a unit under the supervision of its principal.

Teachers attend faculty meetings; they belong to various professional associations. Some attend college courses in the evening at local universities. Many hold a second job after school. Teachers assist in civic and church organizations. Curriculum development and improvement under the present plan require additional meetings, more small meetings between the general meetings, added study and work which place a heavy burden on teachers' time. This causes some to say that we keep the *status quo*, that we do not change the way things have been done.

The basic problems in curriculum improvement are those of preventing overloading the teachers with long, tedious meetings; of spreading the work; of helping teachers see the value in meeting, in discussing, in stating opinions, in arriving at agreement; and of developing together a program that fits the needs of the community. To help overcome a feeling of uselessness, special efforts have been made during the past five years to use all teacher-developed materials—to mimeograph and distribute them to other teachers; to report through newsletters and group meetings contributions made by teachers; and to give full credit to those who worked on the material.

By asking every teacher to participate in the program, the

evolvement of a course of action comes slowly. It has been found difficult to measure achievement from group action when some written manual or course of study was not produced. But the time allowed for meetings is not always sufficient for outlines and units to be fully prepared, for supplementary materials to be included, or for provisions for different levels of pupil achievement to be made. There is not time to have the material adequately edited for printing. Up to this time, therefore, nearly all teaching guides have been broad outlines of the subject or grade.

PROJECTIONS

The School Board of the Galena Park Independent School District, in meeting with curriculum coordinators, has made proposals for continuing the development of guides for teachers in all schools; for providing more supervision of classroom teachers; for preserving balance and individualizing instruction; and for encouraging an evaluation of the present organization. With such a progressive group setting the policies for the schools, Galena Park is very fortunate. The members of the board know that curriculum development is a slow process. Like a giant kaleidoscope twirled by a space-age Paul Bunyan, like an intricate mosaic—curriculum programs emerge slowly, continuously, steadily. It is a process similar to a giant prism whose varied rays reflect different colors and different degrees of light. It is a dome of many-colored glass!

11

BELLEVUE, WASHINGTON

THE BELLEVUE STORY *

BELLEVUE is a school district where last week's population figures are always out of date and probably will be for the next twenty or more years. The reason for the school district's great growth is the rapid expansion of industry in the Puget Sound region and the opening of a floating bridge across the waters of Lake Washington which connects Bellevue with the busy Puget Sound city of Seattle.

Until 1940 Bellevue was a sleepy, rural, unincorporated community of 1,500 people. It was a shipping station for small truck farmers and dairy producers of the area. It was also a suburban retreat for Seattle executives and professional persons who did not mind the ferry trip or the extra twenty-mile drive around the north end of the lake to reach their homes.

When the floating bridge was completed across the lake in 1941 Bellevue was placed within fifteen minutes of downtown Seattle by automobile. This opened the town to a future that it had only faintly anticipated. The opening of the bridge also

---

* This chapter was written by GEORGE BRAIN, Superintendent of Schools, Baltimore, Maryland; formerly Superintendent of Schools, Bellevue, Washington.

created a school district problem that typifies and yet somehow dwarfs the growth of a thousand suburban communities. What makes Bellevue different from many communities in similar straits, however, is the method Bellevue people and their school staff have courageously and imaginatively planned for the community's explosive expansion.

A long-range planning program for the Bellevue Schools was considered by the Board of Education for some time previous to launching the actual program. The district was faced with many problems in regard to the proper development of an educational program and the proper expansion of educational plant facilities.

In 1949 the Board of Education authorized the Superintendent of Schools to contact Dean Zeno B. Katterle of Washington State University regarding a complete survey of school district needs. Dr. Katterle explained that no plan, regardless of its technical accuracy, would be workable unless it expressed the local community's wishes. It was also his feeling that an effective plan could be developed by the local citizens and the educational staff with professional help and assistance from persons trained in the field of school and community planning.

Certain principles and policies were established to make clear the duties and responsibilities of the various participants in the planning program. General objectives were established and adopted by the Board of Directors. The purposes of the long-range planning program were identified as follows:

1. To provide for the best possible educational opportunities for the youth of the Bellevue community.
2. To evaluate the present educational program and facilities.
3. To plan a long-range educational program with the counsel and assistance of the community.
4. To keep the community continually informed of problems encountered by the schools.

These purposes were broad in nature and served as a guide to action for the entire community study.

Bellevue continues to grow. In a period of ten years the school district population has increased to more than 60,000. The plan has served as an effective guide to both school and community development. The Bellevue plan is a long way from fulfillment and no one knows this better than the people who reside there. But they recognize that the plan gives purpose to what they are doing.

UNDERLYING GOALS AND VALUES

The traditional idea that the educational planning had to be done by experts was discarded in favor of the philosophy of involving local citizens in a team with professional educators of the community. The original long-range plan, *The Bellevue Story*, established a philosophy for cooperative development of the school program. Schools cannot and will not be any better than the citizens of the community wish them to be. It was the feeling of the people of the community that good schools don't just happen. They are the result of hard work through joint study and a willingness to make the necessary investment to obtain good schools. It was recognized that the educational job is one done by many persons in the community in addition to the classroom teacher; parents, churches, and youth organizations are teachers also. In short, the actual job of teaching is recognized as a community effort, and the philosophy of the educational program is based on this concept.

In the area of curriculum improvement, the teacher is considered the key individual. All improvements which occur among teachers in perceptions, values, competencies and knowledge will create improved conditions for learning and, therefore, ultimately will improve learning. In Bellevue the curriculum is defined to include all the experiences which children and teachers have together under the auspices of the school. The importance of subject matter, with such a concept, is not minimized; neither are the ways in which youngsters learn to react and to act upon the various facts which they acquire and the feelings which they display and modify.

CURRICULUM GOALS

The major purposes of the program are to transmit the values and knowledge important to our culture and to enhance continually such values and knowledge. A major purpose of the curriculum for schools which serve free peoples who have set democracy as their goal is development of those understandings, skills, and habits essential to the free choosing of those who govern. Our schools should strive to develop citizens dedicated to such ideals as freedom to initiate change; freedom to seek equality under the law; freedom to participate in the religion of one's choice; freedom to express points of view that conflict with those of the majority; freedom to choose an occupation and to follow and progress in it; the freedom of minorities to participate fully and without prejudice in all aspects of life and government; and freedom to promote the cause of peace throughout the world.

These goals include most specifically the experiences which will develop in the individual a self-realization, self-conception, and self-acceptance of his potentialities and limitations. It is, therefore, important that the atmosphere of the school and the classroom enhance sound mental health and the development of self-respect. If these goals can be attained early in the formal educational structure, the acquisition of the basic skills in reading, arithmetic, writing, and the application of fundamental learning tools in the area of the arts and sciences will be more fully realized.

Self-confident and self-acceptant individuals will be able to contribute to the long-term goals of education and readily accept society's efforts in their behalf. These long-term goals may be simply stated as the transmission of the values and the purposes of the culture with a view toward its continuing improvement. In Bellevue these long-term goals are intimately interwoven with the yearning for human freedom through democratic procedures. It is assumed, thereby, that the dignity of mankind may be realized more nearly in our culture than through any other humanly developed concept or planning.

Within the framework of such goals, emphases in curriculum improvement in Bellevue have included guidance, reading, modern foreign languages, spelling, handwriting, science, art, music, physical education; improved utilization of community resources in the classroom; programs for the handicapped; reorganization of the primary grades for guidance and instructional purposes; arithmetic, and social studies.

INITIATION OF CURRICULUM IMPROVEMENT

Theoretically, anyone may initiate a question about curriculum improvement which may lead to an investigation of any segment of the program. Provision is made in the organizational structure (coordinated by the district Guidance and Instructional Planning Committee) to open all ways of communication so that students, teachers, and all other school personnel may submit inquiries or supply information which may become the basis for some examination or improvement of learning experiences.

Districtwide programs such as Bellevue's science and social studies programs were requested by a majority of the faculties of the schools. Other changes have been brought about by students who, for example, in a follow-up program at the high school, emphasized the need for more speech instruction. As a consequence, specific speech instruction has become a requirement for graduation. Questions from parents concerning certain aspects of the junior high school program in art, industrial arts, and home arts have created the impetus for reexamination of the basic offerings in these areas. Other instances of the suggestions of school personnel which have contributed to the improvement of educational experiences within the schools could be cited.

The pivotal positions in the curriculum improvement program are the school building principalships. Each principal is considered the director of guidance and curriculum within his school community and is assisted in his work by the knowledge and direction of special service and central administrative staff. Implicit in all improvement is a never-ending alertness to professional education's contribution to the growing body of research being accumulated both in the field and in the university.

There are numerous ways in which a program may be initiated, but the centrally coordinated organization for curriculum improvement in Bellevue leans heavily on the leadership given by principals in the various school buildings. They, in turn, are provided able and positive leadership by an assistant superintendent in charge of guidance and instructional services, who coordinates their endeavors.

DETERMINING AREAS OF IMPROVEMENT

Every method known to personnel relations, and proven by research techniques, is utilized in Bellevue in an effort to discover subjects of concern to educators and patrons in determining areas in which curriculum improvement will be studied. Follow-up of students, questionnaires sent to parents concerning specific parts of the program, discussions and determinations of faculties with respect to the district as well as building- and grade-level programs are but a few of the ways in which the relations between school and community are ascertained in so far as they concern curriculum improvement. In addition to research projects of various kinds, many group meetings involving parents, teachers, and administrators afford a means to the selection of areas for study. The in-service activities of colleges also assist in alerting personnel to problems.

Emphasis through the entire school system is placed on the child's increasing awareness of the current social and contemporary problems surrounding him. This effort culminates at the high school level, where current problems in the critical issues of our times are defined. The discussion of controversial issues is welcomed, provided all facets are represented and the teacher does not draw conclusions for the pupils.

INTERCHANGE OF IDEAS

No curriculum improvement program can exist in a vacuum. International, national, regional, state, and county educational efforts affect local planning through the interchange of ideas brought about by the sharing of curriculum guides, other materials, and informed community resource persons. The proposals of organizations which sponsor scholarship programs, of test and textbook publishers, and of similar groups can be inimical to local curriculum improvement if the procedural plans of these various groups limit the local program. Thus, foundations sponsoring programs based on preconceived conclusions shrouded as hypotheses may not serve the purpose of creative experimentation as they avowedly intend, but rather may limit the program in terms of their own preconceptions. The restriction that can be imposed by the use of tests which are used and normed nationally is also apparent. Similar limitations may exist within the regulations surrounding scholarship programs or in the unimaginative use of textbooks. Bellevue has been eager to define local concerns and needs and has attempted to use the various resources mentioned above as servants of this concept. Achievement tests, for example, are given in the fall so that the results can be used by the teachers as they commence their program, rather than at the end of the term simply to measure the content which may or may not have been covered.

OBJECTIVE OF IN-SERVICE ACTIVITIES

The major function of Bellevue's special service program—which does not connote supervision in this district—is the improvement of classroom instruction and curriculum experience in an intimate and personal sense. It is a generally accepted principle that the greatest improvement in classroom learnings will result from modification in the behavior of the teacher who is in charge of the classroom program; therefore, it follows that teachers should be helped to develop better understandings, insights, and instructional methods for themselves if the teaching of pupils is to be improved.

Curriculum projects, as they are initiated and pursued, help to define the necessary skills. With identification comes the need for study and understanding. It is then that understandings are developed through study and in-service activity. Summer work at college is also designed to promote such understandings. If this in-service growth is not continuous throughout the entire teaching life of the instructor the program will become stultified by routine and repetition. No amount of publication in the curriculum area can substitute for the face-to-face and group relationships of in-service activity.

PARTICIPATION IN CURRICULUM IMPROVEMENT

All professional staff members are involved in curriculum improvement, but in varying ways in accordance with the project being developed and the needs being expressed. "Curriculum improvement" is a general term and as such is sufficiently inclusive to encompass those contributions toward the betterment of teaching and learning which may be made by any member of the community. The way in which curriculum is organized and developed in the school system and within the classroom, however, should be reserved for the professional educator who is qualified to translate program plans into actual practice.

To the degree that their contributions are applicable, all may be said to participate. Every avenue of communication within the community is used in order that participation may be general. It is true that selected key individuals will accept organizational assignments in accordance with their particular skill or responsibility as the need arises. Thus, definitive attempts to improve the curriculum, such as the development of guides, will entail a committee organization to fit the demands of the job to be accomplished.

Involvement is both voluntary and required, but the voluntary spirit of cooperation is encouraged. By virtue of their offices the various administrators and special service personnel are required to give consultant assistance to curriculum effort. Major leadership for curriculum improvement comes from the superintendent of schools. Practical leadership develops from the offices of the various principals in cooperation with the assistant superintendent responsible for instructional and guidance services. Encouragement in specialized areas comes from the special services which are designed to develop wider competency in particular areas.

CENTRAL OFFICE STAFF PARTICIPATION

Emphasis is placed on the essential commitment of every member of the professional staff to curriculum improvement. No other job is as important or fundamental if the work of the schools is to progress.

Consultants from the district's special services as well as consultants and resource persons from other school systems, college staffs, and persons competent in various areas of human endeavor are brought into the project or event as the need may indicate. Consultants and resource persons assist the staff personnel in an in-service capacity so that staff personnel may actually change their own behavior as the learnings are taking place. Only in such a manner will curriculum changes eventually emerge as improvements in learning experience for children in the classroom. Consultants and resource persons are oriented to their responsibilities by the assistant superintendent in charge of instruction and guidance. A working relationship between staff personnel and the consultants and resource persons is established and communication is effected.

LAY PARTICIPATION

The cooperation of specially qualified lay groups in a consultant capacity and in certain portions of the curriculum is desirable. A very real problem, however, is the mistaken assumption of competency in areas outside the field of the contributor. Many lay individuals volunteer for activity, but without prearranged criteria such a system may lead to displacement of learning material. In Bellevue, however, laymen are welcome participants in an advisory capacity, in assisting in the development of surveys and in obtaining questionnaire responses from various segments of the community. The Citizens' School Advisory Council has been established as a liaison agency in the initiation, conduct, and coordination of these endeavors. The school, the community, parents, churches, and other groups and individuals—all participate in the basic educational program for each child. The ultimate test of all guidance and instructional work is the degree to which children are actually affected in each classroom.

STAFF ORGANIZATION

As in the days when *The Bellevue Story* was written, every member of the school staff has a role to play if the total guidance and instructional program is to achieve maximum benefits for all concerned. If the best guidance and instructional program is to be developed, it is necessary to build an efficient organization. (See chart on p. 281.)

Criteria for the development of staff organization which have been used in Bellevue include the following:

1. Total staff participation must be attractive.
2. Specific organization for action must be developed.

3. All individuals and groups must work on phases of the guidance and instructional program only in relation to the total program. (A good program continually maintains balance and understanding at all levels.)

4. Every staff member must feel a responsibility for sharing in the success of the total guidance and instructional program.

5. Leadership must be a developmental process.

6. The jobs to be done must be carefully analyzed. (Specific goals to be achieved must be set forth so that all teachers and principals are kept informed and enabled to make creative contributions.

Current district thinking emphasizes the unity of guidance and instructional activity. The purpose of guidance is the development of each individual pupil to the maximum of his ability, and instructional services fulfill their obligation when they meet the needs for individual guidance. Hence, the unitary nature of guidance and instructional services is personified in the assistant superintendent in charge of guidance and instructional services.

THE BUILDING PRINCIPAL

The building principal remains the key figure in the development of the guidance and instructional program. He continues to be the professional leader in his school building. There is ample evidence that, with able leadership on the part of the building principal, the building faculty will work cooperatively toward the fulfillment of the objectives of the educational program. The principal must be ever-growing in his job, no matter how broad his experience or extensive his training, because no man can assume that he is fully prepared for his task.

Each teacher in the school unit, as a member of the Bellevue staff, has a part to play in the development of the total program. A genuine attempt is made to utilize the special abilities and experiences of each staff member when needed, and to give each teacher adequate recognition for his contributions. Similarly, the abilities of the district administrators and special service personnel are continuously focused on the improvement of instruction through involvement in the planning of the guidance and instructional program.

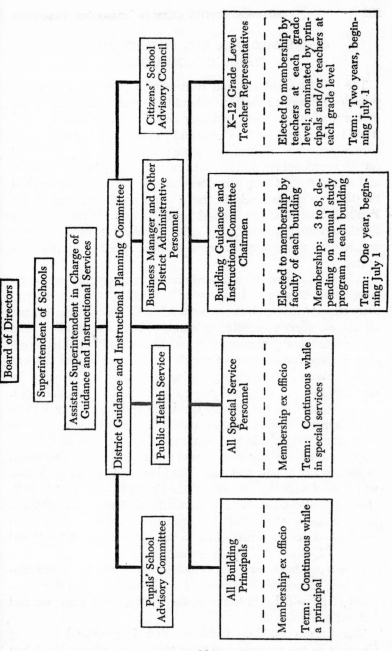

STAFF ORGANIZATION, BELLEVUE PUBLIC SCHOOL SYSTEM

THE GUIDANCE AND INSTRUCTIONAL
PLANNING COMMITTEE

The district Guidance and Instructional Planning Committee provides a means to combine all guidance and instructional committee work into a single working unit. From the chart (p. 281) it can be seen that the Guidance and Instructional Planning Committee comprises all building principals (ex officio), all special service personnel (ex officio), chairmen of the Building Guidance and Instructional Committees, teacher representatives for each of the thirteen grade levels in the schools, representatives of the Pupils' School Advisory Committee, and representation from the district's central administrative office. It selects its own chairman and recording secretary for terms of office specified by the committee.

With such organization a maximum amount of time can be reserved for planning and improving instruction, which is the primary obligation of each classroom teacher. Communication among all staff members concerning guidance and curriculum efforts and progress is thereby greatly enhanced. Greater opportunity, moreover, for the involvement of pupils and citizens in the district's guidance and instructional planning is further implemented by means of the organizational pattern which is shown in the chart.

The function of the district Guidance and Instructional Planning Committee is to receive and discuss all recommendations from either individuals or committees or groups, and to delegate responsibilities and organize special committees for specific study, experimentation, and planning. The plans and recommendations which meet with the approval of the Committee are sent to individual Building Guidance and Instructional Planning Committees. If the majority of the building committees approve, the recommendations are then passed on to the superintendent for Board action and approval if this is germane.

An attempt has been made to include administrative representation from all schools and from all grade levels so that the viewpoint of all will be in terms of the thirteen-year guidance and instructional program.

The various Building Guidance and Instructional Planning Committees are composed of three to eight members, depending on the requirements of each faculty's annual study program. The building committee elects its own chairman who serves on the district body. A recording secretary is elected so that a report of each building committee meeting may be made available to all teachers and other interested personnel throughout the district. The chairmen of the district and the Building Guidance and Instructional Planning Committees are responsible for developing the agenda for each meeting and for assuring that communication of the work of the committees is accomplished.

Whereas the Bellevue plan of organization makes it possible for action to be initiated by pupils, citizens, special committees, teachers, principals, and the members of the district office staff, final decisions on all action and suggested policies affecting districtwide progress come from a simple majority vote of all the building faculties. Each building's faculty is entitled to one vote in such action. A building faculty is defined as that group of instructors which is under the jurisdiction of a given principal.

COORDINATING IMPROVEMENT EFFORTS

The district Guidance and Instructional Planning Committee proposed that only one workshop at a time should be held in the district. The problem of conflicts in times of meetings was raised and the following schedule was proposed: Monday, workshops; Tuesday, faculty meetings and building projects; Wednesday, grade-level meetings; Thursday, districtwide curriculum meetings; Friday, reserved for pupil activities. Meetings involving staff members from various schools are cleared by a central committee so that conflicts can be avoided. Participation on district committees takes precedence over professional committees such as those designated by the local education association.

One of the cogent reasons for the development of the district committee was the abundance of enthusiasm and activity that had been prevalent for a number of years in the guidance and instructional areas. Unbridled and unorganized enthusiasm and effort, however, may produce duplication and inefficiency. A centrally coordinated organization avoids this.

Under the Bellevue plan of organization total staff participation is enlisted; the time of teachers is saved; maximum progress is possible; channels are defined for all individuals to choose in developing the program; the district committee insures the proper maintenance of relationships within the total program; each teacher feels a definite responsibility, as well as opportunity, to contribute; more leadership is called forth than in the usual organization; and the selection of individuals for special assignments is suggested by many different persons rather than a limited few.

With better organization it is possible to obtain budgeted funds for substitute teachers when certain problem needs arise and studies are necessary. Teachers cannot be expected to spend hours of their own time working on problems that may not affect them directly. The people of Bellevue understand the important provisions which guidance and instructional services demand.

Every member of the school staff has a role to play in the guidance and instructional program. Widespread community participation is encouraged as is total staff participation. Specific organization for action is necessary. Every attempt has been made to have all staff members feel a responsibility for sharing in the success of the entire program of curriculum improvement.

Leadership must be a maturing process; hence, the emergence of leadership within programs is carefully encouraged. The wide range of opportunities for active participation in the program provides many circumstances calling for the exercise of leadership. Individuals who demonstrate organizational skill and effective leadership in curriculum improvement projects are marked for consideration as candidates for promotion. Such persons are enabled to experience a variety of leadership responsibilities, and to forge in practice the leadership skills necessary for positions of wider responsibility within the school system.

PROCEDURES AND TECHNIQUES

Varied procedures and techniques of curriculum improvement are used for different purposes. These include group planning, staff meetings, workshops, demonstrations, case conferences, intervisitation, exchange teachers, demonstration teaching, field trips, experimentation and research, curriculum revision, bulletins and handbooks, an instructional materials center, a professional newsletter, a summer study consultive service, and encouragement of travel. Work committees, workshops, study groups, clinics, institutes, and research studies are employed. The liaison between the school district and various institutions of higher learning has been notable. Members of the staff affect college affairs through participation on boards of trustees, through summer teaching assignments and special lecture activities. Also significant has been the development of a Psychological Services Program at one college specifically to meet the needs of the Bellevue school district.

Presently, most staff participation and curriculum improvement activities are conducted in after-school hours or during the summer. Selected personnel, such as those on the counseling staff, special services, and administrators, are tendered extended contracts. Arrangements have been made to use a part of this extended contract time in curriculum improvement activities and projects. Physical facilities for such purposes will be improved with the establishment of a new administrative center. An excellent district curriculum library is being developed under the direction of the Instructional Services Office. Resources for curriculum improvement are made available and are considered as necessary budget obligations. Efforts are made to develop the skills, insights, and understandings essential for effective participation in curriculum improvement by the learning experiences gained while on committees; by various in-service activities and classes; and by the utilization of communication through faculty meetings, district-wide meetings, memoranda, and bulletins.

COMMUNICATION OF ACTIVITIES

The district Guidance and Instructional Planning Committee, along with the various building Guidance and Instructional Planning Committees, provides the vehicle for communication of curriculum improvement activities. These activities are reported in a monthly publication entitled *Keeping Abreast*. In addition, various administrative, faculty, and special service meetings further communicate curriculum improvement activities. Grade-level meetings throughout the district also increase the possibility of communication although, without proper guidance, grade-level committees may become an avenue of communication of poor instructional practices as well as excellent ones.

The development of guides, courses of study, minutes, memoranda, the districtwide bulletin, and reports of meetings are used to communicate information wherever pertinent. When policy is affected by a Board of Education decision, it is the Superintendent's responsibility to communicate such action effectively to all members of the staff concerned.

PREPARING INSTRUCTIONAL MATERIALS

Instructional materials and their development and use are important auxiliary tools to planning. The statement has often been made that as soon as a document is completed it is time for revision to begin.

Careful criteria for the selection and preparation of materials are emphasized in the district. The use and placement of materials are subjected to testing and evaluation when possible. For example, the placement of various experiences in the recently developed science guides was established after a study of the knowledge and readiness of pupils for the various learning activities. This resulted in lowering, by approximately one grade level, many of the science experiences which were previously provided at a higher grade.

In the past four years the office of the assistant superintendent in charge of guidance and instructional services has developed guides in reading, personnel records, handwriting, spelling, junior and senior high school English, arithmetic, speech therapy, community resources, and science. Art, music, physical education, senior high school social studies, and kindergarten guides are in process. The Bellevue school district has pioneered in the use and development of educational television. Plans for the use of language laboratories in the elementary as well as the secondary schools are under consideration.

EVALUATION OF LEARNING

Evaluation is seen as an integral part of every learning situation. The learner has a central role in evaluation with the instructor and parents also playing important parts in the process. The district leadership places high value on an increased command of the skills, concepts, attitudes, information and ways of behaving which are required to deal efficiently and competently with the persistent situations which are a part of living. Parents and other laymen interested in curriculum improvement do not always agree that these long-range goals are valid and tend to see specific and short-term answers to both general and specific problems which may, in themselves, be ill-defined.

Fundamental to evaluation is the stating of goals in terms of the changed behavior of the learner. The value of learning a fact or having an experience cannot be perceived unless evidence is given of the learner's ability to apply the knowledge, generalizations, and the skills he has acquired. This basic, central, and specific core of any evaluative process is too frequently missed by modern critics of the educational scene. They would substitute the acquiring of facts in a catechistic sense for evidence of changed behavior. For example, there is currently much discussion in the Bellevue school district about the value of the home arts course.

Evaluation is a continuous process and is based on evidence which is gathered as teachers and learners work together, and as parents, other laymen, and administrators together consider the educational program in developing behavioral responses of children and youth.

An overwhelming professional problem, however, is the appropriate accumulation of data and their integration so that consistent evidence of progress in an objective sense is properly pursued. Emphasis is placed on all the modern scientific tools of testing and appraisal. Comparative data, such as those from the Educational Testing Service tests and numerous other devices, are utilized. Careful record keeping, especially in the elementary school years, has been maintained. Pupil progress is reported by written records and parent-teacher conferences, as well as through general explanations of goals to be pursued. Nevertheless, there is a keen awareness that more needs to be done than is being done. A director of research, properly trained and oriented, is a desperately needed personnel addition in the district.

In addition to the foregoing types of evidence of pupil achievement and growth and the development of the materials alluded to on page 286, there are many other indications of the vitality and effectiveness of Bellevue's organized plan of school program improvement. Studies to improve instruction are being made along many lines: arithmetic teaching aids; the Continuous Growth Program (an experiment in ungraded primary classes based on reading achievement); elementary school guidance; the rapid learner; outdoor education; teacher-parent conferences; elementary and secondary school integrated classroom programs; the development of a written philosophy of education for the Bellevue school system; a study of the junior college program in extended secondary education; expansion of adult education; the establishment of junior-senior high school counseling and guidance services; follow-up studies of junior and senior high school students; establishment of an annual art and science exposition; scholarship counseling at the senior high school level; the operation of a summer school; and improvement in the methods of textbook selection and warehousing.

FUTURE ACTIVITIES

Attempting to forecast the major emphases in curriculum improvement activities in future years is rather difficult. If the reactionary attitude of a vocal minority of laymen becomes a successful force in curriculum improvement, program development in the Bellevue district, as in many others, will be in for some very difficult times. Of major concern are the problems of growth. As a system grows communication becomes increasingly difficult, and real participation may be reduced to a myth.

Widespread interest, probably a reflection of concerns of our times, is shown in the social sciences at this moment. Improvement in the organizational pattern of the elementary school, particularly a rethinking of the approach to the teaching of arithmetic will also be emphasized. Theoretically speaking (and what is more practical than sound theory?), secondary education must seek ever-widening possibilities for the integration of information. The definition of these objectives for the secondary school must be in terms of those changed behaviors that are appropriate in men and women of the twentieth century.

The hysteria which reached a high point shortly after the launching of the first Sputnik resulted in a pressure to alter the content of the school program to make room for more mathematics and science. There was a strong hue and cry to eliminate courses in the humanities and social sciences which were described by some as the "frills" of public education.

At this point, it appears that some Americans are "running scared." Bellevue seeks to avoid ill-conceived "crash programs" by organized and continuous evaluation and planning, to provide its children with a balanced, constantly improving learning program.

THE INSTRUCTIONAL PROGRAM

Bellevue has made a number of assumptions about the kind of instructional program that should be available for its school children. Some of these are:

1. We respect the individual dignity of each child in our community and we earnestly seek the realization of his individual potentialities through our educational endeavors.

2. Each individual pupil is the focus of all our educational efforts and his purposes and progress are more important than buildings or teachers, textbooks or subjects to be studied.

3. Education is a community effort involving parents, churches, teachers, youth organizations, and other individuals and groups.

4. The educational plan for children determines the nature of the financial and building programs.

5. All administrative activity recognizes the primacy of the relationship between the teacher and the pupils assigned to him for guidance and instruction.

6. The educational program is designed to develop pupil understandings so that they may change their ways of doing things. The instructional program is dedicated to helping pupils comprehend their heritage from the past, understand the present, and be prepared to live in the unknown future.

Out of these assumptions have developed certain observations, some of which are:

1. All children and their instruction are inseparable both in terms of concepts and procedures.

2. In developing personnel practices the guidance of each child should entail the use of the best procedures that have been made available by the science and art of education and by psychological research.

3. The curriculum includes all the experiences the child has while attending school. The curriculum, although affected appreciably by subject-matter organization as perceived by specialists, is not identical with subject-matter organization as defined by scholars.

4. The guidance of each child into self-realized acceptance of himself in the role of contributing citizen in our democracy and in the world is a primary function of all our services and efforts.

5. Curriculum is a fundamental tool of guidance activity.

6. The instructional services of the schools include all the personnel, environmental influences, and materials that will help assure each pupil enriched opportunities to acquire changed behavior and to attain the objectives of the Bellevue public schools' educational program.

7. A school district which identifies and appropriately serves deviate behavior of pupils also identifies and serves normal behavior of pupils.

8. Good guidance and good instruction will emphasize individual variation in performance which will appear increasingly significant as the pupil progresses through the program.

It is toward these ends that the Bellevue school district's instructional and guidance program moves.

APPRAISING CURRICULUM
IMPROVEMENT PROGRAMS

12

IMPROVING PROGRAM QUALITY

PART I

A SUMMARY AND GUIDE

THE PROGRAM descriptions in Chapters 5 through 11 include a variety of practices and procedures used by schools to improve the quality of their educational offerings. Although each of these programs is unique in its design and operation, a number of common threads run through the accounts, having reference to the initiation, structure, and operation of curriculum improvement activities. From these it is possible to formulate guidelines for those concerned with programs for improving the quality of education in public schools. Illustrative practices drawn from the foregoing descriptions of curriculum improvement programs help to make these guidelines more meaningful and helpful.

1. Curriculum improvement is viewed as a process of changing teachers' perceptions and teaching behavior. The degree of vigor with which curriculum improvement is undertaken in a school system is to a large extent dependent on the insights and competence of the system's administrative staff. The chief administrative officer and his staff set the tone for the improvement program and determine the organizational framework within which it operates. Administrative decisions are, in turn, affected by the staff's concept of the curriculum and by their understandings of the process by which it is changed. The conceptions of curriculum and of the nature of the improvement process influence many of the administrative choices with respect to organization, techniques, and procedures.

The concept of curriculum which apparently underlies the improvement efforts of the programs described herein is that the curriculum consists of all the experiences children have under the guidance of the local school building personnel, acting within a clearly stated framework of systemwide objectives and policies. In Bellevue, the definition of the curriculum "includes all the experiences which the children and teachers have together under the auspices of the school." Similarly, in Lewis County, "the curriculum means any and all experiences which affect the development of the pupil as a self-directing, thinking, responsible citizen." With such a definition, it is natural to find considerable flexibility in the instructional program. In Denver, "the program of instruction . . . is flexible from school to school and even from classroom to classroom. That is, beyond the basic program, instruction is adapted according to such factors as the pupils, the parents and community, the facilities of the building, and the size of the school."

Under a broad conception of curriculum, improvement is a complex and difficult task. The most prevalent operating definition of curriculum has been that it consists of specified subject matter to be learned by pupils. Changing such a curriculum is primarily a matter of changing the subject matter. This could be done for the entire school system by an "expert" or by a small, well qualified group. To improve the quality of the learning experiences in his classroom, however, a teacher must acquire motivations, insights, skills and understandings which cannot be communicated solely by rewritten courses of study, by supervisory bulletins, by verbal exhortations, or explanations. No expert or group can change a teacher's personal perceptions or his basic pattern of instructional operation; he can only be helped to do this for himself. It is for this reason that the Dade County "Guidelines for Curriculum Improvement" include such statements as:

> Curriculum improvement is basically a social change which results from growth within people who cooperatively participate in the development of the educational program. . . . The participation of the classroom teacher in the curriculum improve-

ment activities is indispensable to the effectiveness of the educational program.

The premium placed upon such widespread participation is evident throughout all the accounts. In Denver, the educational authorities operate on the assumption that "an instructional program or practice or change is in fact put into operation only to the extent that the principal and the teachers in the school see a need for it, understand it, recognize its value, and undertake energetically and intelligently to use it."

Teacher participation in curriculum improvement activities is based on sound psychological principles. The improvement of any educational program requires continuous learning on the part of the professional staff of better approaches to the quality of learning experiences.

2. Extensive participation by all staff members in program planning and operation is encouraged through widespread use of committee structure. Extensive teacher participation is provided for in the organizational patterns of all the improvement programs described. No difference between current curriculum development programs and those of earlier generations is more clearly evident than the difference in their organization. When curriculum development was conceived of as course-of-study preparation or revision, organization was simple, centralized, and involved relatively few people. The programs described in this volume are characterized by broad participation, attempting to enlist the thinking of the entire instructional personnel. Each program is centrally coordinated, but there is considerable decentralization or diffusion of authority and responsibility for curriculum planning.

Participation is both direct and indirect. Directly, teachers, principals, and others participate in appraising the adequacy and needs of the educational program, in defining objectives, in developing instructional methods, and in providing useful materials. Such participation is aimed at helping staff to develop a commitment to the planning which emerges; to acquire valuable insights from one another from the process of forging new approaches to learning; and to gain personal satisfaction from contributing to a worthwhile enterprise.

Indirect participation is provided for by such means as the ICP

Steering Committee of the Illinois Curriculum Program, the County and Area Curriculum Councils of Dade County, the Area Committees on Instructional Policy in Denver and the Executive Boards of those Councils, Galena Park's Central Curriculum Council, Bellevue's District Guidance and Instructional Planning Committee, and by the numerous special-purpose committees alluded to throughout all the program descriptions. The central planning and coordinating committees provide for representation of all staff members in the formulation of systemwide policy. Presumably, teachers participate directly in discussion of the issues upon which policy is formulated. Such participation takes place among the representatives' "constituents" in staff meetings within the building units.

Good planning is, of course, a *sine qua non* of any effective program of curriculum development. The many kinds of careful planning which take place at all administrative levels are described throughout the preceding accounts of curriculum development programs. Central office personnel engage in continuous planning of the over-all program. In some instances, this takes place in meetings of an "administrative cabinet," consisting of persons with systemwide responsibilities. In smaller systems, meetings include the building principals as well.

It is important to note, however, that planning is not the special preserve of central planning and coordinating bodies. In every program described, planning activities permeate the entire school system and involve personnel at all levels. This is consistent with the concept of curriculum as guided experiences of children. To do an insightful job of improving the quality of educational experiences, teachers need to participate actively in continuous curriculum appraisal and planning. There is growing evidence that teachers recognize this and desire some part in the planning process.[1]

The functions of planning are far from simple. Not only must instructional leaders plan but they must also plan to plan—that is, make possible and facilitate the cooperative efforts of personnel

[1] A study of teachers in twenty school systems from all sections of the United States clearly revealed that they desire participation in determining curriculum objectives, content, and materials. See Chiranji Lal Sharma, "Practices in Decision-Making as Related to Satisfaction in Teaching" (Unpublished doctoral dissertation, Chicago: University of Chicago, 1955).

at all levels of the school system. From broad-based planning comes better educational experiences for children, a curriculum characterized by consistency with diversity, and enhanced staff morale.

In addition to the overarching planning and policy-formulating activities, a variety of "working committees" are described. These committees address themselves to specific tasks in the improvement of the educational program. In reviewing the several accounts, we can identify several types of such committees: vertical committees, horizontal committees, special subject committees and *ad hoc* special-purpose committees.

Vertical committees are groups dealing with problems comprising a range of grade levels. In Dade County, such a committee addressed itself to the improvement of guidance in all grades, while another worked upon sequence in the development of science concepts in grades one to six. In Bellevue a group of such committees, consisting of representatives from all grades, worked on the task of improving the sequence of offerings in the elementary schools.

Horizontal committees are those which are concerned with problems at a given grade level. Such a committee was the Twelfth-grade Social Studies Committee in Dade County. This committee developed proposals for improvement of the objectives and organization of the twelfth-year social studies program, which resulted in a new curriculum guide. The Galena Park account tells of released time for grade-level meetings of teachers.

Special-subject committees may be either of the vertical or horizontal type. For example, the Bellevue vertical committees, concerned with learning sequence, were organized by subjects. The Dade County Social Studies Committee, referred to immediately above, is an example of a horizontal special-subject committee.

Ad hoc committees are constituted to deal with aspects of the instructional program which do not fit into the established organization. In the Illinois program, an *ad hoc* committee was appointed to devise operational plans for a program suggested by the ICP Steering Committee. Other special purposes for which such committees may be formed include formulating recommendations for the scheduling of curriculum improvement activities; developing plans for a program to improve audio-visual methods of instruction; gathering data to determine whether to work on a program to provide television instruction; clarifying the functions of the schools in contributing to the reduction of the incidence of juvenile delinquency in the school district.

Direct participation is also provided for in the meetings of the faculties of the individual schools. Indeed, most of the accounts revealed clearly that the local school building staff is the functional unit of participation in improving the quality of the educational offering. It is the local staff's understanding of, and commitment to, proposed changes and improvements that will determine whether and how the improvements will be incorporated into classroom practice. Accepting the viewpoint that the curriculum is what happens in classrooms rather than that which is in course-of-study outlines, direct participation is then essential. Provisions for all levels of participation are well illustrated in the preceding seven accounts of curriculum improvement efforts.

3. Proposals for curriculum improvement can emerge from almost anywhere in the school system or community.   A variety of techniques for channeling suggestions to the point of decision-making has evolved. Most procedures involve some form of organized face-to-face discussions (by teachers, supervisors, administrators, counselors, and community members) of needs, and specific avenues for communicating the results of deliberations to those responsible for initiating and administering the curriculum development program.

Needs and purposes are ascertained in different ways, with a number of the descriptions emphasizing the desirability of providing many channels for communicating problems requiring study and improvement. In Denver, for example, central office personnel meet annually with the principal and instructional leaders of each school staff to review the program and identify future points to be emphasized in curriculum work. In some instances, community leaders and parent representatives are also present. As a result of these conferences, a publication titled *Points of Emphasis* is prepared to guide individual building and systemwide curriculum improvement activities.

In some systems school personnel may be enlisted in a self survey of the program. One such survey is described in the

Galena Park account. Other school districts, such as Bellevue, have enlisted the assistance of outside experts and agencies. In Lewis County an extensive study of pupils' needs was made by means of a reaction inventory complemented by a follow-up study of graduates. In addition, the principals met in conference with the central office staff for clarification of instructional goals and their implications for the existing curriculum.

Almost all accounts referred to the use of standardized evaluation instruments to ascertain aspects of the instructional program in need of attention. In Newton there is not only increasing use of standardized tests, but of systematic analysis of results. Among other purposes, this is necessary to appraise the success of the experimental programs which are part of the improvement process. In the Galena Park account, an extensive and comprehensive minimum testing program is outlined. As part of its "quality control," Denver makes widespread use of such tests in both its Minimum Testing and Survey Testing Programs. Test results are subjected to both an item and an error analysis. The former helps to identify weaknesses and strengths in areas of learning, while the latter helps reveal needed emphases within areas of learning.

In testing programs, care must be exercised to prevent the tests from imposing objectives or limitations on the instructional program. Teachers can easily slip into the error of overemphasizing the teaching of the objective facts and skills which these instruments test for, to the neglect of equally important learnings which are neither readily nor validly evaluated by any of the available standardized instruments. The seven programs described herein seem to attempt to avoid this in at least two ways. First, the staffs identify the goals they wish the instructional program to achieve; then they seek instruments and techniques to appraise their achievement. Second, it will be noted that most of the tests are given early in the school year, so their results can be used in improving the instructional program. In other words, they are used diagnostically, not as means to pass judgment upon children.

In the curriculum programs described, many channels of communication flowing in all directions are provided. There is both vertical and horizontal communication up and down the "line" as well as definite "fields of communication" arranged for in the planning together by persons from all levels of a system's organization.

In seeking to identify program improvement needs, suggestions may emanate from any person in the system. In Denver, the three major sources from which ideas are capitalized include "the grass roots or general interest among professional staff or the community at large; instructional leaders in status positions; and the continuous program of curriculum development whenever there comes a time when it is desirable to bring up to date the instructional program in a given area." Free flow of communication is, of course, only partly a function of organization. Other factors combine to bring about the climate which facilitates effective communication. Still, the nature of the organization can do much to help or hinder communication, and can help channel it into productive accomplishment.

The supervisor is viewed, in many systems, as an important agent in "up-the-line communication" in identifying instructional improvement needs. By visiting many schools and classrooms, talking with teachers and other staff personnel, the supervisor plays a key role in identifying and transmitting program improvement needs to the central office. Throughout the foregoing accounts there is ample recognition of the attention given to facilitating thoughtful communication in identifying curriculum improvement needs.

4. The local school building is generally viewed as the basic unit of participation in program development. All the school systems whose programs are described in this volume seem to be committed in some degree to this point of view. For example, in Denver, "the principal's considerable authority and responsibility mean that curriculum changes are made a part of classroom practice at different times, in different degree, and in different manner from school to school and sometimes from classroom to classroom." Similar statements will be found in almost all the other accounts. While all are apparently committed to a "broken front" approach to curriculum development in which each school determines its own emphases and proceeds at its own rate, definite administrative leadership is provided in seeking out systemwide and local school needs.

In practically every instance, the primary importance of the local school building faculty in curriculum improvement is

stressed. Perhaps this is most formally recognized in the School
Curriculum Councils of Dade County, but a persistent refrain
runs through all accounts, emphasizing the responsibility of the
school building principal and his faculty for curriculum planning
and development.

**5. Systemwide coordination of curriculum improvement activi-
ties is essential, particularly where the single school has considerable autonomy.** Good coordination is essential (a) for attaining reasonable consistency in objectives and content throughout the system, while providing flexibility for adaptations to local
needs and conditions; (b) for avoiding overlapping and wasteful
effort in the improvement program; (c) for developing and maintaining a suitable learning sequence.

Although the local building staffs have considerable responsibility for the improvement of the school's educational program,
each of the systems represented in this volume emphasizes the
necessity for systemwide coordination of curriculum improvement
efforts. In Dade County the belief is expressed that the purpose
of "systemwide curriculum organization should be to provide
guidance to, and coordination of, the total program." In Bellevue,
the District Guidance and Instructional Planning Committee coordinates curriculum work: "An attempt has been made to include
administrative representation from all schools and from all grade
levels so that the viewpoint of all will be in terms of the thirteen-
year guidance and instructional program offered by the district."

Most of the school systems report providing for coordination by
means of a representative body. In Bellevue, districtwide coordination of planning is handled through the District Guidance and
Instructional Planning Committee; in Denver, by the Executive
Board of the Committees on Instructional Policy. In the Illinois
program, there is the ICP Steering Committee with representatives from professional, industrial, agricultural, service, labor and
business organizations, and public and private educational institutions. Dade County has a County Curriculum Council, and
Galena Park a Central Curriculum Council composed of faculty
members representing all levels. In Lewis County, coordination
is provided by central office personnel who arrange meetings of
key personnel (such as building principals and instructional super-

visors) and organize other systemwide activities and schedules. In the larger school systems, bigness is combated by the establishment of regional planning groups, with representatives from the individual schools. Denver's Neighborhood Committees on Instructional Policy and Dade County's Area Councils are examples. Each school system has worked out a plan which its personnel deems most suitable to its goals and circumstances. One of the chief reasons for their success is undoubtedly the care with which the efforts have been organized to assure effective coordination.

6. Responsibility for general guidance of program improvement efforts is assigned to an individual or an office while emergent leadership of specific aspects is encouraged. Desirable as broad participation is, responsibility for synthesizing the total program must be vested in some individual or department. Otherwise, the old axiom that "what is everybody's responsibility is nobody's responsibility" may be apparent. In each of the programs described one person is charged with responsibility for the entire program. Other individuals in the organization have specific assignments within the organization and overlapping authority or responsibility are guarded against. In all programs, the principal is assigned considerable responsibility for instructional improvement in his own building, and central office specialists work through him so as to reduce to a minimum the likelihood of conflict of authority and responsibility.

In Bellevue, for example, "each principal is considered the director of guidance and curriculum within his school community and is assisted in his work by the knowledge and direction of special service and central administrative staff." In Newton, "responsibility for the coordination of these specialized central office services within each school rests with the principal." In Galena Park, "those engaged in coordination enter school buildings only with the principal's knowledge and consent. Unless previous arrangements are made, a coordinator will not visit a school when the principal is away." Clear understanding on the part of each person of his role and responsibility in the organization is essential for effective working relationships.

In a relatively small system with just a few central office personnel such as that of Lewis County (although the geographical area covered is extensive) responsibility may be kept in the hands of the superintendent or the assistant superintendent. In larger school districts a member of the superintendent's staff is generally delegated this responsibility: Director of Curriculum and Instructional Services (Bellevue); Director of Instruction (Newton). This officer is usually directly responsible to the superintendent who, in turn, is responsible for the entire educational program of the school system. In the Illinois program, responsibility is assigned to the Director of the Program.

In addition to assigning definite responsibility for the leadership of the total program, and making clear that the building principal is responsible for the improvement program in his own school, each of the programs provides for what might be called "emergent leadership." In the conduct of the various components of the improvement enterprise (e.g., committees, grade groups, study groups, coordinating and planning groups) opportunity is provided for many staff members to exercise leadership functions. In Bellevue, for example, "the emergence of leadership within programs is carefully encouraged. The wide range of opportunities for active participation in the program provides many circumstances calling for the exercise of leadership. . . . Such persons are enabled to experience a variety of leadership responsibilities, and to forge in practice the leadership skills necessary to positions of wider responsibility within the school system." Similarly in the Newton program it is observed that, "Leadership is where you find it, not where you bestow it. A wise status leader is one who is quick to recognize a functional leader and is able and willing to work with him. Opportunities to display leadership capacity are many—in the activities of the Teachers' Federation, the PTAs, the committee structure of the schools." Thus, a well-conceived program not only designates clearly the responsibilities of the status leaders; it also provides for the identification and nurturing of leadership ability throughout the staff.

7. Each school system's organizational pattern is related to its size, concept of curriculum, nature of its personnel resources, and objectives of program development. Several of the accounts in this volume include the observation that the organization and conduct of the curriculum improvement activities are well suited to the system under discussion, but would not necessarily be appropriate to any other system. Although we can make generalizations which apply to most or all the programs, the various authors stress that each system's efforts were tailored to fit indigenous concepts and conditions. In other words, it would be a fallacy to attempt any prescriptions for the organization and conduct of a program, but from these accounts one may harvest a wealth of suggestions, and formulate guidelines such as those proposed here.

Although the seven accounts seem to reflect the concept that the curriculum consists of the learning experiences children undergo in school, this seems to have some differences in meaning from place to place. In the Lewis County description, for example, considerable effort is placed on ascertaining pupils' needs, problems, and viewpoints. An earnest attempt is made to develop instructional program and evaluation procedures in terms of behavioral goals. The following statement from the Lewis County description is illustrative:

> For example, one of the goals selected was: "the pupil should be able to assume an adequate citizenship role." The goal was examined in terms of a ninth-grade pupil, and involved delineation of what could be reasonably expected of a fourteen-year-old boy, i.e., what kinds of behavior should the school expect of him? Details of classroom experience were described and their meanings explored . . . opportunities for more extended experiences were explored as the group sought for behavioral outcomes and more specific types of performance than those limited by textbook knowledge. The group kept asking, "Is this goal something which can be observed and evaluated?"

Such an orientation inevitably is reflected in the nature of the improvement program. Activities in Lewis County included follow-up study of former students, gathering data on problems of present students, and analysis of students' study habits so that they might be helped to improve this important area of behavior in different classes and for different purposes. Throughout the program, there is heavy emphasis on taking account of children's needs in program improvement and on development of more effective behavior.

Some of the other descriptions seem to focus more upon children's problems and needs in subject-matter learning. In such programs more use is made of standardized subject-matter tests, many committees are organized around the improvement of curriculum guides in specific subjects (such as mathematics or social studies), and considerable emphasis is placed on devising interesting experiences which are related to children's maturity levels; experiences which will illuminate, enrich, make more meaningful and arouse interest in certain categories of subject matter. One can easily see that the organization of a program oriented to these objectives would differ from the Lewis County organization.

A number of differences are attributable to size. Organization in small-school systems can be simple, and often gains by its informality. Systems of the size of Dade County and Denver, on the other hand, of necessity must devise a more complex and formal organization in order to provide for broad participation, for working groups sufficiently small to be effective, and to facilitate communication and coordination.

Furthermore, larger school systems tend to have more supervisory and specialized personnel. The organization and operation of a system which is well provided with such resources will be designed to capitalize them as leaders in workshops and study groups, and as consultants to faculty groups and to planning and production committees.

The Illinois Curriculum Program is a good illustration of the relationship between personnel resources and program. Because of its small staff, considerable use had to be made of voluntary leadership and resources throughout the state. The limited resources were seen in some respects as an advantage: "Were the program to have a large full-time staff coupled with a large budget, it would run the very real danger of doing curriculum work *for* the schools instead of working *with* them and encouraging them to work with each other." The resulting organizational and operational patterns are directly related to this point of view and to the nature of the staff.

8. Lay participation is encouraged, with clear definition of its functions and limits. Every one of the seven accounts mentioned the involvement of laymen in some aspect of the improvement process. Various levels of involvement were discernible. Perhaps the simplest level is that of meeting with parents to inform them of reasons for, and characteristics of, the school's program. In Lewis County, the showing of "a series of ten films on behavior and child growth followed by discussion did much to increase parent understanding of the complexity of the modern school program." Other parents met for a series of ten discussions of the school program in relation to the needs of boys and girls.

A second level is that of soliciting information from parents or other laymen to assist in planning. In Newton, the PTA and professional staff cooperated in conducting an extensive survey of parent opinion concerning elementary and junior high school education, with the result that "much worthwhile information derived from the elementary survey has provided substance for PTA meetings in the schools. It also has pointed the way to a reconsideration of certain school policies." Denver, likewise, solicited layman reaction to a proposed social studies program; twenty thousand citizens took part in the discussions throughout the city.

A third level of involvement is afforded when laymen are invited to assist in some way in the school program. This may take the form of helping in the library, assisting in field trips, or in contributing special knowledge, skill or experience as a resource in classroom instruction.

Most of the accounts spoke of the participation of laymen in an advisory capacity. Newton conducted a "Little White House Conference" which eventuated in advisory recommendations. Galena Park, Bellevue and Denver enlist the help of citizen advisory committees. Such groups have as their function the making of recommendations concerning school system policy or objectives, but a clear distinction is made between their responsibility and that of the professional staff. In the description of the Illinois program, it was pointed out: "Over the state an increasingly large number of citizens' education councils are being set up in local school districts. These councils generally act in an advisory capacity to boards of education." In Bellevue the position concerning the role of laymen in the improvement program is that "Curriculum improvement is a general term and as such is sufficiently inclusive to incorporate those contributions which may be made by any member of the community who contributes to the improvement of teaching and learning. The way in which the curriculum is

organized and taught in the school system and within the classroom, however, should be reserved to the professional educator
who is qualified to translate curriculum needs into actual practice." The statement concerning the role of laymen in the Denver
program makes the distinction clear. "There are two points at
which Denver school people believe lay citizens can and should
take active part in curriculum development. The first point might
be described as lay citizens joining with school people to state
their aspirations for children and youth—what they hope will be
accomplished through education. The second point at which lay
citizens should help is in evaluation—giving judgment as to how
fully their aspirations are being realized." To accomplish these
objectives, lay members are included on program committees, lay
advisory committees may be organized for individual schools,
and discussions such as those described above are held. Denver
also conducts a triennial survey of public opinion to discern how
well the Denver populace believes the schools to be attaining their
objectives. The clear implication throughout most of these accounts is that the only laymen officially qualified to make educational policy decisions are members of the board of education in
their corporate capacity; and that decisions concerning specific
learning experiences, content, and instructional method are properly the province of professional educators.

**9. Experimentation is considered an integral part of the improve-
ment process.** In all the accounts there were descriptions of
experimentation of one kind or another. In the Galena Park program, "the application of scientific methods of problem-solving,
participation in the solution of problems by all who are concerned,
and testing of the solutions against the realities of the classroom
or school program" represent the kinds of activities which should
be promoted by those responsible for coordinating the program.
Experimentation was so much a part of the Illinois program that
research-training clinics were conducted for teachers. The effectiveness of these clinics was evaluated and "the evidence gathered
on practitioner research indicates that teachers can learn necessary
research techniques and put them to good use in a surprisingly
short period of time." The Newton account tells of experimentation with the use of television teaching techniques, with outdoor

education, with different patterns of staff utilization, with patterns of organization and grouping, and describes a study of the causes of underachievement and overachievement in reading. These are simply illustrative. In these and other accounts there were many descriptions of experimentation, and of data gathering of a research nature for program improvement purposes. Much of this activity is of the type commonly termed "action research," stemming from a point of view which maintains that people are most likely to change their behavior (in this case, teaching behavior) when they participate actively in attacking problems that are of direct concern to them.

10. Many kinds of administrative arrangements are made to provide time and resources for curriculum improvement. Practically all the procedures for carrying out plans and purposes described in Chapter 4 have been illustrated in the program descriptions and will not be dealt with again here. Essentially, the task of the instructional leader is to help select appropriate techniques and procedures and create the conditions which will facilitate their successful use.

From an administrative viewpoint, a major responsibility is that of providing the time and resources to achieve objectives. In the program descriptions preceding this chapter, there are many ways in which time was made available for curriculum development. Some accounts mention the utilization of substitute teachers to release regular teachers for curriculum work. The school day was sometimes shortened or, in some instances, the school was closed for an occasional entire day. The Newton and Dade County reports indicate that some qualified teachers are employed during summer vacation periods for curriculum work. In Newton, teachers may be transferred temporarily to the Division of Instruction in order to facilitate progress at strategic points in program development. In several of the systems it was found advantageous to schedule curriculum planning conferences prior to the opening and/or immediately after the close of the school year. Such conferences range from a few days to two weeks in length. In Newton and Bellevue, each afternoon in the week is specifically reserved for certain types of meetings. In Bellevue, for example, Monday is for workshops; Tuesday, for building faculty meetings and projects; Wednesday, for grade-level meetings; Thursday, for districtwide curriculum meetings; and Friday for pupil activities.

Well illustrated in these accounts are the ways used to provide personnel resources. In Denver, fruitful relationships were established with the University of Denver, the Horace Mann–Lincoln Institute of School Experimentation of Teachers College, Columbia University, and with the College Entrance Examination Board, so that resources from these organizations could assist with the curriculum program. Lewis County also worked with the Horace Mann–Lincoln Institute and the Citizenship Education Project of Columbia University's Teachers College. In addition to cooperating with the Citizenship Education Project, Galena Park used the services of the University of Houston and of the Texas Education Agency.

All these systems also employed specialized personnel to assist the staff in the improvement of the quality of the educational program. Guidance workers, curriculum specialists, writers, and resource consultants, both from within and from outside the school system, were reported in one or another of the program accounts. Also mentioned were various kinds of material resources, such as audio-visual materials, professional libraries, science materials centers, tests (including marking and analysis services), television and language laboratories. The administrative authorities have worked toward establishing conditions which will not only make possible, but will encourage, dedicated and creative effort toward improvement of the educational program.

11. Evaluation of the curriculum improvement program and activities is still a somewhat neglected area. The one aspect of the improvement process which is not well illustrated in the program descriptions in this volume is evaluation of the curriculum improvement program itself. It is true that there were evidences of program evaluation of some types. In the Illinois program, for example, workshop participants were asked to indicate their satisfaction or dissatisfaction with the workshop program, and to indicate reasons for their feelings, on a "Personal Classification Indicator," a form of postmeeting reaction sheet. The summary of the strengths and weaknesses of the Newton program includes evaluative judgments of the program. The Board of Trustees of the

Galena Park Independent School District has made proposals "for encouraging an evaluation of the present organization," although it is possible that this refers to evaluation of organization of the schools rather than of the organization of the improvement program. The accounts made numerous references to informal evaluations which used, as criteria, the productiveness of committees and working groups in compiling curriculum guides and resource materials; the amount of teacher participation in the program; and the number of innovations and improvements in the educational program resulting from the improvement activities.

Although there were many evidences of attention to evaluation of the different aspects of the instructional program (e.g., testing programs, studies of drop-outs, action research activities, surveys of public opinion), there was very little mention of deliberately planned and "built-in" measures by which the organization and operation of the improvement program could be evaluated. Almost all evaluation of this type is apparently casual and desultory.

Evaluation of the improvement program itself would seem to be as important for its improvement, as is evaluation of the learning program to the improvement of teaching and learning. Not only should the improvement efforts be related to program results (which is certainly important); they should also be subjected to evaluation against carefully devised criteria of good organization and procedures employed in furthering the improvement process. Some such criteria are presented in the checklist which follows. They are intended primarily to be suggestive to a school system undertaking to build its own criteria for assessing the improvement program.

PART II

CRITERIA FOR EVALUATING THE CURRICULUM IMPROVEMENT PROGRAM

THE most valid evaluation of any program for curriculum improvement is, of course, the degree to which it results in enhancing the quality of children's learning. It is difficult, however, to isolate the direct consequences of any one of the many factors which affect quality of learning. Hence, the evaluation of the curriculum improvement program must be primarily in terms of those characteristics which theory, experience, and research indicate to be effective and desirable in yielding better teaching and learning.

The criteria appearing below are of this type. They deal with the dimensions of program improvement and only indirectly with assessment of student learnings. They are intended to provide a guide to judging the effectiveness of a program for improving the quality of education.

They are suggestive only, for each school system must develop criteria suited to its philosophy and objectives. These criteria are derived from an analysis of the foregoing accounts of curriculum development programs, and from the experience and convictions of the authors, who believe that the more the following conditions and characteristics are present in a curriculum development program, the better it will be.

I. Scope and Objectives of the Program

1. *The program is comprehensive in scope, dealing with all aspects of the educational needs of the community served by the school system.*   Current conceptions of program improvement include attention not only to the content of learning, but to all factors which affect the environment for learning. Furthermore, a comprehensive approach is likely to avoid overemphasis of some aspects of the learning program and hasty crash programs result-

ing from contemporary pressures which may throw the program out of balance.

2. *The program improvement objectives—both short-range and long-term—are clarified to guide organization and activities.* The specific objectives to be attained by each activity—the aspects of the educational program to be upgraded and the means to accomplish this—are clearly stated.

3. *The concept which guides program improvement is that the curriculum consists of the experiences children have under the direction and guidance of the school; improving the quality of the program means improving the quality of those experiences.* With this viewpoint, curriculum improvement activities are designed to help teachers and other professional staff members improve their competence in fostering better quality learning experiences.

4. *The curriculum improvement program is based on the premise that educational quality will change only as the perceptions, attitudes, values, understandings, and skills of staff members change.* Such behavioral changes will take place only through active involvement on the part of the staff members in the planning of changes and programs they are expected to carry out in their classrooms.

5. *There is common direction and purpose to the separate components of the curriculum improvement program.* So that the many diverse activities and efforts may complement one another, they are related to common goals, thus fostering program consistency and contributing to unification of the educational program.

II. Initiating Program Improvement Activities

1. *Channels are provided for communicating curriculum problems to a central planning and coordinating group.* Significant curriculum problems and program needs may be identified in various ways by different individuals and groups. They are informed clearly of the means for bringing these to the attention of the central committee or group so that ideas may be capitalized, program balance maintained, and unnecessary duplication avoided.

2. *Materials are sent to individuals and groups to keep them abreast of new developments.* Publications of all types are examined and circulated for suggestions and information which might have program improvement implications. Central office supervisory personnel are assigned particular responsibility for systematic reviews of professional and instructional materials and for their being brought to the attention of the appropriate individual or group.

3. *Regular opportunities are provided for individuals and groups to have contact with new ideas and practices through conferences, professional meetings, and school visits.* Teachers, supervisors, and other staff members are encouraged and assisted in participating in many different kinds of activities which bring them into contact with sources of information.

4. *Periodic evaluation of learning and teaching are analyzed for leads to improving program quality.* Carefully selected standardized tests are included in a regular evaluation schedule to provide information about particular kinds of student achievements. Surveys are made to determine unmet educational needs as these relate to program improvement.

5. *Classroom and school conditions—e.g., climate for learning, personnel and material resources, teaching methodology—are appraised regularly.* Classroom practices and procedures are studied to gather pertinent information about the quality of the educational program. The quality, availability, and use of instructional resources (e.g., library, audio-visual materials, resource specialists, art supplies) are evaluated.

III. Administration of the Curriculum Improvement Program

1. *Trained leadership is provided for curriculum work.* Those responsible for the organization and conduct of the improvement program are provided with specific preparation in the principles and techniques of curriculum improvement and in the skills and understandings necessary to successful group leadership.

2. *General responsibility for all services related to curriculum and teaching is assigned to a single administrative officer or department.* Unless responsibility for the teaching and learning pro-

gram is clearly designated, problems of overlapping responsibility and duplication, with resultant damaging conflict, are almost certain to arise. One central office should be responsible for over-all direction and coordination.

3. *The central office staff provides resource specialists to assist in developing the programs of the various schools in the system.* Since "art is long and time is fleeting," teachers cannot be expected to be experts in all the aspects of the improvement program. Specialists in subject-matter, in method, in resource materials, experts in psychology and child development, all are essential to a well-conceived curriculum program. These may be regularly employed specialists and/or resource persons brought in from outside the school system.

4. *Supervision functions as a means of instructional improvement, part of the broader plan of the curriculum program.* Supervision is considered to include all those activities which are designed to help teachers improve the teaching-learning situation. Hence, supervision is an integral part of the total program of curriculum and instructional improvement.

5. *The individual school is the operational and planning unit for curriculum improvement.* Only as the individual building staffs participate in study of the learning program, and in the planning for ways to improve it, will teachers improve their perceptions and skills, and enrich the learning experiences of children of each unique school-community. All activities do not take place in the building itself, but the school is the basic unit for planning.

6. *The central office functions to encourage and aid the staff of individual schools to develop a unified curriculum adapted to the particular neighborhood and pupils served.* Although local autonomy and appropriate variation are encouraged, individual school improvement efforts are coordinated within a framework of systemwide policies and objectives. Attention is focused on the interrelationships among the various aspects of the curriculum (to avoid its unnatural fragmentation) and among the different parts of the improvement program.

7. *There is a central professional committee for the development of general policies and for the coordination of activities.* Such

committees are representative of the different school levels and of administrative-supervisory-instructional officers.

8. *Time and facilities are provided for committees and individuals to engage in program improvement activities.* Effective achievement of program objectives and considerations of morale require that adequate time, meeting places, materials, reference resources and clerical assistance be provided.

9. *Funds are budgeted for program improvement activities.* Curriculum improvement is too important an undertaking to be conducted on a shoestring, and entirely with volunteer work. Funds are necessary to provide clerical assistance, to purchase necessary materials, to engage specialist consultants, and to pay teachers for extra working time spent on curriculum improvement activities during vacation or summer months.

IV. Organization for Curriculum Planning

1. *The organization reflects the goals and purposes of the school, helping to create conditions for program planning similar to those at which the school is aiming in instruction.* The improvement program incorporates those kinds of learning conditions which staffs should be fostering within individual schools. These include cooperative planning; extensive and active participation; careful gathering of evidence; testing of generalizations; evaluation; and provision for the contributions of all and for able leadership for the various parts of the organization.

2. *Individuals and groups at each planning level are supported and encouraged so that they can contribute effectively to the improvement of the total program.* All persons and groups are helped to feel that their contributions are respected and receive serious consideration. Beyond that, the organization reflects active encouragement for all to contribute their talents.

3. *Responsibilities of individuals in the organization are clearly specified.* Careful distinction is made between authority and responsibility for decision-making and implementation on the one hand; and responsibility for providing advisory, consultant or resource assistance on the other. The scope of any individual's

authority is made clear so that personnel conflicts and wasteful effort are avoided.

4. *The organization facilitates coordination of diverse activities of planning and action groups.*   The relationships of committees to one another, and their responsibility to the larger instructional staff and to the central office is made clear in the organizational plan and in committee assignments. Provision is made for each specific curriculum planning assignment to be reviewed by the coordinating and planning group.

5. *Communication among the various individuals and groups working at program development is facilitated.*   Through such means as representatives who act in a liaison capacity, through definite provisions for committees and individuals to report back to the larger group, through written communications, and through systemwide meetings communication is facilitated. Provision is made to check the degree to which the communications are understood.

6. *Assignments for committees are clearly stated, and the committees are discharged when their work is completed.*   Committee members understand clearly the scope of their responsibilities: to gather data; to formulate recommendations; and/or to put plans into effect.

7. *The activities of individuals and groups preparing curriculum plans and materials are organized to facilitate adaptation and use by the other personnel.*   Provision is made for communicating to the staff the progress of working groups. Numerous opportunities are provided the staff to review tentative materials, participate in action research projects, and discuss tentative proposals, so that they may understand the rationale underlying changes, and feel some identification with, and commitment to them.

8. *The organization is effectively related to local conditions.*   A variety of factors such as size of school system, size of schools within the system, types of specialized and leadership personnel available, type of community and its educational expectations, the nature of the educational program in operation, and the characteristics of the staff are taken into account in determining the organization.

V. Participation in Curriculum Planning

1. *Provision is made for those who will be affected by the policy or action decisions which may emerge from the work of the group to participate at some level of planning.* Not all staff members can or need to participate in each stage of planning but those who must eventually change the instructional program are involved at some point of policy determination or decision-making.

2. *Those individuals whose classroom practice is expected to change as a consequence of the improvement program are encouraged to participate.* Those individuals who will affect instruction by changes which emerge from such participation are involved in planning on the basis of their potential contribution to a better learning situation.

3. *The emergence of leadership at all levels of planning is facilitated.* Individuals with a competency or resource which is or will be required for effective functioning and goal attainment by the group are involved in planning. Effective use is made of personnel resources in the school, the community, or elsewhere for upgrading teaching and learning.

4. *Lay persons, including parents and students, are involved in the processes of curriculum development wherever they can contribute their special competencies.* The particular roles lay persons can take because of their specialization, experience, education, or leadership responsibilities are made clear and they are involved on this basis.

VI. Procedures and Techniques Used in Curriculum Improvement

1. *A variety of activities are provided in order that each member of the instructional staff may participate in the program in a way recognized by him as being of value.* Diverse techniques and procedures make it possible for each individual to deal with his assignment, as an individual or as a group member, in ways which will enable him to make his greatest contribution.

2. *Professional staff growth is considered the primary avenue of curriculum improvement.* Procedures and techniques are

selected for their promise in fostering staff growth in skills, insights, and understandings. The procedures contribute to desired growth of staff by facilitating work on specific kinds of curriculum improvement tasks.

3. *Provisions are made for the development of skills necessary for undertaking curriculum improvement activities.* Effective participation in program improvement requires certain skills if maximum individual contribution is to be realized and training for needed skill development provided. The skills, competencies, and knowledge required for effective participation and leadership in a particular procedure are studied and, where necessary, training sessions are provided for extending these. When consultant help is required for particular activities it is either available or can be obtained.

4. *Separate strands of curriculum work are interrelated to build a consistent, comprehensive educational program.* Procedures and techniques are quite diverse for the achievement of different purposes but they are coordinated to build a unified program.

5. *Effective communication among individuals and groups involved in planning, as well as others who are concerned, is maintained.* Systematic efforts are made to inform individuals and groups about work in process as well as after its completion.

6. *Ways for translating plans into practice are constantly considered.* As work proceeds, the policies and procedures for implementing program plans are kept visible throughout. Focus is maintained on instructional implementation rather than on the curriculum improvement activities.

7. *Products, other than changed behavior of individuals, are developed on a tentative basis to be tested.* Curriculum and instructional materials are issued experimentally to be tested and evaluated in a way which encourages continued improvement and revision rather than adoption of a fixed pattern. Appropriate instructional materials are used as a means of aiding teachers to do better work with pupils rather than as an end goal in themselves.

VII. Evaluation of Curriculum Improvement Programs

1. *Continuous evaluation of the procedures in the improvement program and of the changes which result is made an integral part*

of the curriculum program. Evaluation of process is approached in various ways: surveys of staff opinion, postmeeting reaction sheets, staff discussions of procedures, appraisal of the over-all design and operation of the program by the coordinating body or by the central office personnel (in terms of such criteria as those suggested here), or by outside-the-system consultants. The measurement and assessment procedures used are appropriate to the kind of goal development being evaluated.

2. *Techniques of evaluation employed are consistent with the principles accepted for curriculum development.* If goals are expressed primarily in terms of changed behavior, modified program, and improved techniques, evaluation stresses these rather than the production of materials, number of meetings, or prestige persons participating. Behavior changes of staff, and the nature and effectiveness of program activities designed to foster behavior change are appraised.

3. *Provision is made for the practical testing on a limited basis of ideas for curriculum improvement and for the dissemination of results.* Action research projects and experimentation are encouraged in individual classrooms and in building units. Communication of results is fostered and replication of studies is encouraged. Application of findings to other classrooms and schools is facilitated.

4. *Systematic gathering and appraisal of evidence serves as a basis for determining need for changes in curriculum planning and improvement activities, and for consequent modifications.* Changes in procedures are not undertaken whimsically, without attempting to ascertain whether there is good reason for change; change activities do not simply result from the convictions of one person or small group.

5. *Evidence is sought of the effectiveness of curriculum planning in changing the quality of instruction.* There is systematic effort to ascertain the nature of the learning experiences fostered in school classrooms, and to discover relationships between improved quality of experiences and the curriculum improvement activities undertaken.

6. *The objectives of the program, both short-range and long-range, are specified in terms of* (a) *the changes sought in the edu-*

cational program and (b) *the changes sought in staff perception and operation.* The production of materials, the amount of participation, and the time and resources expended on the program are considered means to the achievement of instructional objectives, not as objectives in themselves. Objectives are formulated in terms of behavior changes, and evaluation is in these terms.

CONCLUDING STATEMENT

In no period of our history have educators, lay citizens, government officials, and almost all other groups, been as concerned as they are at the present time with the quality of education in public schools. The concern for quality has become, some speakers have declared, an issue of national policy. One educator has warned: "We run the grave risk . . . that the term 'quality,' as applied to teaching and learning, will become merely another educational catchword." [2]

Improving the quality of educational programs has been a continuing need which has challenged the public school almost since its founding. The program descriptions found in Chapters 5 through 11 are presented to indicate varied, stable approaches to devising programs of curriculum development and improvement which will yield highest dividends in the development of human potential. They underscore the desirability of giving attention to diversified problems, and the importance of attempting to build balanced programs rather than yielding to pressures of the moment to institute "crash programs" in a single aspect of education. The systemwide programs presented in this volume represent curriculum improvement with sound conceptual bases, not sporadic frantic efforts intended to assuage vocal critics. None of the descriptions is offered by its author as a panacea for program quality. None is even offered as a blueprint for another school system. Each represents a thoughtful analysis of the way a system is studying the forces and demands for curriculum change, appraising its curriculum, and steadily improving the quality of education provided for its children and youth.

[2] Arthur W. Foshay, "The Search for Quality in Education," *Horace Mann–Lincoln Institute Interim Report* (New York: Teachers College, Columbia University, 1959), p. 1.

SELECTED READINGS

ASSOCIATION FOR SUPERVISION AND CURRICULUM DEVELOPMENT, *Action for Curriculum Improvement*. Washington, D.C.: The Association, NEA, 1951.

ELSBREE, WILLARD S. and McNALLY, HAROLD J., *Elementary School Administration and Supervision* (rev. ed.). New York: American Book Company, 1959.

NATIONAL SOCIETY FOR THE STUDY OF EDUCATION, *Inservice Education for Teachers, Supervisors and Administrators*, Fifty-sixth Yearbook, Part I. Chicago: University of Chicago Press, 1957.

SAYLOR, J. GALEN and ALEXANDER, WILLIAM M., *Curriculum Planning for Better Teaching and Learning*. New York: Rinehart and Company, 1954.

SHANE, HAROLD G. and YAUCH, WILBUR A., *Creative School Administration*. New York: Henry Holt, 1954.

SMITH, B. O., STANLEY, W. O., and SHORES, J. H., *Fundamentals of Curriculum Development* (rev. ed.). Yonkers-on-Hudson, New York: World Book Company, 1957.

STRATEMEYER, FLORENCE B., FORKNER, HAMDEN L., McKIM, MARGARET, and PASSOW, A. HARRY, *Developing a Curriculum for Modern Living* (2d ed. rev.). New York: Bureau of Publications, Teachers College, Columbia University, 1957.

INDEX

INDEX